The New Slavery

The New Slavery
Accounts of Human Trafficking in Eastern Europe

KATE TRANSCHEL

McFarland & Company, Inc., Publishers
Jefferson, North Carolina

ISBN (print) 978-1-4766-9516-7
ISBN (ebook) 978-1-4766-5441-6

Library of Congress cataloging data are available

Library of Congress Control Number 2025030297

© 2025 Kate Transchel. All rights reserved

No part of this book may be reproduced or transmitted in any form or by any means, electronic or mechanical, including photocopying or recording, or by any information storage and retrieval system, without permission in writing from the publisher.

Front cover image: © Wirestock Creators/Shutterstock

Printed in the United States of America

*McFarland & Company, Inc., Publishers
Box 611, Jefferson, North Carolina 28640
www.mcfarlandpub.com*

To the Rev. Master Serena Seidner,
the Rev. Master Meian Elbert,
and the Buddhist monastic community
at Shasta Abbey,
without whose wisdom, compassion, and support
I could not have done this work.
In their dedication to ease suffering,
they are the ears of Avalokiteshvara,
hearing the cries of the world.
With deep bows of gratitude.

TABLE OF CONTENTS

Acknowledgments	ix
Glossary	xi
Preface	1
Introduction	5
Part I. Interviews with Modern-Day Abolitionists	19
1. Lena Sheraun	21
2. Irina Titarenko	37
3. Svetlana Laletina and Svetlana Bazhenova	52
4. Alina Budeci	66
5. Stella Rotaru	81
6. Oksana, Lena, Yulia, and Natasha	97
7. Ion Vizdoga	115
Part II. Interviews with Survivors of Slavery	129
8. Igor and Anatoli	132
9. Anya	144
10. Alexei	161
11. Nadya, Viorika, and Lida	170
12. Lila	185
13. Sasha and Andre	197
Conclusion	211
Appendix: What You Can Do	217

Chapter Notes 219
Bibliography 235
Index 241

Acknowledgments

I have no words big enough or strong enough to express my immeasurable gratitude to all who were willing to tell me their stories, even when it meant revisiting the darkness and the pain. I am awed by their courage and generosity. It is a debt I can never repay.

I also am deeply indebted to the individuals and organizations who freely shared with me their time and expertise. Huge thanks to LaStrada International in Chisinau, Moldova, and Kyiv, Ukraine, and especially to Alina Budeci, who was instrumental in helping me arrange interviews in Moldova. Also, much thanks to Ana Revenco, Tatiana Fomina, and Tetiana Taturevych. My deepest gratitude goes to the International Organization for Migration (IOM) in Chisinau, Kyiv, and Moscow, especially to Stella Rotaru and J. Blaec Kalweit, who offered advice, direction, and friendship while providing contacts and context. I would have been lost without them. Also, Ghenadie Cretu, Martin Wyss in Moldova, Ahn Nguyen, Irina Titarenko, Oksana Horbunova in Kyiv, and Maria Melnikova and Kirill Boychenko in Moscow. I am grateful to the Organization for Security and Co-operation in Europe (OSCE) in Moldova and Ukraine, especially to Judy Hale and Tetyana Rudenko. I thank Daria Fane at the U.S. Embassy in Moldova for her insights and her compassion. I am deeply indebted to Ion Vizdoga, whose knowledge and courage are breathtaking. Many thanks to Dr. Norbert Cyrus, Dr. Elena Tyuryukanova, David Blood, Yana Sharun, Neli Babcinci, Svitlana Belyaeva, and Oksana Alistratova, without whose generous help and careful insights I could not have completed this project. I am also deeply grateful to Mimi Chakarova and Siddarth Kara, who modeled a deeper kind of courage for me, and for their ongoing activism.

A big debt of gratitude goes to Dr. Bob Cottrell and Dr. Char Prieto, who read and commented on the manuscript, and to Heather Schlaff, who helped edit all three versions. I also want to thank Anya Turner, who helped with transcriptions and translations from Russian, as well as Evelina Trinchuk, who helped with Russian and Ukrainian transcriptions.

Thanks also to Dr. Greta Bucher, who has been a steadfast friend and willing ear all these many years and who listened to my descriptions of various aspects of my research with great patience. I am forever grateful to my friend and mentor Donald J. Raleigh, who provided lots of great advice and tons of encouragement when I needed it most.

Without the unwavering support of my friends and family over the years, I would not have been able to do this work. Special thanks to Jim and Peggy Ralls, who always reminded me of the important things. Much gratitude to Cristóbal Nava, who kept me upright and moving, even when I didn't want to be. Heartfelt thanks to my good friend Concha Nava, who helped me find the light in the darkness. And my deepest, most sincere thanks to my husband and soulmate, Dee Randolph, who was and is my courage, my partner, and my shoulder to cry on through it all.

This work was supported by the Lantis Endowment at California State University, Chico, and the International Research and Exchanges Board (IREX) Short-term Travel Grant.

Glossary

ILO	International Labour Organization
IOM	International Organization for Migration
john	a man who pays a for sex, a prostitute's client
krai	a regional subdivision in Russia slightly larger than an *oblast*
MVD	*Ministerstvo vnutrennikh del*, the Ministry of Internal Affairs in Russia
NGO	nongovernmental organization
Interpol	International Criminal Police Organization
oblast	a regional subdivision in Russia slightly smaller than a *krai*
OSCE	Organization for Security and Co-operation in Europe
PCM	Communist Party of Moldova
pimp	someone who controls prostitutes and arranges johns for them
propiska	a mandatory permit to live in a particular location in the Soviet Union and some post–Soviet states
recruiter	one who makes initial contact with a victim—the setup
Romeo pimp	a man who woos or marries a woman so that he can gain her trust and then sell her
TIP	U.S. State Department Trafficking in Persons Report
UAE	United Arab Emirates
UNICEF	United Nations International Children's Fund
UNODC	United Nations Office on Drugs and Crime
USAID	United States Agency for International Development
USSR	Union of Soviet Socialist Republics
ZAGS	*Zapis aktov grazhdanskogo sostoyaniy,* or civil registry

Preface

This book intertwines three kinds of stories—narratives of men and women who survived human trafficking and enslavement in Eastern Europe; stories of the service providers who rescued and rehabilitated them; and my own story of how and why I obtained these interviews. It joins a growing body of narratives that trace the existence of slavery in the twenty-first century.[1] However, only a very few of the current narratives include the voices of those who work directly with survivors of slavery.[2] Without these voices, only part of the slave experience can be understood—that of bondage. Yet, there is much to learn from those who work to rescue, repatriate, and rehabilitate slaves. Collectively, the accounts presented here detail modern-day slavery and its effects directly from those who experienced it and escaped it, and those who facilitate recovery from slavery's horrors. It also highlights the amazing resiliency of human beings, and that those who have endured such traumas are not defined by the experience—they are much more than this thing that happened to them.

In all, I conducted sixty-two interviews between 2008 and 2012—forty with service providers and twenty-two with survivors. I include in this volume interviews with ten survivors, one lawyer working for victims' rights, and nine people working in various anti-trafficking non-governmental organizations (NGOs). I chose to include these interviews because they represent trends and experiences that repeated throughout the various interviews. Each story documents an individual's experience with slavery—either their own enslavement or that of their clients. Those that were not included in this book nonetheless inform my study. Indeed, my informants reflect the full range of trafficking experiences. Some were enslaved in their home country, but most were trafficked across international borders.

About 20 percent of my total interviewees are male, and nearly one-quarter were trafficked as children. They come from Moldova (including Transnistria), Ukraine, Latvia, or Russia and were either trafficked or

1

worked in a nongovernmental organization dealing with trafficked victims between 1993 and 2012.

I crafted the book as documentary prose to record as faithfully as possible my interviewees' *experience* of slavery, rather than focusing on documenting the facts of slavery.[3] Hence, it departs from oral history methodologies in several ways, largely because of the risk and danger for all involved, including myself.

Following my first research trip abroad in 2008, I received numerous threats after an article about my work on human trafficking was published in a local paper. Since many of the areas I traveled to were quite dangerous, or the authorities were complicit in the trafficking of persons, I took my husband, Dee Randolph, to most of the interviews to provide me with a level of security and comfort. I acknowledge that his presence may have complicated things but, oddly enough, it actually helped to build trust with my interviewees. I mention this because, in interviewing trafficking survivors, I gave them the option of speaking to me in the presence of someone who would make them feel more at ease or supported, such as a psychologist, service provider, or friend. It was entirely their choice and most of them opted to have someone present during the interview. I told them that I gave myself the same option, and in just about every case, I sensed that they understood my own fear and anxieties and therefore agreed to Dee's presence.

Moreover, in making every possible effort to minimize the risk for my informants I employed another technique not commonly practiced by oral historians. Aside from most of the service providers and lawyers, who already have a public presence, I gave most of my informants pseudonyms to maintain their anonymity. Further, I deleted or changed information that came up in an interview that could identify an informant, thereby putting them or their families at risk. This practice deviates from good oral history practices but makes this type of written documentary possible. Without these provisions, this book would not exist.

I located my informants through local NGOs engaged in anti-trafficking work. I asked the rehabilitation professional or psychologist if any of his or her clients might be willing to talk to me. Before I ever approached a survivor of slavery, I first secured assurance from the caseworker or psychologist that the potential interviewee would not be harmed by the interview process. I asked nonprofit institutions to recommend only those survivors who had expressed a desire to share their stories. Nearly all my informants had already given their stories to journalists or researchers, and all of them expressed some kind of relief at being able to talk about their experiences, no matter how difficult that was. For most, their main motivation was to help others—to focus attention on what can happen to migrants, or to warn people about slavery. Since I worked through local NGOs, left out of this project are those who had no access to support or services from an NGO, those still trapped in slavery, those working in governmental organizations and law enforcement, and those who have not identified themselves as trafficking victims.

I never interviewed a minor, although some of my informants were minors when they were trafficked. I always kept the safety, privacy, and comfort of my interviewees as my highest priority. I crafted each interview around a set of basic questions that I asked every informant, such as their social background, education level, age, birthplace, and the like. But I was also careful to give each person the time and space to talk about what they thought was important. I asked them how they understood their experiences, and what, if anything, they would like to communicate to readers of this book.

As a result, many of the interviews were much richer, more personal, and took directions that I had not anticipated. For example, one of my first interviewees was a survivor from Moldova. Anya thought she was in Greece when she jumped out of a sixth-floor window to avoid being sold to the highest bidder at a slave auction. It was only when she came to consciousness in the hospital that she discovered she was in Istanbul. At the end of the interview, I asked her if there was anything that she would like to say to those who might be reading this book. She said, "Tell them we are human! … You can't sell human beings. Tell them we are HUMAN!"[4]

The goal of this volume is to provide to the reader, as accurately as possible, the remembrances and lived experiences of those who have endured or witnessed slavery firsthand. Even though these interviews took place well over a decade ago, the information is still relevant today. There are several reasons why so much time has passed between my first research trip and the publication of this book. Transcribing, translating, and editing the interviews was a multi-year process. Further, it took me several years to find the right publisher for this work. In the meantime, the people I met and the stories I heard weighed heavily upon me, and I felt I needed to do something to help bring attention to this horrific crime. I therefore dedicated myself to public outreach and awareness, working with local law enforcement, service providers, and civic clubs organizing anti-trafficking conferences, giving public talks, and advocating for potential victims and survivors. This work seemed more urgent, and it delayed the completion of this manuscript. But, in February 2022, when Russia invaded Ukraine, I watched in horror as millions of women and children fled into Poland to escape Russian bombs and tanks. At the Polish border, thousands of well-meaning Europeans met these refugees, offering them transport to safety. I know (and subsequent research has proved) that some of those waiting at the border were traffickers, ready to entrap and enslave hundreds of women and children. It convinced me that now, more than ever, these interviews are relevant. Besides, the stories contained in this volume are not mine—they were given to me in the hopes that others may not have to suffer the same fate. In the last fifteen years, national and international efforts at monitoring, documenting, and prosecuting human trafficking have improved exponentially. Yet so, too, has the ability of traffickers to prey upon and exploit vulnerable populations. Sadly, not much has changed in the business of modern-day slavery. If anything, it has gotten worse.

Introduction

> *We have thankfully watched the fall of the Berlin Wall, but unfortunately the wall fell on women's heads.*—comment by a participant in the Russian State Duma meeting on the status of women in the Russian Federation, 1993

My story begins in Moscow, Russia, in 1998 when I first met Lena, a Russian woman who claimed to have been enslaved in a brothel somewhere in the Balkans. She was in her thirties and was tall, thin, and very blond. My friend Marina had introduced her to me. Lena was trying to get sober in the Moscow Beginners group of Alcoholics Anonymous. She had managed to stay sober for about thirty days. Marina was letting Lena sleep on the couch in her flat until Lena was a bit less shaky. At the time, I was in Moscow researching alternative youth cultures under Brezhnev. Even though Lena didn't fit the type of interviewee I was looking for, Marina thought I might find the story interesting.

"They say I am prostitute. I am no prostitute" was how Lena started our conversation. She then told me a story of how, five years earlier in 1993, she thought she was going to a modeling job in Europe, but instead was forced into prostitution in Bosnia. She related a harrowing tale of escape with the help of a john[1] and then finding a truck driver who smuggled her back into Russia. She told me there were dozens, if not hundreds, of girls like her forced into prostitution in Bosnia.[2] She was proud and defiant and intense, and I did not believe a word of it. I had never heard of such a thing. In my professional arrogance, I thought if this were really happening, surely I would have heard of it before now.

But in 1998 I had not heard of human trafficking—few in the public had. I believed that slavery had ended in the nineteenth century—that there were laws and international conventions that prevented the practice of slavery. Consequently, I did not know to ask Lena how she was recruited or how she was transported to Bosnia, what conditions in the brothel were like, and who her traffickers and johns were. I did not ask her where the other girls were from, or how many times she was sold. I did not ask about the details of her escape, or how she was reintegrating. I just thought she was a dramatic and intense young woman with an alcoholic past and an overactive imagination. She did not fit the profile I was looking for at the time, so I paid little attention to her story.

However, there *was* something compelling about her that made me very uneasy with my own readiness to dismiss her story. Despite her defiance, there was something fragile and broken about her that I could not quite pin down. I never saw Lena again. She got drunk—again—and Marina had to ask her to leave. I will never know the end of her story. But for the rest of that summer, I could not get her out of my mind. I kept returning to her story of the forced prostitution of dozens of women and wondering, "What if it were true?" What if, indeed.

When I returned home, I resolved to find out if Lena's story had any merit. I started scouring newspapers for evidence of vast numbers of women forced into prostitution. Scant attention was paid in the media to human trafficking in those years. However, I found one article in the *New York Times* that related the story of young girls trafficked from Mexico and forced into prostitution in New Jersey.[3] Another told of 1,500 Ukrainian and Russian women trafficked into sexual slavery.[4] As I dug deeper, it became clear that hundreds of thousands of men, women, and children were being trafficked and sold into slavery around the globe each year.[5] This book presents some of those stories.

Defining Modern-Day Slavery

People often want to know how many slaves there are. Unfortunately, that question cannot be answered with any kind of accuracy. The very nature of human trafficking as an underground, illegal activity makes it nearly impossible to know the real scope and details of the trade. Numerous international organizations and researchers have tried to estimate how many people are trafficked and enslaved each year. Conservative estimates place the number of slaves in the world today at 27.6 million.[6] The 2023 report by the Global Slavery Index places the number of slaves at 49.6 million in 167 countries.[7] Of these, at least 10 percent come from the former Soviet Union.[8]

Further complicating the estimation of "how many slaves" is the issue of definition. Terms such as *human trafficking, modern-day slavery, sexual slavery,* and *smuggling* lack clarity and hence have become controversial against the backdrop of highly contested international debates on how to define human trafficking and its relationship to prostitution and slavery.[9]

Scholars, policymakers, advocates, and activists do not agree on a single definition of human trafficking or slavery. Nonetheless, a significant proportion of academics, lawyers, political leaders, and those working in NGOs generally follow the definition of human trafficking as adopted by the so-called Palermo Protocol. The Protocol defines human trafficking as "the recruitment, transportation, transfer, harbouring, or receipt of persons" by means of "threat, use of force or other forms of coercion, of abduction, of fraud, of deception, or the abuse of power or of a position of vulnerability" for the purpose of exploitation. Integral to this definition is control over another person for the "purpose of exploitation," which distinguishes it from human smuggling.[10] As defined by the Palermo Protocol, human trafficking is the process by which persons become enslaved.

For the sake of language variation, I use the terms *human trafficking* or *trafficking* interchangeably with *slavery*. While doing so is somewhat controversial, the U.S. Trafficking Victims Protection Act defines trafficking as a "contemporary manifestation of slavery" and includes "obtaining a person for labor or services through the use of fraud, force, or coercion."[11] According to this definition, holding or obtaining a person through force or coercion to exploit their labor constitutes slavery. The sale or transport of a person is not a necessary component. Since *human trafficking* is often confused with illegal human smuggling or the international transportation of victims, the term *slavery* is more precise in describing the lived experiences of many of my interviewees. Both are parts of the same phenomenon—the buying, selling, and exploiting of persons.

Scholarly literature on what constitutes slavery is voluminous, and yet this term is also problematic.[12] In describing modern-day slavery, scholars prefer to use terms such as *bonded labor, forced labor, unfree labor, labor exploitation*, or *debt bondage*.[13] However, the interpretation and application of these terms is often politicized to fit the varying agendas of those working and researching in anti-trafficking circles, thereby making a precise definition of *slavery* elusive.[14] Historically, the term *slavery* has been used to describe a multitude of modes of human exploitation in vastly different contexts, giving it broad and sometimes contradictory meanings. Further complicating the use of *slavery* in a modern context is that the common understanding of the word is the practice of owning human beings and treating them as property, or chattel. Chattel slavery, like what existed in the United States in the seventeenth through nineteenth centuries, implies legal rights of property ownership, the existence of a master or owner, and the powerlessness of the slave.[15]

Further, the word *slavery* carries a strong political and emotional charge.[16] Much of the academic controversy over use of the word is related to a deep respect for the experiences of African and African American victims and survivors of the transatlantic slave trade. The horrors endured by enslaved peoples and the injustices suffered by their descendants must be acknowledged and honored. At the same time, the restriction of a person's freedom, the violation of their right to self-determination, and the exploitation of their labor as occurs today must also be called *slavery* because that is precisely what it is.

Author and activist Kevin Bales argues that today there exists a new type of slavery in which people are so cheap and easy to obtain that they are disposable, making it distinct from earlier forms of slavery. He asserts that the exercise of control over a person is tantamount to possession and that possession is *de facto* slavery, even if the situation is not one of formal legal ownership of a person.[17] Laura Murphy correctly asserts that use of the word *slavery* compels one to "articulate the common denomination that characterizes it over time and space," and serves as a reminder that the work of abolition is still incomplete.[18] Professor, author, and activist Siddharth Kara contends that slavery is "a system of dishonoring and degrading people through the violent coercion of their labor activity in conditions that dehumanize them."[19]

Every one of the survivors who chose to tell me their stories would easily be recognized as slaves under these definitions: They were trapped in systems of servile labor exploitation (including sexual labor) that included a measure of violence and coercion that severely dishonored and degraded them.[20] Sometimes the violence did not necessarily take the form of physical abuse. Forms of violence my interviewees endured included threats or harm against someone they loved, verbal or psychological abuse, and deprivation of basic human necessities, such as food and water. Many were forced to live in deplorable conditions that further dehumanized them and stripped them of their dignity and humanity. All of them had their freedoms restricted and none of them were free to leave. When they did try to leave, the words they used in telling me their stories are *escape* and *rescue*. What would this be, if not slavery?

The service providers whose stories are also included in this book confirm the experience of slavery of their clients. Those engaged in the rescue, repatriation, and rehabilitation of trafficking survivors often have a broader view of human trafficking. They tend to have a deeper understanding of what survivors are likely to have endured, and what it takes to recover from the abuses of slavery. In talking about their enslavement, many of my interviewees had difficulty expressing and reliving the pain of that time in their lives. Instead, many of them focused on the period in their lives just before being trafficked, the process of being trafficked, or on their lives after escaping or being rescued. However, the service providers engaged in rehabilitation services can often more directly bear witness to the effects of slavery upon their clients. Many of these men and women were themselves vulnerable to trafficking, and often have sacrificed a lot in order to help others. Their stories are as compelling and revealing as the slave narratives contained in this volume. Without these voices, only half the story can be understood.

Why Post–Soviet Eastern Europe?

Lena's story, along with the stories of millions of trafficked Eastern European men, women, and children, began with the collapse of the Soviet Union in 1991. The end of the Soviet Union ended seventy years of centralized social, political, and economic controls that guaranteed employment and social security for all citizens. These controls also served to insulate the population, shielding individuals from crime, poverty, and the excesses of capitalism. The Soviet state and its satellites limited international migration and traced internal migration through a system of passports and residence permits known as *propiski*.[21] Strict border controls, along with military patrols of perimeters, ports, and airports, minimized the flow of people, goods, and even ideas into and out of Soviet-controlled countries. Consequently, when the Berlin Wall fell in 1989, thousands of Soviet Bloc citizens marched through the Brandenburg Gate and elsewhere like a victorious army, pushing aside the Iron Curtain with absolutely no idea what dangers or pitfalls awaited them.

Human trafficking from the former Soviet states is intricately linked to economic changes that occurred after 1991. Most post–Soviet states underwent a rapid shift from a state-controlled economy to a market-oriented one. As communist states shifted from centralized command economies, there were no regulated infrastructures, nor regulatory bodies to oversee the privatization of state-owned industries and resources or business transactions. The result was the flow of billions of dollars' worth of state capital into the pockets and offshore accounts of those closest to the centers of power.[22] In trying to characterize what happened in the post–Soviet Russian economy, experts have coined terms such as *kleptocracy* and *mafia state*. The problem by 1991, then, was not so much a rise in crime and organized criminal groups, but rather the criminalization of the entire Russian and most post–Soviet economies.[23]

Many authorities in these criminalized states profited from human trafficking and other forms of exploitation, either through direct involvement or through payoffs and bribes, and hence were reluctant to admit there was a lively trade in humans.[24] Often, state agencies refused to recognize trafficked persons as victims, arguing instead that they were

Map of European Russia. Source: Nations Online Project. https://www.nationsonline.org/oneworld/map/russia-political-map.htm.

voluntary workers, prostitutes, or criminals.[25] In one surreal conversation I had in Riga, Latvia, the head of the international human trafficking division demanded, "Show me a victim! Show me! You say there are victims—I see none. Show me a victim!"[26] It is not surprising, then, that under such conditions organized criminal groups engaged in human trafficking with impunity. According to the Ukrainian Ministry of Internal Affairs, the number of organized crime groups in Ukraine grew from 260 in 1991 to 960 in 2000.[27] And the Global Organized Crime Project claims that by 2000 there were 200 Russian organized crime syndicates operating in 58 countries, distributing Eastern European women all over the world.[28]

The collapse of the Soviet Union and the establishment of criminalized states coincided with a decade of severe economic decline. Thus, post–Soviet governments ended or greatly reduced many social programs and benefits, such as housing provisions, guaranteed employment, and family assistance. Further, with the move toward market economies, these states abolished the communist-era fixed-price systems and ended state subsidies on everything except for a few food items. Prices rose precipitously overnight, followed by triple-digit hyperinflation. Families were left to survive on their own. And women, as the primary caretakers, were responsible for feeding and sustaining the family. The result, especially in the first years following the collapse of the Soviet Union, was the rapid and dramatic collapse of economies, soaring prices, widespread unemployment, the sudden disappearance of state subsidies and aid, and the feminization of poverty.[29]

One of my interviewees, Natasha, described to me what it was like living in St. Petersburg in what she called "the hungry winter of 1993." She was attending St. Petersburg State University and received a small student stipend of seven rubles a month, enough to buy two to three loaves of bread. That was all the money she had for food for the month. She told me that she was always hungry and lightheaded, so much so that her studies suffered. Her overcoat was thin, and her shoes had holes in them. She was constantly looking for ways to get food or money to buy food, including at one point running afoul of a street gang by trying to sell an old pair of tennis shoes on *their* street.[30] Natasha told me that her engineer mother, having not received a salary for several months, took a job at a local kindergarten. While it paid practically nothing, at least her mother could scrape up the children's lunch leftovers and take them home to feed the family. Natasha remembered having enough kopeks once to buy an egg—one. And she described the old woman in line in front of her that day who did not have enough money for a whole hotdog. The clerk sold this old woman one half of a tiny hotdog, and wrapped it up in gray butcher paper for her to take home. That was the day Natasha decided to go abroad to find work, no matter what it took.[31]

Women and children were hit the hardest in the immediate post–Soviet economic chaos. At the beginning of the transition from a socialist economy to a market-oriented system, women's salaries were about 70 percent of men's.[32] After 1991, as these economies contracted or collapsed, women were the first to lose their jobs. According to numerous international agencies, throughout the 1990s and early 2000s women in post–Soviet societies made up somewhere between 60 to 90 percent of the unemployed. When you consider that 80 percent of single-parent, single-income households were headed by women, and that up to 80 percent of these were unemployed from the 1990s well into the twenty-first century, it is easy to see why traffickers found a steady supply of desperate women to exploit in post–Soviet Eastern Europe.

At the same time, millions of men faced a similar lack of economic opportunity in emerging post–Soviet states. Large numbers of these men migrated (and still migrate), falling prey to traffickers and those who exploit their labor. The International Organization of Migration (IOM) was one of the first international agencies to focus on the trafficking of men. Established in 1951, the IOM is the world's leading intergovernmental agency in the field of migration. With offices in over 100 countries, it was one of the first international organizations to recognize and track human trafficking. According to their research, as well as research conducted by the United States Agency for International Development (USAID), most trafficked adult men are married with dependent children. They have some education and technical skills but do not receive salaries in their home countries sufficient to support their families.[33]

In addition to creating economic chaos, the collapse of the Soviet Union coincided with the advance of globalization and the rise of the internet. Marked by an increasingly integrated global economy, globalization in the *fin de siècle* involved free trade, free flow of capital, and the search for cheap labor that transcended the boundaries of nation-states. Taking advantage of more porous and sometimes nonexistent borders, rapid broadband communication, and political and economic chaos, traffickers operated freely within the margins of mass migrations of people and preyed upon the most vulnerable. The men and women whose lives and livelihoods collapsed with the Soviet Union sought opportunities abroad to improve their lives and unwittingly made human trafficking a prominent feature of the post–Cold War era.

At the same time, human trafficking was not only a consequence of globalization, but in the former Soviet Union, it also was the first evidence of it. As Ghenadi Cretu, a migration specialist at the IOM in Chisinau, Moldova, explained to me, until the mid–1990s the Soviet Bloc had been a closed social system with limited economic contact with the West.[34] But with the first breach of the Berlin Wall in 1989, migrants flooded out of Eastern Europe as opportunists flooded in. This is when integration into a global system began in Eastern Europe, one hallmark of which was the rapid increase in human trafficking.

Trafficking is a complex issue, rooted not only in the economic and political development of post–Soviet states, but also in the social and cultural detritus of the Soviet era. One such factor is a history of domestic violence and sexual abuse. Post–Soviet societies tend to tolerate a certain amount of violence toward women. For example, at the start of the new millennium an estimated 14,000 Russian women were killed each year, on average, by partners or other family members, according to a Russian government report to the Committee on the Elimination of All Forms of Discrimination Against Women.[35] That is nearly one per hour.

In the late 1990s, the Russian Ministry of Internal Affairs (MVD) estimated that close to 36,000 women in Russia were beaten by their spouses or partners every day.[36] In Ukraine, according to a 2010 joint EU/UN Development Program report, nearly half of all Ukrainians have experienced domestic violence.[37] Until recently in Ukraine, law enforcement and society regarded men's violence against women as a "private family matter."[38] Repatriation experts at La Strada International estimate that seven out of ten rescued women endured domestic or sexual abuse before being trafficked.[39] Founded in 1995 and headquartered in Amsterdam, LaStrada is a network of European anti-trafficking NGOs and the leading organization engaged in trafficking prevention, repatriation, and victims' services. LaStrada's client profiles suggest that as women fled violence at home, they became vulnerable to trafficking.

Further, in most emergent post–Soviet states, the law contained weak definitions of, and very mild punishments for, rape. In Moldova, for example, if a victim of rape agreed to marry the perpetrator, all charges were dropped. A few of the women I interviewed were forced into marriage with their assailants by family members trying to save the family's "honor" and by law enforcement officials hoping to "solve" a crime. One of my interviewees from a small village in Moldova was forced to marry her rapist. She was sixteen and had become pregnant from the rape. Village justice demanded that he marry her, which he did, and then he continued to abuse her and their daughter until she sought escape abroad and ended up trafficked. It is not unusual for women attempting to flee abusive situations to come under the control of a trafficker.[40]

A history of labor exploitation, combined with a weak understanding of civil liberties, aids the traffickers. Many of the survivors I interviewed had little or no sense of their right to fair pay for labor rendered and felt no outrage—only embarrassment—at being trafficked. They internalized their experiences and blamed themselves for not being smarter. One such person was trafficked from Moldova to Uzbekistan in 1994. He was sent to Central Asia to deliver a shipment of lumber. But once there, he discovered that he had been sold to a man who owned a newly privatized farm.[41] He was physically abused and forced to work with no compensation. When I asked why he didn't try to escape, he merely shrugged:

> I had no documents, no money. Besides, where would I go? As bad as life was on the farm, working in Moldova was no better. There we had no money, no food, and no help. At least on the farm, they fed me so I could work.[42]

A Moldovan woman who was trafficked from Chisinau and forced into slave labor in the flower industry in southern Russia expressed similar sentiments—abuse by the state or abuse by a private farmer amounted to pretty much the same thing.[43]

Who Are the Victims of Human Trafficking?

Anyone can be trafficked and enslaved, and victims come from everywhere and from all socioeconomic classes. No one and no place is immune from slavery. However, trafficking from the former Soviet sphere has some noticeable distinctions. The first victims of trafficking identified from Eastern Europe in the early 1990s were relatively well-educated women from urban areas. As mentioned above, as socialist economies collapsed, women were the first to lose their jobs in disproportionate numbers. Many of these were educated, professional, often bilingual women seeking professional careers abroad. Local NGOs report that the first victims of trafficking were female teachers, university professors, and mid- to high-level bureaucrats who were forced into sexual slavery. The privatization of central-command economies resulted in state agencies, public schools, and institutions losing the ability to pay their employees. Many of those with the most marketable skills sought employment abroad and hence became vulnerable to trafficking.

But around the year 2000, people from different socioeconomic backgrounds started to emerge as trafficking victims—rural men and women with little education, as well as individuals from the middle class who had some technical training or vocational skills.[44] Several factors can account for this shift. By the early twenty-first century, several NGOs, such as La Strada and the IOM, launched numerous prevention programs, making information about human trafficking more available. However, these campaigns were largely concentrated in urban areas—much of the information did not get out to the villages. Urban men and women considering going abroad had more knowledge and more tools to assess the potential risks. Further, until the 2008 financial crisis, many former Soviet republics saw the emergence of a small but growing middle class. As the various economies began to stabilize, there were better—if limited—opportunities for highly skilled or professional jobs in urban areas. Consequently, highly educated or skilled professionals had more information about the hazards of migration and had more professional opportunities at home. But those with less education, who were lower on the socioeconomic chain, or who came from rural areas, were often left behind in the emerging post–Soviet economies. These became the populations most vulnerable to trafficking.

It is noteworthy that nearly all my interviewees who were trafficked for labor exploitation had some kind of trade, technical, or vocational schooling, as well as previous work experience. Also, all of them came from working-class families with average incomes, and most of them came from provincial towns, not large urban centers. Their decision to migrate was not made out of desperation, nor because of dire poverty. It was based on a lack of employment opportunities in their home countries, as well as an assumed lack of future opportunities. Many perceived the standard of living to be higher in Russia or Europe. It was this perception of life abroad that was a major determining factor to migrate despite the risks.

One of the most important factors in the shift in victim demographics was a change in strategies used by the traffickers and recruiters. In the early 2000s traffickers began recruiting aggressively in small towns and villages, promising jobs, money, and opportunities abroad. Across all the former Soviet republics, representatives of NGOs reported suspicious advertisements for work abroad appearing in newspapers and on billboards. Having read dozens of such ads in Russian, Ukrainian, and Moldovan newspapers, I noticed several red flags. Almost none of the job announcements required knowledge of English or the language of the destination country. None of them required a specific type or level of education. All of them offered higher-than-average salaries for the source countries (typically 500 to 1,000 Euros a month), and most boasted flexible working arrangements. Many of these ads offered government contracts, and noted that visa, travel, and living arrangements would be paid for by the company. It was easy to see how someone looking to improve their employment status would answer such an ad.

As law enforcement and NGOs began paying attention to, and warning against, such ads, slavers shifted tactics. Traffickers began operating in employment or tour agencies, or study abroad agencies. The majority of these were registered with the state, and operated as legal, licensed businesses. They promised people jobs abroad and assisted in arranging travel documents. According to several NGOs in Russia and Moldova, the legal agencies were just as likely to engage in trafficking as the illegal ones.

As one prevention specialist at the IOM told me, if everyone who went through a particular agency got trafficked, people would know it was a trap. But in most agencies, both legal and illegal, 90 percent of the time, they actually do send people abroad for school or work. Only about 10 percent of the time do job seekers going through any specific agency get trafficked, so people are willing to take the risk.

About half of my interviewees went abroad via an agency of some sort. They were recruited through legitimate-looking advertisements on billboards, in newspapers, or on the internet that mimicked offers for legal migration. They thought they had made legally binding agreements with reliable companies or employment agencies. Several interviewees with signed contracts had their travel arrangements paid for. However, once they reached the destination country, they were locked in a room or on a compound and forced into slave labor or prostitution. Others were told that they owed thousands of dollars for the travel documents and had to pay off the debt before they could go free. But the traffickers kept adding charges for food, housing, medicine, and clothing, ensuring that the debt never got paid off. Still others were forced into prostitution until the debt was paid.

One of my interviewees from L'viv, Ukraine, worked in an anti-trafficking NGO. She knew all the risks and dangers. And yet, when offered a job abroad through a legitimate-looking agency, she took it. I interviewed her just before she left for this "job" in Europe. I asked her why, knowing all that she does, she would risk it? She shrugged. "Yes, I know the risks. But I also know that I have a good chance of actually getting a job. For me, it is worth it."[45] I never heard from her again, although there were rumors that she did find employment in Europe. I hope so.

A multitude of studies, including assessments by international NGOs and individual governments, have pointed to the international and multifaceted character of trafficking rings. However, my research suggests that a significant number of victims are recruited and sold through small, informal criminal networks that are opportunistic and fluid. Most of the people I interviewed who were forced into slavery were recruited by a friend or a family member who promised to secure them employment abroad. Others knew they were traveling across borders illegally, but they trusted their recruiter. When they arrived at their destination, their documents were taken, and many were beaten, raped, and sodomized, and then sold. Or they found themselves in debt bondage, forced to work off huge bills and fines with no hope of escape.

It has been over twenty years since I met Lena at Marina's apartment in Moscow and got my first introduction to modern-day slavery. And it has been more than a decade since I conducted these interviews. Sadly, the information in this book is still relevant—little has changed in the business of human trafficking. All the people whose lives you are about to enter wanted to tell their stories in the hopes of effecting change. Some wanted to warn of the dangers inherent in migration. Others wanted readers to know that slavery can and does happen to anybody. All of them expressed a hope that their experiences could somehow shield others from the pain of being sold. In the end, they all thanked me for listening to their stories, understanding that change can only come through awareness. I am humbled by their courage.

PART I

Interviews with Modern-Day Abolitionists

> *I will not allow my life's light to be determined by the darkness around me.*—Sojourner Truth, African American who escaped slavery in 1826 to become a prominent abolitionist and women's rights activist

Who answers the phone when someone trapped in slavery manages to call an NGO for help? And what happens next? What is it like to work with law enforcement when you know many in the system are complicit in human trafficking? Who would choose to enter a profession where, as one service provider put it, "There are few success stories"?[1] In trying to secure prosecutions of traffickers, do case workers risk their lives? How safe is it to work in anti-trafficking in areas where the law is fluid and corruption is high? These are questions that went through my mind as I began interviewing my first trafficking survivors. Having befriended a few service providers while trying to locate informants for this project, I began to informally ask some of them a few such questions. Their answers very quickly made me realize the importance of their experiences in understanding modern-day slavery and how to combat it.

As far as I know, there are no scholarly studies that look at the lives of anti-trafficking workers—those in the trenches engaged in the rescue, repatriation, and rehabilitation of survivors.[2] What I discovered anecdotally is that a large proportion of those drawn to survivor assistance are themselves survivors of trafficking or have come very close to being trafficked. Several of the service providers you are about to meet fit that category.

I chose to present the interviews of those working in anti-trafficking NGOs first—not to diminish the importance of what the survivors have endured, but because these interviews provide the reader with a better understanding of human trafficking and the conditions within which it happens in Eastern Europe. The stories you are about to read are from some of the most courageous people I have met. Some of them were trafficked, some nearly missed getting trafficked, and most don't even recognize themselves as modern-day abolitionists. But they are.

1

Lena Sheraun

Anti-trafficking activist
NGO: Road to Life
Kharkiv, Ukraine
August 27, 2010

I decided to place Lena's interview first because she is a survivor of sex trafficking and later became a service provider and an anti-trafficking activist. She had been enslaved in a brothel in Belgium and at the time of the interview she ran a very effective anti-trafficking NGO that was a leader in prevention and protection in eastern Ukraine. Her story is horrifying and, at the same time, typical of survivors of sexual exploitation who have benefited from successful reintegration efforts. Nonetheless, in speaking about her past, Lena mentions that not one day goes by that she does not remember what happened to her. She is remarkably candid when talking about her experiences. As a service provider, she understands more than most what her clients are going through and how best to help them.

Road to Life, the NGO that Lena founded and ran, was the largest anti-trafficking NGO in eastern Ukraine before the Russian invasion in 2022. With support from the International Organization for Migration (IOM), Road to Life reached beyond the city of Kharkiv and conducted prevention and outreach programs in every corner of the *oblast*.[1] One reason for the NGO's effectiveness is Lena's personal experience with trafficking. Having been enslaved and exploited herself, she is uniquely situated to understand what victims need for successful reintegration, and how to approach them.

As I waited for her to finish a phone conservation outside her office so I could interview her, I reflected upon how much she resembled her home city of Kharkiv. Both have endured unspeakable abuse and tragedy, and yet emerged from it amazingly resilient and vibrant. Kharkiv, located

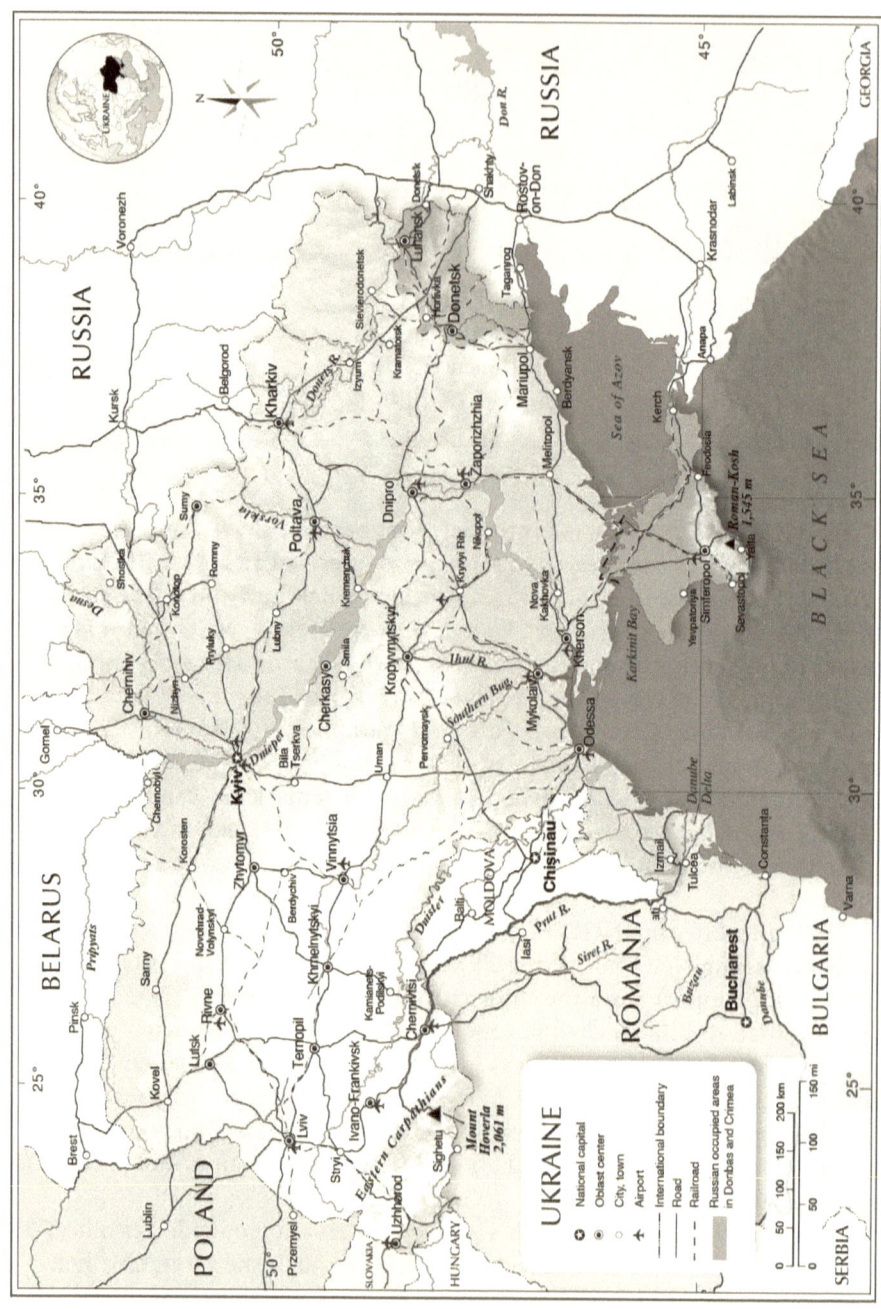

Map of Ukraine. Source: Nations Online Project. https://www.nationsonline.org/oneworld/map/ukraine-political-map.htm.

just twenty-five miles from the Russian border, has a complex and dramatic history. The city suffered tremendously from the Stalinist purges in the 1930s only to be devastated by Nazi occupation during World War II.[2] By the end of the war, 70 percent of the city was destroyed, and tens of thousands of Ukrainians had died in the battles for the city. Further, while Kharkiv was under Nazi occupation, the Germans murdered over 30,000 civilians, half of them Jewish, dumping their bodies in a mass grave known as Babi Yar (grandmother's ravine). Despite these atrocities, Kharkiv rebuilt and once again became an important cultural, intellectual, and industrial center.[3] This is the Kharkiv that Lena grew up in and that existed until the Russians invaded again in 2022.

When Russia launched a full-scale invasion of Ukraine on February 24, 2022, Kharkiv Oblast was one of the first areas invaded and occupied, and the scene of some of the fiercest fighting. During over six months of nearly constant shelling, the Russian army destroyed or damaged over 18,000 facilities, 4,000 apartment buildings, 6,000 private houses, more than 800 educational institutions, 270 healthcare institutions, and 350 cultural institutions in the *oblast*.[4] Observers noted that the atmosphere was like it had been in the 1930s and 1940s. Lena's NGO was in one of the neighborhoods that had been heavily shelled. I have heard nothing from or about her since the invasion. The physical rebuilding of Kharkiv will once again take tremendous effort and many years.

Lena's life has followed a trajectory similar to that of the city she loves. Having survived the brutalization of her body and the death of her sister, Lena emerged from the experience willing to face down her traffickers in court and fight for the rights of those still trapped in slavery. One can only hope that Lena, and her many clients, managed to survive the Russian invasion and can once again rebuild their lives.

But on that hot day in 2010, Lena finally finished her phone conversation and turned her attention to me. "Shall we...?" she said, extending an invitation to go into the building. As we trudged up the four flights of stairs to her office, I was remembering our first meeting two years prior. At that time, in a matter-of-fact voice, she related how she and her sister endured over six months' imprisonment and sexual slavery. Having survived trafficking, repatriation, and rehabilitation, they believed they could help other trafficking victims. They also decided to testify against their traffickers. Typically, victims don't testify for fear of retribution.

However, before the case came to trial Lena's sister died in a suspicious car accident. Rather than being defeated or intimidated by such a stunning loss, Lena strengthened her resolve to confront her oppressors and help other victims. Her NGO, Road to Life, became a leader in public information and outreach. At any time of the day or night, one of Lena's three cell phones might ring, sending her off to God knows where to meet another terrified woman who managed to escape enslavement.

I have thought about you many times over the last two years. Last time we met you shared your story with me, and if you don't mind, I would like you to talk about it some more.
Lena: Of course.

Okay. Last time we met, there was already a criminal case started against your traffickers. Has that been resolved? Has it come to trial?
Lena: [*Sighing*] No, not yet. I did receive some compensation, which I filed for under the article for Material Damages—or is it Moral Damages? I can't quite remember which of the two I filed for—it was so long ago.[5] So my attorney was able to get some money for me. My parents still don't know what happened to me.... I am married now and have two children—the oldest is already five.

The court notices still come to my home address. God forbid that anyone finds them at my home. My husband knows what is going on and he gives me all kinds of support. But if, for instance, his mother finds the notices at our house, God forbid—that would really be unpleasant. Even though she really loves me and might be able to understand ... still, I do not want her to know.

Now, my attorney is handling everything—I have no time for it. He says the case is just hanging on and on, that they cannot close the case the way it is. I trust him to deal with it. If he tells me I must appear in court, I will appear in court. But I am just sick of the waiting and not knowing. It has been going on for nine years now. My sister died seven years ago ... [*slight pause*]. Yes ... it has been seven years since she was in that fatal car accident. But her death is the reason I will not give up, why I am still pursuing this case. I want justice for all the things that my trafficker did to us.

The Road to Life kind of keeps my sister alive for me—it keeps us together. When we were enslaved in the brothel, there was one other girl there with us, from Mariupol.[6] All these nine years I have stayed in touch with her. She stayed in Belgium under the witness protection program and now has changed her citizenship to Belgian. She went to school there and found a good job. She recently visited Kharkiv, spending nearly two weeks with me. This is only the second time in nine years that she has returned to Ukraine. But we have become close—like sisters—because of our experience in forced prostitution. We text each other all the time and call each other occasionally. I am lucky to have someone who understands what I went through.

Two years ago, you asked me not to use your information in my book. How do you feel now? If I were to change your name and identifying characteristics, would it be okay to use it now?

Lena: Absolutely, you may use my information. And you don't need to hide my identity. I am not ashamed of what happened to me. My husband knows now. I still don't want my children to know—that is understandable—because it is not very pleasant. But I am not ashamed.

When I meet victims for the first time, they tell me that I can't possibly understand what they went through. Then I share my story with them, unless they are children. The kids I meet that have been trafficked really do not understand yet what happened to them. But, if it is a mature woman, I will tell her everything. Everything changes once they know that I have endured this hell too. We begin communicating in a more open and intimate way. They understand that they can trust me. So, yes, you can use any information you get from me in your book, I am not ashamed of it. I am not screaming it from the rooftops, but I am not ashamed.

Great. Thank you. First, I want to ask about your organization, Road to Life.
Has the 2008 financial crisis impacted your organization? If so, how?

Lena: My work is completely funded by the IOM. I am completing different projects for them. Therefore, the international financial crisis has not really affected the functioning of my organization that much. The crisis has, however, greatly increased the number of victims we encounter.

Before the financial crisis, the banks here were giving out credit right and left without asking for income verification. One could very easily buy a falsified income verification document. I know a lot of people who did that. Then when the market got turned upside down and the economy crashed, people started losing their jobs. A lot of people could no longer make the payments on their loans for apartments or cars. Small amounts they could still pay, but a $500 mortgage payment? Who could make that? So, they were forced to leave their homes. They also had to somehow find jobs somewhere. Many people accepted dubious jobs abroad and ended up trafficked.

In terms of funding for Road to Life, before the crisis the government had no money to give us, and now they still don't give us money. They used to give us a few pennies to fund public lectures, and that kind of thing. But the amount was so small, it was laughable. We hardly notice it is gone. The reason the government gave us so little support is because they claim there is no human trafficking in Ukraine.

But if human trafficking does not exist in Ukraine, how come we have so many victims? We have children who are victims, female victims, male victims, victims of sexual exploitation, victims of labor exploitation, victims forced to beg. That means we have all types of trafficking here. Yet the authorities claim these issues do not exist. They sit in their districts and collect their salaries, but they have no desire to do anything. They say that they do not know of anyone who has gone abroad and gotten trafficked. I know they know better. Pfft. I don't even want to talk about it.

That is why so many people come to us—because state assistance is nonexistent. For example, just this morning—first thing—I got a call from a man. He claims he knows some of the victims in our district that we are helping because he was trafficked with them. He said they all were victims of labor exploitation. He himself was too scared to come in two or three months ago, when the rest of the group came in asking for assistance. He assumed that since we promised the victims some sort of compensation it had to be a trap. He figured that if he came to us, we would sell him again, or something bad would happen to him—maybe we would give him back to his traffickers. When his friends got help and he saw that we didn't demand anything from them, that we helped rehabilitate and reintegrate them, that is when he decided to call us. You see, he finally understood that we were trying to help people get on with their lives. That's it. Nothing more.

Are there a lot more victims now than before the financial crisis?
Lena: [*Sighing*] There have always been large numbers of victims. However, the generation over age 35–40 do not self-identify as victims of trafficking. Despite being exploited, they say, "Oh, nothing special happened abroad." Because of their time under the Soviet Union, they do not know what human rights are. They do not understand that they have the right to fair pay, or the right to recourse if they have been abused. These individuals are extremely afraid of border guards and police—so afraid that they will literally crawl under something to hide. They do not trust the police. I think it all comes from the Soviet period.

Plus, the recruiters understand human psychology very well. Several years ago, before the influence of Western movies and TV, recruiters would tell girls that they could go abroad and find work making *piroshky* [meat-filled pastries], or work in a shop. Then, as we got more exposure to Western media, recruiters started playing on images coming from the West. They began telling girls they could go abroad to be models, or dancers, or actresses. Last year we had a guy who opened a modeling agency here in Ukraine. He had contacts with sheiks in the United Arab Emirates [UAE]. He sent a lot of Ukrainian girls to the UAE for "modeling" jobs, when in reality he sold them to the sheiks or to Arab pimps for sexual exploitation. And it was all legitimate: The agency was licensed by the state, he gave the girls contracts, he arranged for their passports, visas, and travel. Everything was so well done, so organized, that the girls never suspected that they were being sold.

Traffickers exploit the girls' situation here to entrap them. The traffickers know there are no good opportunities here for young women in rural Ukraine, so they tell the girls that if they go to Moscow, they will have a beautiful life, make lots of money, and be their own boss. Or they tell girls that they can get a job in Turkey as a waitress in a fine restaurant, wearing beautiful clothes and making lots of money. Or that they can get jobs as hostesses—that they will just have to accompany rich clients to restaurants. The traffickers and recruiters talk about luxury, wealth, advantages, and opportunities that aren't available here.

Before the financial crisis, individuals went abroad to find more, or better, opportunities. But today it is different. People are leaving because they are desperate. The minute they see a job announcement that resembles something they might be able to do, something they might have the skills for, they jump at it. They don't think that it might be a trap, and they don't care. They leave immediately for that job because they just don't want to lose their apartments. But they lose everything anyway when all their bills become delinquent. We can't help them with their loans. And so, the crisis has affected victims tremendously, but we are working pretty much as we worked before.

When I was here in 2008, I noticed a lot of public announcements and posters warning about human trafficking. I saw advertisements in the metro, in some newspapers, etc. Now I hardly see any. Why is that?

Lena: Well, the public has lost interest in trafficking. Now people are more interested in politics and the economy. For example, if we are planning a big public awareness project we will hold a press conference. We invite journalists, newspapers—they all come. They sit through the press conference and ask questions, but none of them report it. They have lost interest in the subject in general. They seem more interested in writing about political scandals—what authority lost his position, who got thrown in jail, who took a bribe, who is doing what and where, who got caught doing what, and the like. Trafficking issues are no longer interesting to the media.

However, about six months ago our local newspaper, the *Kharkiv Courier*, wrote a huge article on trafficking that took up the entire front page. At the time we were working on a project with the support of the European Union to prevent trafficking of minors. The *Courier* was the only newspaper that covered our work.

Two years ago, the majority of victims were women trafficked for sexual exploitation. Has that changed at all?

Lena: [*Sighing*] When we started working with victims in 2007, I had only females and young boys trafficked for sexual exploitation. There were quite a few young gay boys who got exploited in gay night clubs. Also, some transgender people—"lace girls," if you know what I mean.[7]

In 2007, trafficking caught the media's attention, and the issue roared like thunder all over Ukraine. The news outlets began announcing that boys were being sexually exploited, that men were being transported and trafficked from all over Ukraine. We began seeing victims from all the major Ukrainian cities. But the most victims came from Kharkiv, Lugansk, and Sumska Oblasts.[8] Even though they are still mostly women and girls trafficked for labor or sexual exploitation, we now get more and more men and boys.

Just a few months ago we had a new type of case that we had never seen before. I had one client—a male victim who "got hired" along with several other men by a construction firm. When these guys got to the construction site, the "boss" took their documents and locked them up and posted guards. Their captors forced them to work and beat them. They were trafficked, exploited [*sighing*]. But then, the wife of the banker who owned the construction project selected three of the men for herself. My client was one of those. She took them into a room and demanded that they have sex with her. My client refused, so she had the guards beat him. They beat him quite badly, even knocked his teeth out. After that he realized that he had to perform sex with her or get brutally beaten. She always selected three men—always the tall, handsome ones to service her. The guards gave them Viagra or something to arouse them—they didn't know what it was. Two of the victims are clients here. One is a young man twenty-three years old; the other is more mature—forty-six. So, we treat this as both labor and sexual exploitation.

Dual exploitation like this is becoming more common. There are children too, who are exploited for both sex and labor. I am, right now, starting a case where a mother and her son left the country for a job in Russia. When they got there, the traffickers split them up and sent [them] to different barracks. They forced the boy to do horrible, unspeakable things sexually. Both the mother and the boy were exploited for labor and for sex. The boy was only sixteen years old. It breaks my heart. He is such a handsome young kid, with curly blond hair. It is really frightening how brutally these people get treated.

Are most of your clients trafficked to Russia?[9]

Lena: Yes, a lot of Ukrainians are trafficked to Russia. However, earlier, only Moscow and the suburbs of Moscow were destinations for trafficking. But now, traffickers operate all over Russia. I am working with victims trafficked to the Kursk Oblast,[10] to the Caucasus near Krasnodar,[11] to Rostov—that is where the mother and son were trafficked—and to Belgorod.[12] The geographic area where victims are trafficked to has greatly expanded. Maybe that was always the case, and we just didn't know about it. And many victims who come in for help bring more people with them.

In 2008 I interviewed several victims from Ukraine who were held in train cars in encampments and used as slave labor on large construction projects. These individuals claimed that local authorities were involved directly in keeping them enslaved. Have you encountered this?

Lena: You mean that the Russian authorities are involved in trafficking? Of course. The Russian authorities could clean it all up, dismantle the slave-labor camps in Russia, but no one is doing that because there is so much money to be made. I don't know if the authorities are actually trafficking anyone, but they are clearly benefiting financially from trafficking. There is big money involved, and officials can get paid for looking the other way.

It is not like in America. You know, I was in America for six months in October 2009. I was traveling with the program Open World and sharing my experience. We were in Washington, D.C.[13] I was part of a delegation with representatives from the Ukrainian Ministry of Foreign Affairs and three other NGOs. We visited different American organizations that work with victims of trafficking. I got the impression that it is easier for you in the States. Standing behind you and supporting you, you have a government, as well as nongovernmental organizations, and private donors.

So, in that respect, our situation is much worse. You have support. I saw how your organizations work and how your government helps them. I also saw that there were structures in place so NGOs could receive private donations. We don't have that. We must rely only on international donors. As for private organizations, well thank God we can at least collect books and toys for the orphanage. But the victims themselves bring in those contributions.

Can we talk a little more about your personal experience?

Lena: Of course. As I said, I am not ashamed. I mean, if I could influence even just one human being not to go out of town looking for better earnings, it is worth it.

I was recruited and trafficked to Belgium from Kharkiv. Belgium is a closed country—a kingdom. Who would ever think that such a thing could happen in Belgium? Everyone knows that countries like Turkey are selling people, Russia too, even Italy. Everyone is familiar with forced prostitution in those countries. Most people have heard about trafficking in countries like the United Arab Emirates, Greece, Cyprus, where they have strip-tease bars and prostitution. Or even countries such as Holland or Germany. Everyone knows that trafficking is there and that girls go there to work in peep shows and get trapped in forced prostitution. But who knew that in Belgium such things existed?

Was it just you and your sister who got sold to Belgium?

Lena: No. There was one other girl, Rada, whom I told you about earlier—the one who came and visited me recently. She was trafficked with us. But after she was rescued, she stayed in Belgium and got assistance from a Belgium NGO and now she is living and working there. But so are the traffickers—no one has gone to jail for it yet [*long pause as she traces a chip in her desk with her finger*]. When we were there, in the whorehouse, it was on the Flemish side—Belgium is divided into two sides, Flemish and French. We were on the Flemish side. When Rada got assistance, they moved her to the French side, because her traffickers and johns were still walking around free on the Flemish side. So now she is in a place where she should never accidentally meet them on the street, thank God.

And now ... [*long pause*] now ... she is okay, and I am okay, thank God. As they say, one cannot escape one's destiny, no? I have lived through a lot. But what is most important to me is that I did not get infected with AIDS or HIV or hepatitis.[14] I was able to give birth to two healthy children. However, I did come back with some venereal diseases. It was horrible there, in the whorehouse. But the IOM treated me for the diseases in their center and I got cured.

You know, there is not a single day in these last nine years that I do not recall what happened to me. I understand that my job is a constant reminder. But even without that, I would remember it every day of my life. I cannot erase it from my memory. I remember everything—the beatings, the hunger. They did not give us food very often, so we were literally starving most of the time. So, I am grateful for what I have now.

The man who recruited us here in Kharkiv sold us to traffickers in Holland. He was Ukrainian! Our compatriots sold us to traffickers in Holland! And from Holland, we got sold to Belgium. All those people who were involved in trafficking us in Holland are still walking around free. The traffickers in Belgium are free as well.

Our Belgian traffickers, once they knew we were going to testify against them, began intimidating us. The man who owned me would call me and say, "Lena, don't play with me." He meant that if he wanted to, he could make fake documents again, like they made for us before, implying that he could easily buy and sell me again if I wasn't careful. When we got sold to Belgium, they gave us fake ID cards that we were supposed to show the police in case they showed up.[15] But usually, if they thought the police were coming, they would just hide us in the basement. There was an underground passageway at the whorehouse. Our owners would drag us down there. They seemed to always know when the police were going to come. That was really frightening. I was hoping that the police would find us and rescue us. But every time, the trafficker knew the police were coming and managed to drag us into the basement before we could be found. It was almost as if they were getting notified or something—like someone in the police department was tipping them off.

So, that is why nothing really changed. The traffickers are still trafficking, the recruiter is still free, nothing has changed except my job and now I am helping people. Because all of them are free…. ALL of them who sold and enslaved us!

How did you get home?

Lena: After we were there for about six months, the guy who oversaw the whorehouse allowed my sister and I one phone call to my mother. When no one answered, I called my friend's mother. She told me that my mother had been in the hospital for more than three months. When our owners came to the brothel, I told them I needed to go home because my mom was very sick. I told them to do whatever they wanted to me, I no longer cared what happened to me. I wasn't afraid to ask because I had lost all hope—they could do nothing worse to me. I was crying all the time, and my face was swollen because of the tears. No one wanted to buy me like that. So finally, they said okay, but that only one sister could go and the other must stay. My sister said that I should go because I was younger and had more life ahead of me than she did. But our owners made it clear that if I didn't come back, or if I went to the police, they would kill my sister.

They bought me a train ticket to Kyiv. I had no passport, no documents, no money—nothing but 50 U.S. dollars that they gave me to get from Kyiv to my home in Kharkiv. They dumped me at a train station in Germany and left. I had real problems at the German, Polish, and Ukrainian borders because I had no ID. I just begged the border guards to let me go home until they relented. At the Ukrainian border, they held me for three hours while I was begging them to please let me go home. Finally, they let me go. The train had left already, so I had to take a bus. That is how I got to my mother.

When you found out that your mother was in the hospital, you and your sister had to decide who was going to go home. I can't imagine how difficult that must have been. And then, when you got home, what made you decide to risk your sister's life and go to the police?

Lena: [*Sighing*] Something needed to be done. I decided that death for my sister and me was better than what we were forced to endure every day in the brothel. Yet I was really afraid to go there, to the police station—I thought they would arrest me or humiliate me. Public opinion about our police force is very low. But as it turns out, when I got there, I found out that there was a department that deals specifically with human trafficking. The head of that department spoke with me himself and it was clear that there were people working there who really cared about me as a victim. They all did their best for me. Luckily, the Kharkiv police have a good working relationship with the Belgian police. So, the two police forces coordinated a raid. They arrested all of the traffickers and rescued all of the girls. They took my sister to a local detention center in Belgium where she stayed for some time under the witness protection program. Eventually, my sister came back to Ukraine under the IOM's reintegration program.

I was not hurt by the Ukrainian police; they were great. But what really upset me was the Belgian police. They knew we had been trafficked and were enslaved there. They had all the data. They had surveilled the brothel for months! They could see that we could not leave the premises. They could see that the whole brothel was secured by a laser alarm system and a sound alarm system. And there were periodic checkups by the authorities at that place. We were in some kind of elite brothel that was, in theory, well regulated.[16] They later sold Rada to a horrible place—a really scary brothel in a bar. Things were just horrible there. But even in this "elite" brothel things were awful.

The local police knew that I was kidnapped, they saw me in a surveillance photo after I got beaten up by my owner. It is just that whenever they went to raid the brothel, the traffickers hid us so we couldn't be found.

The traffickers beat you?

Lena: Yes. They beat me very badly, saying I wasn't obeying them. Once, I told them I was not going to service johns anymore. That was my attempt to rebel, to fight back. But nothing came of it, except that they beat me up really badly. The Belgian police knew all this. There was even one time, when we first got there, that the traffickers took us to a store so that we could buy "sexy" things to wear. The police had a picture of us taken from the store's surveillance camera when we first got sold to Belgium. Can you imagine how much torture they could have saved us from if they had intervened at that time?

But, according to Rada, in Belgium everything must be proven absolutely. I guess that Belgian police wanted to find the main trafficker—the one on top who was responsible for all of it before they could raid the brothel and save us. Those who bought us in Holland, they all had fake names. So, it took the Belgian police time to find out who was responsible for arranging our fake documents, and who was handling our documents in Ukraine. That is what I cannot forgive—for seven months of absolute hell, they knew what was happening to us and they did nothing. But the Ukrainian police acted on it when I went to them. They went right to work and got us out of there.

When my sister and I got through our psychological rehabilitation, we started thinking about how hard it is for someone returning from being trafficked to resume normal life. You have a lot of STDs and other medical problems. And you don't know where you can go to get help. You can't really talk to your relatives, or anyone, really. I had no idea how to find a lawyer, or how to get my passport and ID replaced. So, my sister and I decided to start looking for trafficked women and refer them to the IOM, so that they could get assistance. That is how Road to Life got started.

You mentioned that you don't receive any support from any government agency. Where do you get support, personally, to deal all day, every day with such human tragedy? How do you not get continually re-traumatized?

Lena: You know, most of the moral support I get comes from my husband. I have such a great husband. Financially he supports my whole family. He is from a very good, well-to-do family. He wants me to keep doing what I am doing because I am helping others who are going through what I have gone through. If I need to travel somewhere, if I need something for Road to Life, if I need to visit a victim, he supports me.

One time I needed to find an underage female victim who disappeared from the shelter. Dima, my husband, drove me 400 km [248 miles] and spent half a day with me looking for her. When we ultimately found her, she had no belongings, nothing. She lost everything when she was trafficked. She was from a really poor family, so my husband and I bought her everything she needed—underwear, shoes, clothes, everything.

Also, my kids give me strength when it feels like I cannot do this another day. Recently I had this client who was fifty-four when she got sold into slavery. She was exploited sexually and for labor for two years. The things they did to her—unimaginable. A real horror story.

Anyway, the day she came to see me for assistance it was eight o'clock in the evening and I had already processed six new clients that day. I was just leaving the office when she showed up. I was exhausted, but I could not turn her away. I listened to her story for two hours, with tears streaming down my face from the horror of her story and the shock. When we finally finished, I walked home sobbing. I realized that I was unable to control my emotions because I had been through most of that myself. But it happened to me when I was young and healthy. This poor woman, she had been stabbed and had a huge wound. She could not even go back home because she had such serious physical and mental trauma. I knew it would be impossible for her to recover.

When I got home, I was totally drained. I sat for about a half an hour just drinking tea. And then, that was it. My kids needed me, and they demanded my attention. Whenever I am around my children, my focus switches to them. So that day, my kids helped the horrific experiences fade into the background.

I also get a lot of support from the victims themselves. They often volunteer to help me both at work and at home. We get a lot of help and input from victims themselves who have received assistance through our organization. Although I do not expect anything, they have so much gratitude for our organization and compassion that they are eager to help.

Do you see this is a lifetime career?

Lena: [*Laughing*] As long as there is enough money to cover all our bills at home. But yes, this is my calling. I didn't even take maternity leave because I could not abandon these victims. I kept working without interruption because I felt that I simply could not trust my job to anyone. I could not allow someone to hurt the victims the way I was hurt, God forbid. If you look at a victim the wrong way or say something behind their back ... [*long pause*]. It only takes one thoughtless second to damage a person, but they must live with that pain the rest of their lives.

And what do you think about the traffickers? Those who buy and sell people? Or the johns who buy women?

Lena: Oy! What can I think about them? Selling people involves really big money. And everybody wants money. But this is not the way to earn it. If you want money, go and work. But selling people...? And the money is instant because so many people here in Ukraine are desperate to find work. They will jump at anything, so they are easy to recruit and sell.

Men get sold for a lot less money than women. One man can be sold for as little as one hundred U.S. dollars. There were even cases where men were sold for a mere fifty U.S. dollars. But this is usually when the trafficker is selling a large group of people—whole buses of people sold at one time. Women are more expensive, of course, because the traffickers can make more money off them. They cost between US$200 to $500.[17]

Currently we are working on two criminal cases in Germany. Several women got trafficked to three different cities in Germany according to their value. The more beautiful ones were sold to larger cities, and the less sexy ones got sold to smaller cities. In Germany the traffickers have their own way of categorizing and pricing women. One human being can net a trafficker over 2,000 Euros!

Why do people risk it? Why leave home and risk getting trafficked?

Lena: When someone is told that they will make US$2,000 or 1,000 Euros a month, they are thinking that they can go and work for a few months and come back wealthy. But it never happens that way. I understand the young victims who have children—they will risk anything to feed those children. I also understand the victims who owe money on their houses—they needed to pay their loans back. If your child is sick, you need to pay the doctor and buy medicine. This is why people take risks and get trafficked.

Those who are selling people, their motives are clear. Those who get sold, their motives are clear too—they simply want to eat.

Oh yes, and the johns. The most horrible ones are the pedophiles. I don't understand how one can rape a child. Forgive me for saying this, but I wish we had a death penalty for abusing children sexually. I really mean it. I see what happens to children who come out of brothels. This is a very painful subject for me because I have two children of my own.

Those men who buy adult women for sex.... Oy! ... [*pause*]. Well, I should not be the one to judge them. But, you know, those men, the johns, who came to the brothel in Belgium? They had no clue we were slaves, that we were being forced into what we were doing. We were supposed to smile, or we would get a beating. Those men thought that we liked what we were doing because in their country prostitution is a legal industry.

In our brothel the johns were not allowed to be cruel. We didn't have it like some girls in other places that allow all kinds of abusive sex practices—places where the johns could abuse.... [*long pause*] any part of your body. We did not have to have anal sex. We did have to have oral sex, but with a condom for protection. In other words, the johns could not hurt me even more ... [*long, long pause as Lena stares off into space*]. That's what I mean by normal people—thank goodness that they were not allowed to be abusive or cruel.

My friend Rada, on the other hand, told me that in the third place she got sold to the johns could do whatever they wanted to her. It was a horrible place. We did not have that. The pimps could beat us, but not the johns.

And even the pimps would beat us and punish us in ways that did not leave bruises. They did not want to spoil our looks, our marketability. Nevertheless.... [*she stares off into space*].

How do you see your experience of being sold? How do you think about it?
Lena: Well, I see everything that has happened to me as important, because without it I would never have been able to do this kind of work. The most important thing to me is to be able to help people. And as for the victims, I have always said that ... [*deep sigh*] that life goes on, that life has not stopped on that painful moment—even when there is a terrible diagnosis, like AIDS. Fortunately, I have only had a few victims with HIV/AIDS. But life goes on and one needs to keep living. I tell them that they will never be able to forget what they went through, but they can use it to help someone else. They need to remember that no matter what happened to them, if they can warn just one person not to leave the country for a risky job, that might save someone's life.

Of course, it is more difficult for older people. I have some older women who are really having a hard time recovering from their enslavement—a really hard time. And it is impossible to imagine that they would get trafficked. One client was fifty-six years old when she got trafficked. They raped her and forced her into prostitution. After that they handcuffed her and cut her very badly with a knife—she still has a lot of deep scars. And even she says that her life goes on. In general, you can see that we who survived all the human rights violations of the Soviet period, we are survivors. We will survive anywhere, no matter what happens. But you know [*sighing*] there will always be trafficking victims, and if God allows, I will be here to help some of them.

2

Irina Titarenko

Reintegration specialist
NGO: International Organization for Migration (IOM)
Kyiv, Ukraine
November 22, 2008, and October 18, 2010

The return, rehabilitation, and reintegration of trafficking survivors is seldom mentioned in the literature on slavery. Ironically, as horrifying as the abuses and exploitation endured by today's slaves are, there seems to be much less interest in how one recovers from those experiences, if at all. Horrifying tales of kidnap, torture, and rape capture the public's attention, selling books and popular movies. However, the mundane business of trying to patch back together survivors' broken bodies and minds does not seem to be as compelling. Even current anti-trafficking campaigns tend to focus on the "three Ps": prevention; prosecution (of traffickers); and protection (of victims). Yet the other efforts that help ensure the long-term well-being and safety of survivors are much less discussed.[1]

For survivors, long-term recovery and successful reintegration back into some semblance of a normal life depends upon what assistance they get in the early months of their liberation. In this interview, Irina Titarenko discusses the challenges facing victims trying to recover physically, emotionally, and economically from being enslaved and abused. She also discusses the obstacles facing those who provide victim assistance. Having worked directly with victims since 2002, she details some of the abuses suffered by trafficking victims, and highlights changes in victim demographics and traffickers' recruitment strategies over the years. In talking to Irina, it became clear to me that given the right resources and support, many former slaves not only recover from their experiences but manage to create new, successful lives for themselves.

Irina was the first person I spoke with who talked about victims that get retrafficked. I had just assumed that if someone survived being bought and sold, that was the end of it. However, I learned that a significant number of persons get retrafficked. Serious research needs to be done to understand the particulars of secondary trafficking—most of the evidence is anecdotal. But there is consensus among anti-trafficking professionals and organizations, as well as academics, on the seriousness and significance of retrafficking.[2]

There are myriad reasons why a person might get retrafficked. Irina intimated that if a survivor does not get sufficient psychological and economic help, they remain vulnerable to trafficking. Some persons are retrafficked as they try to return to their home country after escaping a situation of enslavement. Others get caught and retrafficked by their original captors. Many victims, still needing to find a way to feed themselves or their families, attempt to migrate for work again and get trapped or duped into slavery again. And some of the people I interviewed who were trafficked at a young age felt like they were ruined already, so why not risk it?

Irina had a wealth of information about trafficking and countertrafficking, and I learned a lot from her. I interviewed her twice—once in 2008 and once in 2010. Each time we met she immediately got down to business. Portions of both interviews are included here.

The first time we met, Irina warmly welcomed me into her office in the IOM building on Mykhailvska Street in Kyiv, Ukraine. As the IOM's reintegration specialist, her job is to find resources and assistance to help rehabilitate and reintegrate trafficked victims once they have been repatriated. My first impression was of a young, hip, professional woman who could have been working in any international setting. She was full of energy, speaking very rapidly and with confidence. She was very professional and engaging at the same time. I liked her immediately. We conducted the interviews in English—her English was flawless while my Ukrainian left much to be desired.

How did you get interested in the field of countertrafficking?

Irina: Let's just say it was chance. I was looking for jobs—for pretty much any opportunity. I didn't really know about trafficking. In the 1990s no one knew much about trafficking—it was hard to believe something like that could happen. Anyway, I was reading newspapers for different types of job offers. In one of them I found a job as some sort of waitress in the Czech Republic. It sounded like fun to me, so I was all ready to go. But I had a child. My mother was supporting us financially at the time because my salary in Ukraine was very low. Also, I kept changing jobs trying to find better opportunities. But every job I found paid so little I could not afford to pay rent and buy food. So, I was looking for any kind of job that paid better and I found this one in the Czech Republic that offered a very good salary. Of course, my mother wouldn't let me go abroad. And it was quite interesting when I got involved in countertrafficking and looked back on that job offer [from] the Czech Republic. I thought, "OH MY GOD!" I was ready to take a job that was very likely a set-up for trafficking. I would have gone there if my mother hadn't stopped me.

I learned later that a friend of mine had been trafficked to Poland. She was sold as a slave to a sewing factory. Her parents found out and were able to send her some money, so that when she managed to escape, she could buy a ticket home. I realized that in the 1990s we were all vulnerable to being trafficked. Believe me, anybody can be a victim of trafficking. No matter what kind of education, no matter what kind of family, no one is immune.

Do you think about your own experience when you're helping women?

Irina: Yes, of course. Many of them, especially those with an education, are ashamed, like "how could this happen to me?" I always tell them that this could happen to me, or to you, or to anybody else. It's simply a matter of one day you make a mistake or something bad happens to you and your life changes in a moment. I mean, it's bad, but you shouldn't be ashamed of it, because you were looking for good things. You were not trying to steal, or to kill; you were simply trying to make enough money to live.

You help with reintegrating women. What are some of the challenges and problems that they face coming back after having been trafficked? When you get a phone call to meet a woman at the airport, for example, what do you do? And what does she have to face?

Irina: In 2002, when I first started working here at the IOM, we had a lot of urgent repatriations. We would meet them at the airport as they first arrived back home. For the last couple of years, however, the numbers of urgent cases like that are really very low. We have a lot of people who manage to come back themselves, and then an NGO identifies them as a trafficking victim. For those that we meet at the airport, first, we tell them about the organizations that will be helping them, and what kinds of services we can provide for them. But it is hard for them to believe that something like that would exist in Ukraine. That somebody would just meet them and help them without wanting something in exchange. They don't really believe there can be free help. They don't trust people. Once, for free, someone "helped" them go abroad for work—a trafficker or a recruiter paid for their travel and arranged their documents. And look what happened to them. So now they can't trust that anyone will actually help them without some kind of catch.

After getting some kind of psychological, medical, and/or financial assistance, they begin to understand that we are not asking for something in return. We don't hold their relatives as collateral or blackmail them. In time, they begin to trust us.

We have a lot of clients who were exploited for labor. The first thing they want to do is look for a job. But considering what kind of experience they had when they were trafficked, they usually need some kind of medical help first. When you consider the sort of pain that they have, the kind of health problems they have, and their emotional trauma, they cannot be integrated or employed just anywhere. Most victims suffer from PTSD symptoms—headaches, stomach problems, and the like. So, the first thing we do is get them medical and emotional treatment, and then we can deal with all the rest of the issues, like finding employment.

How long does rehabilitation and reintegration usually last?
Irina: Typically, victims need at least one year of medical and psychological assistance. Even if they manage to get home but don't find out about our program for some time, they still need about one year of assistance. However, if a long period of time passes between when they get back home and when they receive some help, then it is much harder to rehabilitate them—they become chronic cases. It's easier to treat them right after they come home than if they wait for a period of years.

The first three months are the most difficult for the client because any psychological process usually re-traumatizes them. It also takes a lot of time to come up with an individual reintegration plan. During this period most victims simply don't know what to do. They can't look to the future, because they have no idea what they are going to do. The reintegration plan must be very flexible, because one day they want this, tomorrow they will want something else.

Initially, the NGOs that assisted victims provided medical, psychological, and financial assistance. But it became clear that if victims' circumstances don't change, they are vulnerable to retrafficking. So, the NGOs began giving vocational training but it's case-by-case. We have an individual approach for each client. Some of the victims first need legal assistance, much more than perhaps psychological assistance. Sometimes they need more family support—it just depends on their trafficking experience. It also depends upon how psychologically healthy they were to begin with. Some of them can be reintegrated in three months, four months, but most will require one year, some require up to three years. Many of them, after about six months, don't want to continue with us—they feel strong enough to move on and don't want to see anyone who reminds them of what happened to them.

We never push them to talk to us. If they feel they are done with our services, then they are done. However, we try to monitor minors for a longer period, to make sure nothing bad happens to them again. We also try to monitor their families. Quite often victims suffer post-traumatic stress syndrome, depression, nightmares, and suicidal thoughts.

The educational level of some of our clients is quite high. We've had a university professor who was sent into slave labor in Russia. Many of our clients are teachers and medical professionals. The salaries for professionals here in Ukraine are low, and so they travel abroad and end up trafficked. When they come back, it is very difficult for them to return to their professions, especially if they have been through sexual exploitation. It is difficult for some of them to come back to teach children, for example, because they feel like they are dirty. In the case of labor exploitation, most victims we encounter were treated like slaves, or worse—not even treated like human beings. When they come back to Ukraine, they try to find work as soon as possible, because they have no money.

We try to provide them with some ability to generate an income, but we can't afford to give all of them vocational training. Besides, many individuals don't even know what to do. Now we also have a program that helps some clients start very small enterprises, which is fantastic. However, not everyone has sufficient educational background to qualify for this program. They must first prove they are really serious so that we don't waste time and money. They go through very rigorous training and must produce detailed business plans before we can approve them. We are very proud of this program—few NGOs can provide this kind of training.

How has reintegration changed since you started in 2002?

Irina: Reintegration started in 2001, and it hasn't changed much. Victims have changed. Now they are looking more and more for training that can give them a job as soon as possible. More of them want to work for themselves because it is difficult to find jobs. More and more victims are applying for legal assistance, too. Some of them plan to testify against their traffickers and some of them sue their traffickers for civil damages. So, we are helping them find more legal counsel.

Is that changing because NGOs are becoming more effective at letting people know they have legal rights? Or is it a function of more awareness of civil society by the citizens?

Irina: I cannot really say that people are more aware of their rights. It's very difficult for victims to prove that they were exploited. Their legal counsel is more to show them how to initiate a legal case, for example how to send letters to get official answers. They're still afraid of the police, but they are more willing to cooperate with law enforcement if they can benefit from it. One of the first things that NGOs do is inform clients that they have legal rights. We show them what paths they can take, and who can help them. If the trafficked person can provide phone numbers and information about traffickers and recruiters, it will help their case. We can direct them to the right department, like counter-trafficking, rather than let them just walk into a police station and try to get assistance.

Ukraine is quite a big country, and we simply cannot know what is happening to all the victims. Plus, we have an increasing number of clients so we cannot physically visit all of them. That's why from the beginning we created a system of NGOs that worked with each other—like an NGO net. They identify victims from their regions and refer other victims to the appropriate organizations. These NGOs have different programs than IOM, like HIV recovery programs, or programs aimed specifically to help victims of forced prostitution, etc.

We've realized that we cannot do everything by ourselves. In some regions, doctors have been trained to identify victims of human trafficking, and to refer them to the appropriate NGOs. It really is like a net. Nonetheless, we still have gaps and difficulties. In some regions the employment centers are cooperative, and some not. In some areas counter-trafficking units are fantastic, while others are not good at all.

We heard that there are camps in Russia where they keep hundreds of slaves from Ukraine and Moldova living in train cars and exploited for labor. In these cases, the government is somewhat complicit. Have you heard of this?

Irina: Yeah, we've had several such cases. But when we have tried to contact the police to find these people and these camps, the camps suddenly disappear. We think somebody from the police department must leak the information to the traffickers because the criminals seem to know in advance when the police are looking for the camps. There are places where a lot of people are held as slaves for labor exploitation. Some of the women there also must provide sex for the guards or other workers. Some individuals who managed to escape said that they were treated extremely brutally. They were basically fed garbage and threatened with attack dogs. They were also beaten, sometimes in front of the others. We received reports from one of these camps that one girl just disappeared because she caused too many problems for the traffickers.

Another horrific situation occurred in the United Arab Emirates. One girl delivered a baby in the brothel, and as it got older they took its teeth out [*pause*] ... to provide [*long pause*] ... on purpose ... for ... let's say, um, well you know ... [*her voice drops*] oral sex. In that same brothel one group of girls had to provide sex to single clients. Other groups of women were forced to service up to twenty men at one time. Some women were forced to have sex while being filmed for pornography to be posted on the internet.

Does Ukraine have a good relationship with the United Arab Emirates? If you get a call from somebody enslaved there, is it easy to get help for him or her?
Irina: No. We have good working relationships with Turkey and Russia.[3] Because Russia is such a large country, if we call one department, they call another in the region. But it doesn't always work that well. Nonetheless, they try to identify the victims, their locations, and try to get them back to Ukraine. Turkey is also good, especially because they have an effective trafficking hotline. When victims call this hotline, they get rescued very quickly. Turkey has a human trafficking police unit standing by ready to rescue people. So, it's good if a victim can call, especially if the victim knows his or her location.[4]

We also have a good cooperative relationship with Italy. If a woman identifies herself as a victim, the Italians immediately work to help her even without an investigation to prove she was actually trafficked. Some countries are difficult to work with—they don't understand human trafficking. They see exploited women as prostitutes and blame the victims. It takes time to work with these countries. For example, in 2002, we had our first victim from Uzbekistan. She was trafficked first to Turkey and then got deported to Ukraine. In Ukraine, a Moldovan trafficker recruited her and trafficked her to Moldova. The Uzbek Embassy was not cooperative at all. Their attitude was, "Why should we work to help this prostitute?" Many other countries are just as uncooperative.

Prior to the collapse of the Soviet Union in 1992, it is believed that trafficking, as we understand it today, didn't exist in the USSR. However, I'm beginning to learn that people were in fact trafficked within the Soviet Union. Have you encountered any cases of internal domestic trafficking during the Soviet period?
Irina: I remember one case of a man from Donetsk who was trafficked to Kazakhstan, but I don't remember when he was trafficked.[5] He spent decades in Kazakhstan. That is the only one that I can remember.

Why do you think cases of human trafficking from this part of the world exploded as soon as the Soviet Union collapsed? Almost overnight,

thousands of persons were trafficked from the former Soviet republics. Why do you think that is?
Irina: When the Soviet Union broke apart in the early 1990s a lot of people left. First, they didn't know what to do or where to go. The economic situation then was dire. There was nothing in the stores, you could not buy anything, and no one had any money. It was really a perfect time for trafficking to flourish because it was so easy to recruit victims. If you were told that you could make US$5,000 to US$9,000 picking apples abroad, let's say—well, even I would have gone. People didn't understand that those kinds of wages were unrealistic. But back then there were no options or opportunities at home and people were willing to work anywhere doing anything.

In the case of the man from Donetsk who was trafficked to Kazakhstan, I think he went first to Russia in 1975. At the beginning he was simply a migrant worker, but then he was sold. I can't remember why he went to Kazakhstan, but I think somebody from Russia sold him there. He worked in Kazakhstan for so many years that now he really is quite old. When his family in Ukraine learned that he was a slave, they offered to take care of him. So now he is living with them, back in Donetsk.

But even in the last years of the Soviet era, from about 1990, the borders opened, and a lot of people crossed them trying to find a better life. Before that it was always difficult to get out of the USSR because the KGB had thousands of informers that would report you for trying to leave. Also, the Soviet regime prohibited the average citizen from leaving, except perhaps to go to another Soviet Bloc country. But after about 1990 you could just pay a fee or bribe a border guard and cross the border. Even other people could pay for you—it was that easy.

There were also a lot of Western movies, like *Pretty Woman*, that glamorized sex work that suddenly became available in the Soviet Bloc. Such movies made prostitution seem romantic and glamorous. Thousands of young girls aged sixteen or seventeen began to dream about marrying nice, rich men, who would really take care of them, like they saw in the film *Pretty Woman*. Maybe they would have to be a prostitute for a little while, but then they would meet a Prince Charming.

From 1998 to 2000 it was mainly women and girls who were trafficked, and mainly for sexual exploitation. Even before that some people would find work abroad and end up sexually exploited. Single mothers had to find some way to pay their debts and feed their children, so they were willing to take risks. In Donetsk, for example, I had several cases of girls exploited for sexual purposes in Russia. One girl was promised that in one year she would make enough money to buy an apartment back home in Ukraine. Plus, her recruiter told her it was likely that she would meet somebody who really loved her and would buy her a lot of beautiful things. This girl's father was raping her at home, so she really wanted to leave. But what she was promised and what actually happened are very different stories.

The recruiters tell the girls that this is a lot like dating—if you want to go with the john, then you can; if you don't want to, you don't have to. But actually, it isn't like that at all. And now all the wishes and dreams of these young girls are ruined. When you hear their stories, you realize that, even though they didn't have a good life before, their life is even worse after being trafficked. And we never know if they are going to be retrafficked or exploited by their own families.

* * * *

At this point, Irina had to end the interview to attend to a client needing her attention. We agreed that if I could return, she would let me interview her again. As luck would have it, I was able to return not quite two years later. I was happy to see her again. She had not changed, but was the same keen, clear, stylish woman I met in 2008. This interview takes place in October 2010 in Irina's same office in the IOM building in Kyiv.

Hello! So very good to see you again. Has much changed regarding trafficking since we last spoke two years ago?

Irina: Last year, the IOM got funding for a project that focused on identifying and finding minors who have been trafficked. In one year, we have already identified 110 minors. Most of them were trafficked to Russia or within Ukraine. This project works with governmental agencies because we cannot provide services to any underage children without the consent of their guardians or parents. So now, all levels of government are dealing with trafficked children. At first, government agencies did not understand trafficking and did not believe that this was happening to children in Ukraine. Between six and nine months after our new project was launched, they had to accept that children really are being trafficked in Ukraine. And now they are ready to work with us to help these children.

Congratulations! This is good news.

Irina: Yes. Thanks. The whole process of trafficking has changed a little. For all types of trafficking, the destination countries are changing. Russia is the number one destination, followed by Poland and the Czech Republic. And internal trafficking is growing in all those countries.

Also, the length of time a person is enslaved is changing. In the beginning, the period of exploitation was quite long, especially if it was sexual exploitation. Girls would come back with no money, having been enslaved abroad for sometimes several years. Now the traffickers try to obscure the fact that they are trafficking these women. They force the women into sexual exploitation for only two to three months, while the women's visas are still valid in the destination country. The traffickers also now pay the women a little money, like US$150. This way, the victims will not identify themselves as victims of trafficking because they were paid, no matter how little. So, when the traffickers send them back home, the women think, "Okay, I was raped, cheated, and exploited. I was trapped but finally they sent me home and paid me." The fact that they got money makes the situation a little more sensitive for us to identify, because if you ask them if they were paid, they will say yes. But if you ask them how much money they made, or why did they not come back earlier, it becomes clear that they were enslaved. Their traffickers did not allow them to leave until their visas were almost expired and paid them almost nothing.

The same is true of labor exploitation. We have had many cases of men trafficked for labor exploitation in construction. But beginning in 2009, we started getting clients who were enslaved in shipping or fishing. With these individuals it is also difficult to identify, because one of the main indicators of labor exploitation is the lack of freedom of movement. And how can you talk about being held captive if you're on a ship at sea? For them it is more difficult to identify whether they were victims of trafficking, or if they were just cheated. So, we have to ask different questions. But these guys do not like to self-identify as victims. I mean, seamen think of themselves as strong men, and for them to come and ask for even a small amount of help is very hard. It's also more difficult to reintegrate them because they cannot change their jobs. It seems to them that this only happened once, so how can we tell them not to go back? We try to teach them how to check information about different countries. We also advise them to memorize the hotline number in case they need to call. Although usually they call the ITF [the International Transport Workers' Federation] in Britain. I think it's something like a trade union for seamen.[6] We have had six cases of trafficking referred to us from the ITF.

With all of your experience dealing with people who have been trafficked, can you talk about what happens to a person's sense of self after such an experience?

Irina: Not all of them will accept that they need psychological assistance because for Ukrainians it is not common to seek psychological help. We usually only seek psychological help when we know we have had some kind of extreme psychological disorder or severe mental illness. So, if it is something "normal" like depression—everybody get[s] depression—we keep it to ourselves. It is just not part of our culture. This makes it harder to reintegrate victims. They feel very uncomfortable talking to psychologists. It's even more difficult for Ukrainian men to accept that they need a psychologist. That's why it is good to provide them psychological and medical treatment together, like we do in the patient therapy center. There, they get individual psychological counseling and group therapy. However, outside of Kyiv it's more difficult to provide psychological assistance. Most victims come from small villages or towns, but the main offices of the NGOs are situated in the provincial capitals. For many individuals, it is difficult to pay for transportation in order to travel from their village to a therapy center. Sometimes it may take several hours to drive to the NGO for psychological counseling. Most victims will not do it.

So, can I ask you some personal questions about yourself? How do you keep going? What supports you?

Irina: In Kyiv, it's not that difficult. I work with survivors in the repatriation center. They are already getting assistance. But I generally don't work with them where they live, or see their towns, or meet their families. However, sometimes I will go to various regions to monitor how clients are doing and get to see clients where they live. With children it is extremely difficult, especially when you see children who've been brutalized and traumatized and who continue to suffer because of what happened to them. Sometimes they are in government group homes or orphanages, which are not the best places for kids. Sometimes those institutions are not well equipped even for basic needs. When I see those children, it breaks my heart. That's why I ask my colleagues to go there—so I don't have to. It is just too hard on me.

Every time I come from these monitoring trips I tell my husband, "Let's adopt a child." I just learned that there are five-year-old twin girls who were sold by their mother to Russia. I can never understand how parents can do this. I mean, how can they exploit their own children? Sell them like pieces of furniture? So, I came home really wanting to adopt these two girls and raise them as my own children. With the children, the stories are much more difficult to handle than with a grownup.

Some cases are very difficult, like a recent victim of trafficking whom I visited. She has HIV, hepatitis, and a newborn baby. This woman will not live more than five years and her child will be quite young when the mother dies. The grandmother is an alcoholic, and it is obvious that there is no one else who can take care of this child or support it.

Another time I went to where one of our clients was dying. I don't remember what kind of sickness she had, but she was lying there like a log. She had been beaten severely in Italy and the trauma triggered some kind of brain disorder. She went to work in Italy in order to help pay for her children [to] go to university. This case happened in 2004, I think, and I went to see her in 2006 or 2007. Some Ukrainians had helped her get back home, but by that time she already had some severe physical disorders related to the trauma. The doctors said her brain was getting smaller and drier, but she didn't understand. By the time I saw her, she was simply alive, and that's all. Sometimes she'd open her eyes. But it was not a psychiatric disorder. It was some kind of physical degeneration because of the beatings she endured.

How did you find her?
Irina: How we identified her as a victim of trafficking was through a local NGO. Her mother had heard about an NGO that helped trafficking victims. So, the mother went to the NGO, because the victim couldn't talk. In fact, those people who brought her back from Italy told the mother her story. It was awful, because this old lady, the mother, who is nearly ninety years old, is taking care of her forty-something daughter who can no longer talk or even feed herself. Until we got involved, it was just the victim and the old lady—there were no doctors or nurses helping, simply because they had no money. I mean it was awful. Unbelievable.

How do you deal with all of that? You personally?
Irina: I have colleagues I talk to about difficult cases. Also, I try not to take it home with me. My husband is supportive, but I don't think he really understands so I don't really discuss any details about my work at home. From time to time the kind of work I do does come up with friends. And my husband will say, "Come on! You're actually helping prostitutes." And I say, "*Excuse me?*" I mean, sometimes you run into someone who used to be a prostitute in Ukraine, but then she gets trafficked. She is sexually abused or exploited, and not paid, and beaten. When she comes back home it's difficult to prove that she was a victim of trafficking—that she is *not* a prostitute. I don't know why he…. I mean, I thought that my husband understood everything! They're not prostitutes.

What was really funny was that when he saw one of those human-trafficking movies—I think it was an American movie called *Human Trafficking*—he asked if I was helping *those* kinds of people. I said, "Congratulations!" He finally understood. It shows me that we should work more in prevention and education, telling your neighbors, or parents, that their child could become a victim of trafficking. Then perhaps people will be more supportive and consider that someone they meet *might* be a victim of trafficking. It's important to make people understand that this could happen to anybody.

I remember a woman in her forties who was completely surprised when this happened to her. She went to the Balkans on business, at Christmas. She went there to buy some kind of Christmas stuff to bring back here to sell. She went to the market, and it was closed. So, she decided to go back to her hotel. She hailed a taxi, and the driver took her right to a brothel. The traffickers were waiting and forced her into prostitution. When she managed to get back home, she still could not believe that this could happen to her. She said, "I have a twenty-year-old daughter. I am a mother. I am forty years old. How could this happen?" She could not understand it.

One of the things that I am encountering is that older and older women are getting trafficked. Even women in their fifties are used as slave labor during the day, and then exploited sexually at night. Have you encountered this?

Irina: We have a lot of labor exploitation combined with sexual abuse. We try to separate it, but it is mixed exploitation. We don't have statistics on this, but it's quite a big number. Sometimes women exploited for labor are raped once by their owners or guards. Sometimes it is constant sexual abuse. During the day they must work in the field or some other place, and during the night they are forced [to] provide sex for the guards, for example. As labor exploitation becomes more prevalent, we see more and more cases where a person is also sexually exploited. Earlier we didn't have that many cases of labor exploitation.

Why do you think more people are getting trafficked to Russia now?

Irina: I don't know. First, many people in eastern Ukraine still consider Russia their nation. I mean, they speak Russian and believe that the people in Russia live better. When they go to the Crimea on summer vacation, prices there are very high, and the level of service is very low. A lot of people from Russia go there—they can afford it. But for Ukrainians it is very expensive. Some people think that in Russia there must be well-paid jobs, so they want to go there. A Ukrainian can go to Russia without a visa. It is not like a European country where one doesn't know the language, and it's more expensive to buy food, or whatever. It seems safer, somehow, in Russia. However, the police in Russia are actually harsher. If you get caught without an official registration, they take you immediately to prison. And then you're deported. No questions asked. Nothing. Just "get out."

Girls who get trafficked to Russia suffer horribly. These girls endure all kinds of torture there. I mean johns, or traffickers, or guards do all kinds of horrible things. I don't understand how they can do these things. They must have some mental disorder. They pee or defecate on the girls. They beat them and put their heads into the toilet. How can a person with a normal psychology do this to anybody? When they see a person crying or suffering, it irritates them even more. Maybe this makes them feel important. I don't really understand how these people can live knowing what they are doing to others just to make money. Because it is not just the victims who suffer. The traffickers, too, have to somehow live with this and survive it, knowing how they abused and tortured people who trusted them. They know what they are doing, and they know it will catch up to them someday.

What happens to the women who come back pregnant?

Irina: You know, I don't really know how many have abortions. I know of ten girls, for sure, who came back pregnant and have children now. Maybe more, but I don't see everybody. I know a couple of girls who had abortions once they got rescued, and I know that traffickers or pimps often force women to have abortions. Some of our clients had abortions after they began receiving assistance from us, but I do not know exact numbers. Some women gave birth in the brothel and gave the child to the father, the john, thinking that he would be able to give the child a better life. I know a couple of girls who had babies and who maintain a relationship with the john. Who knows? Maybe in the future the john will act like a father to the baby. Sometimes these girls manage to find other men to take care of them and their child.

We also try to educate our female clients about what a healthy relationship looks like. If they have been beaten in their families, and then the traffickers beat them, they consider it normal to be beaten based on their experience. And if they are desperate to have a john or some other man take care of them and their child, they are even more vulnerable. So that's why our psychologists or psychotherapists try to help them understand that violence is not love.

After someone is reintegrated, then what? They've had this experience, but they still must go on living. How do they do it? A repatriation expert in Moldova once told me that there are no happy endings. Is that true in your experience?

Irina: You know, it depends upon their circumstances. You do work in Moldova too, right? From the very beginning, Ukrainian victims have very different profiles than those from Moldova. In Moldova, most victims are from rural areas, with little or no education. Here in Kyiv we have victims with university degrees, and the level of education is much higher. Moldovan victims are mainly young ladies between the ages of eighteen and twenty-five. We have women from twenty-five up to forty years old, so we have a completely different demographic. We have a lot of clients who were trafficked while looking for professional jobs, not looking for work as dancers, or waitresses, or prostitutes. We are more successful at reintegrating people who have a higher level of education and some professional training.

I once went to see a girl who had just returned home from being trafficked. She was seventeen or eighteen years old. This was several years ago. When I saw her, she was not doing well at all. One of my colleagues saw her a year later and told me that she was fantastic—so beautiful and confident. I couldn't figure out how she managed to recover so quickly. I know that we bought her equipment for hairdressing courses, and then provided her with money to pay for the courses. Not long ago she visited our offices, and she really *was* fantastic. Her life is great. Now she has her own shop. We have a lot of good stories about both women and men who make successful recoveries, especially those we can help with micro grants for small enterprises. This really helps them a lot. It's not just funding for a car, or groceries, it really aids them in growing a business.

We have another guy who is forty-five or fifty years old. When I first saw him, he looked like a beaten-down worker. But now he is tall and handsome, working as a construction instructor—teaching guys how to build things. After his trafficking experience he became addicted to alcohol for a while. He told me that recently he renovated his house, which is quite old—from Soviet times. He told me that he did it all himself—all the renovation and he made all the furniture. So, we helped him with a micro enterprise to make furniture, like a small workshop. He stopped drinking and is now fairly successful. I sat on a sofa he made, and I was thinking, "Oh my God! And he is a victim of trafficking?" I mean, I bought my own sofa, and it is a rag! [*Laughs.*] His stuff is high-quality work.

Another time this girl came in, well dressed, quite confident. At first, I thought she was from the government to meet with us. But then I realized that she was one of our clients, a survivor of trafficking. Sometimes it is hard to tell who is and who isn't a former victim once they have been successfully reintegrated. One girl had a university degree in economics before she was trafficked. We helped her open an accounting agency. When you talk to her, it is clear that she has a high level of education and intelligence. You would never know that something dreadful happened to her.

Of course, these people already had some good relationships and work experience, maybe families, and a place to live. So, as you can see, there are some happy endings. Some people are able to reintegrate successfully. It all depends upon the level of support they have, and their inner resources.

3

SVETLANA LALETINA
AND SVETLANA BAZHENOVA

Rehabilitation specialists
NGO: Victims of Human Trafficking Assistance Center
Vladivostok, Russia
September 27, 2010

According to the U.S. State Department Trafficking in Persons Report (TIP), over a million people are living as slaves in Russia. With the number of slaves so high, one might assume that the Russian state would be very motivated to engage in, and support, anti-trafficking work. But that is not the case. Far from being a moral or human rights issue, in Russia human trafficking is highly politicized and contentious. Political scientist Laura Dean points to the lack of policies related to human trafficking, the number of laws passed that aim at closing shelters for trafficking victims, and the promotion of government-sponsored media that politicize trafficking to argue that the Russian government sees human trafficking as layered in political controversies.[1] Indeed, Russia passed its first, and only, legislation regarding human trafficking in 2003. And since 2003, all the other former Soviet republics have passed multiple laws that address new forms of trafficking, or as new information about human trafficking is revealed. Now Russia finds itself alongside Iran, Congo, Libya, North Korea, and Zimbabwe (among others) as a Tier 3 country.[2]

These findings were confirmed by the 2023 TIP Report, which noted a Russian government pattern of forcing thousands of North Korean workers into work camps and exploiting them as slave labor. Since Russia's full-scale invasion of Ukraine in 2022, the Russian government has also engaged in trafficking Ukrainian citizens into a sprawling system of filtration camps and detention camps that include forced labor. There have also been credible reports that Russian officials are forcing and coercing foreign nationals, including children, to fight in Russia's war against Ukraine.³

The 2023 TIP Report also noted that the Russian government engaged in conduct that made certain populations highly vulnerable to trafficking. Most notably, the government separated thousands of Ukrainian children from their parents and forcibly transferred them to Russia. Further, Russia's targeting of civilian populations spurred millions of women and children to flee Ukraine for Europe, leaving them vulnerable to human trafficking.⁴

Russians who were enslaved abroad and then returned home, either by escape, rescue, or release, find a serious lack of support. Because the government is ambivalent at best about human trafficking, anti-trafficking NGOs and victim assistance shelters receive little to no funding or support. Shelters that opened under the auspices of an international agency closed as soon as they tried to transfer operations to Russian control. Between 2006 and 2012, nearly all anti-trafficking NGOs and victim assistance shelters closed due to lack of state support.⁵ Then in 2012, Vladimir Putin approved a law that required international NGOs to register as foreign agents, thus paving the way for the expulsion of internationally funded organizations engaged in anti-trafficking work, including the United States Agency for International Development (USAID). But even before the passage of the law, all shelters save one in Vladivostok had already been closed.

I wanted to go to Vladivostok for a variety of reasons. My attempts to investigate human trafficking by meeting with survivors and NGOs in Moscow led to numerous dead ends. Moscow was too close to the political center, and most of the anti-trafficking NGOs had already been closed or kicked out of the capital cities. I thought that if I could get far enough away from Moscow and St. Petersburg, I would stand a better chance of finding people who were willing to talk to me. Since the last shelter for trafficking victims left in Russia was in Vladivostok, I was very interested in how they managed to stay open. Also, I knew that Vladivostok, being a port city very near the Chinese, Korean, and Japanese borders, was an important point of origin, transit, and destination for human trafficking.

Many of my interviewees in Ukraine claimed that there existed whole settlements or camps full of slaves near Vladivostok. In 2010 it was estimated that over 40,000 men and women from North Korea were used as slave labor in the logging industry. The North Korean regime provided contract labor for logging camps operated by North Korean companies in the Russian Far East. These North Korean companies paid workers less than 15 percent of the agreed-upon wages—if at all—and the workers were not free to leave.⁶ Also, many tens of thousands of Russians were enslaved and exploited in the Far East, especially in agriculture and fishing. Thousands of women from Russia were sold into sexual slavery to China, South Korea, and Japan via Vladivostok, and many tens of thousands of Central Asians have been trafficked and enslaved in Russia's Far East.[7] If any region needed a victim assistance center, it was Vladivostok.

From Moscow to Vladivostok is a little over eight hours by plane. Before I left Moscow, I spoke with Ludmila Erokhina, the head researcher at the Center for Studies on Organized Crime in Vladivostok. She arranged for me to interview Svetlana Bazhenova, the chief executive of the Far Eastern Center for Development of Civic Initiative and Social Partnership, and Svetlana Laletina, both of whom had worked with the Victims of Human Trafficking Assistance Center since it opened in 2009.

In this interview my two informants discussed opening the shelter and how they hoped to make it sustainable. They also talked about being so close to the relatively porous Chinese border and how that fuels a steady flow of migrants and exacerbates human trafficking and slavery in the area. Further, they were in a unique position to illuminate government complicity in slave labor in the region. Borderlands the world over are ripe hunting grounds for traffickers. The two Svetlanas detailed why that is, and how thousands of people are tricked into slave labor in their region every year. They also talked at length about how national diasporas feed the slave trade.

Both Svetlanas graciously agreed to meet me at my friend's apartment, saving me the trouble of trying to find my way around the maze of streets on the hills of Vladivostok. The city calls itself "the San Francisco of Russia" for good reason. Sitting on a hilly peninsula overlooking the Sea of Japan, Vladivostok historically was—and is—an exciting frontier town. Founded as a military port in 1860, it rapidly grew to become an important cultural and economic center of the Russian Far East, despite its status as a "closed city" during Soviet times. In 2010 it remained a vibrant cultural and economic hub, with a population of 750,000, mostly Russians and Ukrainians.

Svetlana Laletina (S.L.) arrived first, and we sat drinking tea in my friend's sunny kitchen atop a hill that overlooks the bay. Svetlana Bazhenova (S.B.) did not know how late she would be, so we decided to start the interview without her.

If you find a victim of trafficking here in Vladivostok, what would happen first? For example, if a woman said, "I am from China and I have been trafficked," what happens?

S.L.: The first thing we would do is to go to the police. If they determine that she came here on her own in order to work, then the authorities would deport her immediately. But if it turns out that she has been trafficked—if she has been beaten or raped, or forced to have sex—then she may need some medical help. In that case, the authorities would put her in a rehabilitation center here. They would also launch an investigation to determine what happened to her. After that, they would either give her documents allowing her to stay in Russia or deport her. Most often it ends in deportation. But I am not certain. We'll have to ask Svetlana Bazhenova. I don't know of any cases where a Chinese woman was allowed to stay.

We have an interesting history in this area with Chinese migrants. Before the Bolshevik Revolution in 1917, there were many brothels with Chinese and Korean women here in Vladivostok. There were whole quarters of the city like that, with Chinese brothels. Under Nicholas II [1868–1918], the last Russian tsar, one of his ministers came here to Vladivostok. He published a report titled "The Yellow Threat" [*Zheltaya Ugroza*], about the relationship between Russia and China. The report claimed that thousands of Chinese crossed the border, legally and illegally, to live in Vladivostok. They worked mainly in construction and in laundries. A few had their own businesses, and of course many were prostitutes.

Under the Soviets [1918–1992], Vladivostok was a closed city. Not just anyone could buy an airplane ticket and simply fly here. And for foreigners, there were really strict restrictions on who could come to, or stay in, Vladivostok. So, for several decades there was practically no Chinese presence here.

My husband grew up here and he studied in a Chinese school—one of our schools teaches Chinese languages and cultures, and that is where my husband went. He told me that when he was a schoolboy, they had a little Chinese museum in their classroom that had only three Chinese objects in it [*laughing*]. That's it—three things. And that was considered a museum! And there was only one actual Chinese person in the entire school—he was the one who taught Chinese language. The restrictions against foreigners were so rigid that Chinese were not allowed in Vladivostok for any reason—not even to teach at a Chinese school!

I was born here in the Primorsky krai.[8] I lived in a village right on the Chinese border. There was a border patrol unit station in my village. When I was a kid, I crossed the border into China several times. The border patrol would let us kids climb up in their tower and use their binoculars to look at Chinese people. We would wave at them, and some of them would wave back [*laughing*]. And that was the only contact we had with China.[9] That is, throughout the 1970s and 1980s we never saw a Chinese person up close. Not until the 1990s, with the collapse of the Soviet Union, did that border open. Then the Chinese poured in.

Very rarely do the Chinese come here out of desperation. They are mostly trying to make money to send home. They don't want to register here legally, which would allow them to become permanent residents. Nonetheless, they work in construction, and they trade in the local markets. But they are vulnerable since they are here illegally.

[At this point, Svetlana Bazhenova (S.B.) arrived and joined the conversation.]

S.B.: I have been working in the field of human trafficking since 2002, mostly in prevention of sex trafficking of women. When I started in 2002, we did not have a systematic approach to identifying victims and offering them protection and assistance. We simply did not have the opportunity to develop such a program because the authorities denied that trafficking existed. They said there were not many cases of trafficking, and in general they blamed it on the victim. They argued that the victims cross a border on their own and then get into trouble: "Who forced them anyway?" and "Why did they go in the first place? *They* all know where this is going to end." Well, these were the kinds of attitudes we had to work with.

At first, we worked on projects financed by the USAID and other international agencies.[10] Those projects focused on spreading information about human trafficking and increasing the economic self-sufficiency of women in small villages and towns. Nonetheless, when we began talking about the problem of human trafficking, local authorities would tell us different "stories," claiming that trafficking did not exist.

And of course, we had cases where victims came to us for help. But at that time, we could not provide them with much more than just some psychological help. However, in 2006 we had a regional event that focused on human trafficking and that began to change our local administration's ideas about slavery. For that event, specialists came from all over the world, and we had a huge international forum on how to stop human trafficking. It was entirely funded by our regional administration.

We had representatives from the United States, and from Korea, Japan, and China. At the end of the event, we drew up a resolution that committed us to taking several actions to address trafficking in the region. That resolution subsequently attracted some serious international funding so that we could start assisting victims of trafficking.

Last year [2009] we opened a small shelter for trafficking victims. It was created as a state institution, so that if international funds run out, we can still get state funding. So, it is sustainable. In fact, our grant ran out in December, but the shelter still exists.[11]

We also have a state-run Primorsky Center for Social Services that has branches all over our region [Primorsky krai]. It provides help to women with children who find themselves in difficult circumstances. The

Center provides counseling services, works with children, assists with domestic problems, helps women with divorce issues, and helps people find work—those sorts of things. We worked very closely with this Center, training its staff.

The only question now that the regional administration needs to address is where to find the money for all this. They do have some money—enough to pay the employees and run the shelter. But not quite enough to feed these victims or provide them with special medical assistance, or to buy them clothes. This kind of assistance the regional administration cannot afford. But we haven't lost hope. I know that IOM has enough money to finance this project for the next eighteen months. So, we have been waiting since January [2010] to hear from the regional administration how they will finance us after that.

For the last year and a half we have also been working with the Primorsky Center, and with other rehabilitation centers and state institutions, to identify children who have been trafficked and to get them the help they need. We work with a great number of specialists, educating them as to the circumstances that lead to children being trafficked. Who are the vulnerable children? How can we help them? How can we protect them from trafficking? These specialists, as a result of our work, are beginning to understand that they need to reach out to children in orphanages, homeless kids, and runaways, in order to identify those who have been trafficked.

So, this is where we are now in terms of solving the problem of human trafficking in the Far East. Recently, we had four victims in our shelter. One was sent to us from law enforcement under the witness protection program. He was exploited in labor trafficking. He ran away from a construction site in the *tiaga*.[12] But the authorities sent him somewhere else from here—we don't know what happened to him.

We then had two underage girls sent to us from Khabarovsk.[13] They were victims of sex trafficking. There is an international investigation going on because a firm in Khabarovsk sold these girls to a Greek firm—they were forced into sexual slavery in Greece. But the firm in Khabarovsk was part of a very well-established pipeline through which traffickers sold girls to Greece, Israel, and several other countries. A significant number of girls were trafficked from Khabarovsk. I don't know how many made it back to Russia. These two girls came for rehabilitation at our shelter because their lives would be in danger if they stayed in Khabarovsk. One of the girls testified against her traffickers while still in Greece and she got help in Athens. Ultimately, she got repatriated back to Khabarovsk, where her trafficker started putting pressure on her and making threats. So, law enforcement sent her here.

She stayed with us for about a month and a half. While she was here, we got her into a training program on how to do pedicures and manicures using Japanese methods, so that she might be able to find work. She also saw a psychologist here.

The other girl from Khabarovsk also got trafficked to Greece. There were actually two of them—she and her twin sister—who got sold together. But once in Greece the traffickers separated them. They sent one sister to a tiny island to work in a brothel, the other they sent to a brothel in Athens. One of the sisters managed to run away, so the traffickers punished the second sister for that. They placed a huge debt on her and forced her to work it off in beastly ways. And then, later, they just let the second sister go. Evidently, a criminal investigation had begun with the first sister as a witness, and perhaps the traffickers were afraid of getting caught. The second sister said that one day the trafficker just gathered her belongings into a suitcase, drove her to the airport, and gave her a ticket to Moscow. She was allowed out of Greece without documents.

The sisters explained to us that the Greek traffickers had connections within the Greek immigration service, so crossing the border in either direction was no problem. In fact, once the twins got to Greece, the traffickers used their connections to get them legal immigration status as *refugees!* This trafficking ring operated a very organized network. The traffickers in Moscow would gather groups of victims and send them to Greece via different airlines. When the victims arrived in Greece, they would be provided with documents that allowed them to enter the country legally as refugees. From there, they were forced into sexual slavery all over Greece. Quite organized.

We had another girl staying here that we helped get out of China. Once we opened this shelter, we were routinely in touch with the vice consul of the Russian Consulate in Guangzhou about various trafficking cases.[14] One day the vice consul called me and said that he had just gotten a call from the police in Sanya, on the island of Hainan in the very south of China. It seems a young Russian lady walked into the police station in Sanya and sat down. She just sat there, not communicating with anyone. The vice consul said that he knew this girl. Last year he helped her get back to Russia from Shenzhen. He said she was mentally ill. And now, a year later, she was back in China.

Her story is a classic story. She is from a small village near Khabarovsk. She went to Khabarovsk to study at the university, but she was not admitted into the free department. She had no money to study in the fee-based department and did not want to return to her tiny village.[15] She is a beautiful girl with long hair and a great figure, so at some point she must have gotten an offer to be a "model" in China.

S.L.: It is quite easy to get into China. Getting a visa is no problem, especially from here.

S.B.: So, she finds herself trafficked to Shenzhen and forced into sexual exploitation. When we were able to bring her back to Russia from China, I spoke with her. As I understand it, in China she began to hear different voices in her head and that she could only lay in bed sick. So, her traffickers abandoned her. The Chinese authorities found her wandering around in a deranged state. She had an expired passport, and she would not speak a word. They put her in jail, but because she had no money, she was not offered any medical or psychiatric assistance. She just sat there, not talking to anyone. After about four months, the Chinese officials took her with a group of illegal immigrants and just dumped them back over the Russian border. Somehow, she got to a hospital in Khabarovsk and started getting some help.

Evidently, when she got released from the hospital, she left Khabarovsk again for China. But how would a girl like that, with no money and no support, get a passport and visa and travel 4,700 kilometers [2,974 miles] to Sanya? Her traffickers must have taken her back to China, that is the only explanation.

Once there, she started acting crazy again and got abandoned again. Yet she had enough sense left to go to the authorities in Sanya—to sit in the police station and not leave. The authorities took her back to the hotel where her passport was registered. But she showed up at the police station again. She just sat there again, not speaking. The police in Sanya called the Russian consul, who got in touch with us. We called the IOM, who bought her a ticket home. We met her at the airport and placed her in a psychiatric hospital right away. She stayed in the hospital for four months, and then she came to our shelter. We got her back to her village, settled in with her parents. However, she is now back in the hospital because her mental illness is quite severe.

One of our most recent cases was a man from Ukraine. We assisted Interpol and the IOM in finding him. They knew through an address listed in immigration that he was here in the Primorsky krai somewhere, but they did not know exactly where. We have good connections with the Department of Internal Affairs, so they helped us look for him. We found him in a tiny village, about twelve hours from here by bus. The district police located him.

It turns out he was among a huge number of workers who were recruited in Ukraine and sent to Khabarovsk to work on the railroad, replacing the ties and repairing the tracks. These Ukrainians were brought here three years ago [in 2007] and used as slaves. There were lots of them—somewhere between sixty and eighty. They were brought by train and occupied an entire rail car. The recruiters divided all these people up into work crews and spread them out all along the railways. This man with his crew got sent to the Primorsky krai. After we found him, he said they were absolutely slaves—living and working in inhumane conditions. They all lived in train cars at a station or base. He said everyone lost twenty pounds right away because they were not getting proper food or water. The traffickers would bring them rotting or spoiled food and gave them no access to clean water. Because of this, workers had to drink from puddles of muddy water and eat bread rather than the fouled food they were brought.

Initially, all the workers stayed because they were promised good pay. But because conditions were so bad, individuals started to leave. In order to stop people from leaving, the crew boss fabricated some story about having to re-register the contract or the documents. He confiscated all their passports. He locked everyone's documents in his office at the station so the workers couldn't leave.

Our Ukrainian victim said that he was "enduring and enduring" until he realized that he could endure no more. He was a small man, and the heavy work was tearing him down. So, he hatched a plan with the other workers to run away. They would cover for him while he ran to the station to steal back all their documents. They were working seven kilometers [a little over four miles] from the station where their train cars were parked. He said he ran the whole way so that he could get to the station before the boss noticed he was missing. When he got there, he broke into the boss's office and took his and all his comrades' passports. At that moment, the boss returned, and the Ukrainian had to physically fight him. Finally, he got away with the passports and was able to give them back to the workers. He took his and ran away.

He didn't go back to Ukraine, however, because there was still no work for him there. He wandered around for a long time looking for work. He came to Interpol's attention because some workers started a suit against the Ukrainian firm that sent them to work on the railroad. That triggered a criminal investigation. So, our Ukrainian was identified as a victim and Interpol began looking for him, and that's when we found him. He stayed at our shelter for a brief time and then the Ukrainian IOM got him tickets to return home.

I heard that somewhere here, not necessarily in Vladivostok, but somewhere in eastern Russia, there are camps that have only slave labor. Is that true?

S.L.: Yes.

S.B.: Such a camp was found near Perm—in Permsky krai.[16]

S.L.: I know that in Krasnodarsky krai there are also slave camps because Sochi is there.[17] There are a lot of Tajiks who go there to work, as well as Ukrainians, Syrians, Armenians, Georgians, and others.[18]

It turns out that the police and the authorities in the Department of Internal Affairs themselves are complicit in getting people trafficked. For example, if a migrant has a job and a contract with a Russian company, he must register with Internal Affairs as a legal migrant. When he goes to register, the authorities demand a US$2,000 bribe in order to officially register him here. However, since the person hasn't started working yet, he has no money. So, they then say, "Fine. You are not registered here, you have no legal right to be here," and they put him in a detention cell. Traffickers know this and will pay the authorities the US$2,000 "fine" for the migrants in order to entrap workers into debt bondage conditions.

And now we are preparing for the 2014 Olympic Games in Sochi, so there are huge construction projects going on. Hundreds of Tajiks and Ukrainians are going there for work. The same is true here in the Primorsky krai. The government is building a federal university with many construction projects. We are also building new bridges and highways. Consequently, we have a huge number of migrant workers here. There are special settlements built to house them all. And the construction companies closely guard those settlements—one cannot just show up and start asking questions. The construction companies have their own security services that don't even let the police into these settlements. The administration is very corrupt, and the migrants are being exploited and mistreated. Probably many of them are not getting paid at all and cannot leave, so they are slaves.

One can only enter the settlements with special permission—high-ranking state inspectors are allowed in. But there is a lot of advance notice, so that when inspectors are allowed on the premises, they are shown that everything is okay. As soon as the inspectors leave, the harsh treatment begins again. People try to flee from these places. Just yesterday I learned that there was a large group of workers brought in and fifty of them fled—they just ran away. For the last five days they have been living at a railway station, waiting for their relatives to send them money to get back home. If the construction site had more or less acceptable living and working conditions, and if workers were getting paid, they would not be running away en masse and asking their relatives for money.

S.B.: Russia is becoming fairly attractive for labor migrants from the so-called "near abroad," such as Ukraine, China, and Central Asia. But since labor conditions here are not transparent, foreign nationals will keep coming and will be subjected to brutal exploitation.

S.L.: I saw some statistics a few days ago. According to our local

Department of Internal Affairs, there are 600,000 registered migrants in our area [Primorsky krai]. However, in reality there are over a million migrants here at times—nearly twice the number of legal migrants. They all live here somewhere. And it is unclear what they do and under what conditions they live. They are predominately Tajiks and Chinese. Some of them come here legally but most just run across the border.

And of course, the authorities know because there are not that many big cities in Primorsky krai. It is mostly small villages. Everything can be easily observed in the villages—everyone knows everybody's business.

S.B.: The local authorities know that waves of illegal immigrants here are being exploited. Such huge numbers couldn't be here without the cooperation of the district police and the local administration. They know these people are being brutally exploited and they do nothing. [*Speaking forcefully with great emphasis*] I don't believe that the head of administration in some district is not aware of what is going on, of what settlements are being constructed, who is constructing them, and how people are being enslaved in his district!

Another serious problem we have with slavery is on fishing boats. The men who work on these boats are exploited as slave labor. The traffickers sell men to the foreign companies that run the boats. Then the men are forced to work in inhumane conditions, catching and processing fish. Most of the time these men are promised that they will get paid at the end of the season, but no one pays them. Then they are stuck here since they have no money to get back home.

For the last several years the individuals working on the fish processing ships are from Ukraine. Russians are less and less interested in obtaining such low-paying jobs. These guys are forced to work in freezing weather, and they are not provided with proper clothes or shoes. It is very dangerous work. There are cases where men are out to sea for six or nine months and if they don't catch enough fish, they literally get paid nothing.

Earlier, working on a fishing boat and processing fish used to be considered good work with good wages. One could go to sea for nine months or a year and then come back with enough money to buy an apartment. One could get married or start a family on the money made in fish processing. However, for the last ten, maybe fifteen years, that is not the case. Now people who process fish get paid very little, if at all. They are being tricked very skillfully. The bosses tell them that they literally cannot get paid at sea. There are no stores or banks. The workers are fed in the ship's cafeteria—sometimes they get decent food, but usually they get fed very poorly. But they endure, believing that they will get paid once they are back on land.

When the boat finally docks, the workers get issued bankcards [like ATM cards] in lieu of a paycheck. The whole crew of three hundred people lines up at the bank to cash in their cards, only to be told, "There is no money in this account." So, they are stuck with no money, no way home, nowhere to go, and no recourse. When the workers sign their employment contract, they are promised really good pay because the traffickers need several hundred men. Sometimes whole villages are recruited to work on the boats, only to be cheated.

I was wondering if I could ask you a few personal questions. You work with people who are going through incredible suffering. How do you deal with it? Who supports you?

S.B: I am fairly new to this, so I have not dealt with dozens of victims. But basically, I see them as people who are in difficult life situations. Even before I started working with trafficking victims, I was helping girls who were prostitutes. Those girls were from very small towns and made the conscious decision to become prostitutes. Many of them were from orphanages and became prostitutes in order to make some money. At that time, we had no shelter, so we were trying to find places for them to live. We managed to get some of them into a rehabilitation center for teenagers, Sail of Hope [Parus Nadezhdy]. We also sent some to the IOM shelter. But a lot of people didn't want to help these girls. Even some of my friends would say, "But they are just prostitutes!"

I was able to convince some of them that prostitutes are human beings, too, and that they also have human rights, despite their life situation. But I did not want to work with young prostitutes permanently because it is hard work—emotionally hard and physically hard.

S.L.: The hardest part of our job is working with the local administration. At least now they can see that our shelter is necessary and will start providing some state aid. But it is always a battle. I am glad that some of the local authorities have finally accepted our program and with our help they have started implementing a regional program for human trafficking victims.

S.B.: I would like to mention one aspect of human trafficking—that of national diaspora. It is something that I observe in our area. We get a lot of foreign nationals from Central Asia—Tajikistan, Uzbekistan, and the Caucasus. Kazakh citizens generally do not come here because Kazakhstan is relatively prosperous. But the Tajiks are very poor, as are the Uzbeks, so we get a lot of them here.

S.L.: We also get a lot of Armenians.

S.B.: Yes, Armenians and some people from Azerbaijan. So, we have a national diaspora here from Central Asia. This area is a popular migration route from Central Asia to Russia because not a single migrant comes here with nowhere to go. They are being recruited in their home countries and enter Russia without a hitch. You see, people from the former Soviet Republics can enter Russia legally and stay for up to ninety days. It is only if they stay longer that they get illegal status. They come here legally, and then start working underground and drop off the authorities' radar. That is when they find themselves trapped in bad situations. Or traffickers will provide them with "legal" documents allowing them to work in Russia. The migrants must pay for the documents and thus become enslaved through debt bondage to the trafficker.

Sometimes migrants get help from their compatriots—those who came here earlier and who already own businesses here. These new migrants must pay for the help with their labor and get trapped in debt bondage. Established migrants bring newcomers here and say, "We will pay for all your transport expenses. First you will work to pay for that, then you will start to earn money for yourself." And of course, the money they charge is much greater than the actual cost of travel. They are exploiting their own people and it never catches the attention of law enforcement. I am sure some of the new migrants who are enslaved would like to ask for help, but they are afraid. They know it will come back to them somehow, if not here then back in their own country. Back home they live in small villages or small towns, and the migrant still has an uncle, or a daughter, or a cousin back home that can be pressured or terrorized. So people are too scared to complain or try to escape. This type of debt bondage slavery is everywhere a national diaspora exists.

S.L.: We also have a large problem of slave labor among foreign nationals in agriculture. A farmer will rent twenty acres of land, for example, and instead of buying a tractor he will use forty of his compatriots to do the work by hand. These migrants live in tents in the fields from spring to fall. The owner of the land has a registered rental agreement, so he looks good on paper. However, how many workers he actually has there, how he treats them, or if he pays them is difficult to ascertain. Even if by some chance the Russian authorities send a police raid to the farm, the workers will not say anything because they are terrified.

In 2002 we had such a case in our krai. There was a man from Azerbaijan who had a farm with livestock that he kept in a cowshed.[19] He made his workers live in the cowshed with the animals. The farmer picked up homeless people or people who had no relatives or acquaintances and put them to work on his farm.

For example, one of the workers on the farm was a twenty-year-old guy from Vladivostok. He was simple-minded—he had a very low level of intelligence, so he was very gullible. His mother had died, leaving him a very good apartment in a very good district. However, one of the district policemen convinced him that he did not need such a large apartment and talked him into selling it and buying a smaller apartment. Well, the policeman and his accomplices sold the apartment and gave the kid a tiny studio apartment in exchange and cheated him out of a lot of money.

Then this kid started working for the Azerbaijani farmer, who talked him into selling his studio. The farmer promised to buy the kid a house in the village with the money he got from the studio. However, the farmer kept the money from the sale of the studio. He told the kid that if he worked on the farm for a year, he would get all his money back. So that's how this kid ended up working as a slave on the farm. When the police raided the farm, they freed five or six slaves, but only two agreed to testify against the farmer. The others simply left, too afraid to testify or get help.

We get hundreds of phone calls for help. But when the caller finds out that they must come in and sign some documents to receive help, most of them just hang up. They are so afraid of retaliation. For example, in the last six months, we received several hundreds of calls, but only forty people have begun the process of rehabilitation.

S.B.: They are all so scared.

S.L.: On average we actually help less than 20 percent of the people who call in because most of them are too afraid to come in. They are afraid of state authorities, they are afraid of the police, and they don't trust the organizations that help migrants. So there is not much we can do.

＊ ＊ ＊ ＊

At this point, the two Svetlanas noticed the time. We had been chatting well over an hour, and they both had to get back to work. They were both so knowledgeable, I wished we had many more hours to chat. I have often wondered what happened to them and their shelter. Did the state come up with funding? Did the local authorities really support them into the future? Unfortunately, the U.S. State Department in the 2017 TIP Report appears to hold the answer to my questions about the fate of the Victims of Human Trafficking Assistance Center. It states:

> A similar shelter established by an international organization in cooperation with Vladivostok authorities remained closed following its loss of funding in the reporting period. Similar to the previous reporting period, the government took steps to limit or ban the activities of other civil society groups, including some dedicated to anti-trafficking activities.[20]

4

Alina Budeci

Psychologist
NGO: La Strada International
Chisinau, Moldova
October 24, 2008

Moldova's geographical location makes it a prime country of origin to traffic persons in several directions. Traffickers can take their victims into Europe either west through Romania, north through Ukraine, or south through Bulgaria to Turkey and then on to Asia or the Middle East. Further, because Moldova is one of the poorest countries in Europe, there is an endless supply of people desperate enough to risk migration to find a job. In 2008, the average monthly salary in Moldova was US$230, explaining why huge numbers of people were eager to leave. At that time, it was estimated that nearly 25 percent of the working-age population was working outside Moldova, leaving large numbers of children behind.[1]

It was in Moldova that I first heard the term "social orphans"—meaning children who had parents working abroad, leaving them with no one to care for them. These children often live in orphanages or in boarding schools where traffickers know they can bribe officials to obtain kids for sex, slave labor, or forced begging. Moldova is also a destination for child sex tourism. Sex tourists target orphanages and bribe orphanage administrations to gain unsupervised access to the children.[2] It is little wonder that child trafficking for sexual exploitation or for labor exploitation remains a huge problem in Moldova. Aided by a very high level of government corruption and very few protections for vulnerable populations, traffickers operate with seeming impunity in the villages and small towns in Moldova.

When I heard that there was to be the first multinational conference on human trafficking in Chisinau, Moldova, in the fall of 2008, I jumped at the chance to attend. The conference brought together all the anti-trafficking NGOs and international organizations working in the area. It was at this conference that I first met Alina Budeci, who worked for La Strada International.[3] After the conference, she graciously agreed to let me interview her. In this interview Alina discusses child sex trafficking at length. She also discusses how official corruption aids the traffickers. Because she had been working with trafficking survivors since 2001, she was able to provide a unique perspective on changes in trafficking schemes over time, as well as changes in law enforcement strategies to subvert those schemes. This interview made me realize the unimaginable cruelties one person can visit upon another.

During our first interview, Alina recounted, in a matter-of-fact voice, some of the horrors she has witnessed. She told me that recently victims were showing up with their teeth bashed out by traffickers so that they could more easily give oral sex. As the barbarity of that started to sink in, the phone rang. She was called away from the interview. She had to go to the airport to meet a woman and her baby who had been rescued from a brothel—both were being used for sex.

In addition to working as a psychologist with victims of trafficking, Alina ran the hotline twenty-four hours a day. She explained that at any time, day or night, she might get a call from a terrified trafficking victim. She then must either arrange with local police to find and rescue the caller, or, if Moldova does not have an agreement with the country where the victim is calling from, she must figure out how to reach the caller through a series of informal contacts which include local NGOs and local police networks.

At the time of the interview, Alina had been trying to locate a woman who had been trafficked and used as a sex slave. The woman kept calling the hotline at 3:00 every morning. However, she was clearly terrified and would hang up before Alina could get any information that would help her locate the victim. Over the course of two weeks, Alina was able to figure out that the woman (who did not know where she was) was probably somewhere in Turkey. Distressed that it was taking so long to locate the woman, Alina mentioned that in terms of human trafficking two weeks is a very long time. Anything could happen to this woman at any time: she could be resold, she could die by suicide or murder, or she could simply disappear.

In this interview, Alina discusses many aspects of trafficking in Moldova, including recruitment methods the traffickers use. She also talked about how traffickers' methods of intimidation have changed. Traffickers initially used extreme violence and cruelty, but this resulted in people willing to risk everything to escape—even death or suicide. Now, the traffickers used a mixture of brutality, coercion, and psychology. They played on stereotypes of the West and fed the fantasies of desperate men and women wanting a better life.

One of the things that disturbed Alina the most was the trafficking of children. Typically, children trafficked into sexual slavery are between the ages of twelve and seventeen. Younger boys are sometimes used for sex, but they are more often forced to beg. Alina told me that parents often unwittingly "sell" their children into slavery. They sign the required documents for the child to be taken across state lines either out of ignorance or because they are promised the future earnings of the child by the recruiter.

At the end of the interview, I felt as if I had just taken an intensive seminar on human trafficking. I decided I would follow Alina's suggestion and go out to the villages. She subsequently helped me find survivors who were willing to talk about their stories. Without her help, my experience in Moldova would not have been nearly as rich. In the ensuing month, we had several conversations, and shared a few meals.

Has trafficking changed in the last seven years?

Alina: Yes, it has changed a lot. It seems every time law enforcement figures out how to thwart or capture the traffickers, the traffickers change tactics. Over the last several years recruitment procedures have changed, as have the techniques for manipulating victims and traffickers' strategies.

For example, recruitment has changed. We have a very popular newspaper, *Makler*. It is full of want ads, especially help wanted ads. This is the primary place people look if they are seeking employment. In 2001, *Makler* very openly advertised positions for young girls to work as strippers, or in bars in Turkey, Cyprus, and elsewhere. The ads said they were looking for girls "with passports and no complexes." In 2001, we could explain to people that responding to such an advertisement could be very risky. Now you won't find this kind of advertisement because the recruiters have changed their tactics. They did so because the public became too aware of human trafficking. Now all advertisements include the claim that it is a "legal job" or "legal opportunities," and that potential employers will sign a legally binding contract, which in many cases is patently false.

Not long ago, *Makler* ran advertisements for jobs in Japan. These ads included all the information we used to tell people to look for in order to determine if a job was legitimate. We would tell people to ask about a contract, to ask about time off and to ask if the job included provisions to call relatives back home—those sorts of things. Well, these ads stated that they would provide a work contract, opportunities to call relatives back home, time off and opportunities to travel, etc. But it was a setup. A lot of women who answered those ads were trafficked to Japan.

Another thing that changed is the way the traffickers transport their victims. Several years ago, you would see groups of people, especially young women, leaving to go abroad together. Minibuses full of women headed to Romania or Ukraine, none of them knowing exactly where they were headed. For border guards and for us, it was obvious that this was probably a trafficking situation. We were able to stop a lot of people at the borders, especially if they did not know the name of the town or city they were going to.

But this method of transport required a lot of control and a lot of money. A trafficker would have to find a driver willing to take people across the border illegally. He or she would have to have another person meet the victims on the other side of the border, in Romania or Ukraine, for example. Then more people were needed to get victims across more borders and into Europe or Turkey. So, the traffickers needed a lot of people to organize, and that all takes time. In the meantime, the victim might figure out that something was amiss, or a driver might say something that would make someone realize what was happening to them.

Now, recruiters tell the potential victims that the "firm" or "agency" will arrange and pay for their passports and visas, and that they can pay the agency back once they start working. The recruiter tells them to just wait, that it will take a little time to arrange everything, but that the victim will get a phone call when everything is in order. Then he calls the victim and says, "OK, everything is done. You will leave tomorrow." This way, there is no time for the victim to think, or to question, or to figure out what is going on. It all seems legitimate—they have a work contract, and now a visa and a passport, and they are trapped before they even know what is happening to them.

Sometimes, especially for women from very poor families, the recruiter will give them a little money as an "advance" so that they can buy food for their children. The recruiter assures the women that once they start working, they will have a lot of money to send home. But this is pure manipulation. A desperate woman will go to the airport and be in another country all within a few hours. She never even thinks to ask why she isn't told the name of the person who will meet her when she lands. She has never flown before, and she often doesn't even know what city she is in when she lands.

Also, traffickers have changed their manipulation techniques. Several years ago, traffickers used a lot of violence to terrorize their victims into submission. Now they use psychological manipulation, providing the victim with a false sense of freedom. One of the first things a trafficker used to do was confiscate the victims' passports under the guise of holding them for "safekeeping." This would ensure that the victim could not run away. From the start, victims would get suspicious, or try to resist. But now, in the construction field, for example, traffickers tell the workers, "We will hold your passports for safekeeping, but here is a copy for you in case you need it. You must work for six months and then we will pay you your full salary." So, the workers keep working, thinking that they will get paid, and believing that they are free to come or go as they wish. But then the boss will tell the workers that the project is shutting down and no one will get paid. Or they will tell the workers that they will get paid tomorrow, or the next day, but they must keep working if they want to get any money. So, victims work six, seven, or more months and then get tossed aside with no money and no way to get home.

Are more people being exploited now for labor than for sex?

Alina: I think it's about the same ratio as before. Several years ago, people were not talking so much about labor exploitation. "Trafficking" referred almost exclusively to sexual exploitation. Generally, people who are trafficked for labor exploitation do not self-identify as trafficking victims. They think that since they did not provide sexual services, or were not kept in a brothel, that they were not trafficked. They think they just didn't get paid.

From everything I've read, about 8,000–9,000 persons from Moldova have been trafficked since 2001. How many of those do you think were for sexual exploitation?

Alina: I can only judge from our own statistics. About 80 percent of them were trafficked for sexual exploitation. According to our data, about 5 percent of these are men. When we look at children that have been trafficked, about 5 to 6 percent are boys. In most cases, children are trafficked for begging, for agricultural work, or for physical labor. The girls, of course, are sexually exploited as well. The youngest child that we assisted was four years old, and the oldest was eighteen. In some cases, children are trafficked together with the entire family. Moldovan kids are typically trafficked to Russia, Ukraine, and Poland for forced begging. For agricultural work, they usually get sent to Ukraine. There are a few cases of internal trafficking, but very few.[4] We have one case of a woman trafficked internally and held as a slave for twenty-six years. She was exploited for labor and for sex.

Do you have any cases of trafficking before the collapse of the Soviet Union?

Alina: Yes. Based on victims' testimonies, we have people trafficked as early as 1985, and into the early 1990s. But these are relatively few. After the Soviet Union collapsed [in 1992], trafficking from this part of the world exploded, as you know. The main reason for this is economic. It is all about migration. People needed jobs and money, and they were willing to migrate to find them. Not everyone who went abroad got trafficked, so there are those successful migration stories. Each time someone goes abroad and returns having made some money, more and more people are willing to risk it.

Also, very often recruiters will exploit images from movies that people have in their heads. They play on fantasies that movies create. For example, one girl who was trafficked to Cyprus was told that she would be working in a casino. She told me:

> You know, I never thought this would be risky because the first image that came to me was of Las Vegas, like I had seen in the movies. And this is how the recruiter explained to me what my work would be. She said there will be a lot of beautiful, rich people, and a lot of bright lights. She said that I will wear a beautiful uniform and I will provide beverages for people who are gambling. I thought I would be so happy—like living in a Hollywood movie.

This is what some people thought they were going to find when recruiters told them that they will be working for a family and taking care of houses. A lot of people here watch soap operas, especially those from Spain and Portugal. What they see in the soap operas are big, beautiful mansions with glamorous servants. They think they will wear a very nice uniform, live in a beautiful house, and take care of fabulously rich people. For you, it may be laughable. But for someone who grew up in a small village, who has never been out of the country, or to a city even, this looks like paradise. They *want* to believe this is the way things are.

You need to go out to our villages. You will see some very disturbing poverty. Hire a car and go talk to these people. If you say that you have a job for them and will provide the money for a passport and visa, you will draw a large group of people. You will see how many people will say, "Yes, take me!" It is not because they want to leave, but because they have heard some success stories, and they want to make money.

Right now, border guards report that they have a lot of cases of the Roma people taking children across the border. Roma have distinctive features—they have dark hair and eyes, olive skin. They are taking fair-skinned children with blond hair and blue eyes over the border, telling the authorities that these are their children. It is impossible, but we cannot stop them because their documents are in order. And the kids are so young, they cannot communicate with the border guards.

Are these kids kidnapped?

Alina: No. Well, sometimes they are kidnapped. But more often the child is bought for a bottle of wine or cognac. They are from very poor families, so the Roma know that parents will never come looking for the child. If they get stopped at the border, they tell the authorities that they are gathering children up to help them in their homes, or in their fields in Moldova. The parents have already signed the documents giving the Roma permission to take the kids, so the border guards must let them go.

And it's not just the kids that are leaving. Go to any village and you will see that our villages are emptying out. Our volunteers go to villages to do seminars, and they report that some villages have only the very old and the very young left. In some villages, you will see nobody between the ages of eighteen and forty-five years old because they have all left. The old folks generally take care of the young ones, although there are cases where the kids are just left alone. As you walk through the villages you will see some beautiful new houses being built. But these houses are empty because the owners are working abroad and sending the money home for the houses to be built. This is all about migration. If you want, you can go to the village Maximovca, it is about a half an hour from here, about 30 kilometers [18 miles due east of Chisinau]. We have had a lot of girls from that village trafficked to Turkey. Very bad situations.

It is very easy to manipulate people when they have a fantasy in their heads. And even if they know about trafficking, they think it will not happen to them. They have heard one hundred success stories of people making a lot of money abroad, and one horror story about trafficking. So, most villagers are willing to take that chance.

In Russia, many women leave as mail-order brides. Is that common here in Moldova?

Alina: Not really. Our hotline volunteers also monitor those websites, the ones looking for mail-order brides. There are also some ads for this type of marriage in the newspaper, *Makler*. But we really haven't had so many cases of mail-order brides.

You can't move vast numbers of people across international borders without cooperation from some of the local authorities. Have you found that police and border guards are colluding with the traffickers?

Alina: We can only surmise from the information we get from people who were taken illegally across the border. We don't have any reports of people actually seeing a border guard getting a payment. But all of our clients report that their traffickers knew the route very well and appeared to know many of the border guards by name. Sometimes victims had to wait until a certain border guard was on duty to cross. So that suggests that at least some border guards are working with the traffickers.

Also, usually to obtain a passport one must do it oneself—nobody can get a passport for you. But we have reports from numerous victims that they never went to the passport center, the traffickers arranged passports for them. This suggests that someone, or even several people from within the government passport center are complicit in helping the traffickers.

It is illegal to take a child out of the country without legal permission. The parents must go to the notary office and sign specific papers. But we have so many cases where people transporting children across the border have never met the parents. For example, we are working on one case now where the parents of three girls have been in France working illegally for the last ten years. They have not seen their children for ten years. The parents left the girls under the care of the grandparents. But now the parents are in the process of getting legal residency and work permits. Understandably, they want to bring their children to France. We got involved because the police called us and said that a woman was trying to take these three girls over the border, but the parents were not there. She had papers for the children, but the border guards were suspicious. Svetlana went to the border to meet them because it is our responsibility to determine if these kids are victims of trafficking.[5] In this case, the parents hired someone to get their children to France. But because she was trying to take the kids across the border without a parent, she is being held in prison for smuggling the kids. The kids are in custody as well. Even the parents did not know this woman who agreed to smuggle their kids across the border. She was a friend of a friend of someone they knew.

You can see how the parents would be desperate to bring their children to France, but not be able to do it themselves. They still have no legal right to be there, so they cannot just leave the country and get back in. If they get legal immigrant status in France, they can then apply through the embassy for permission to bring their children into the country. However, if they do that, then the French authorities will discover that the parents have been in France illegally for ten years. Under such circumstances, I doubt they will issue visas for the children. So, the parents' best option was to hire someone to smuggle their kids into France. But now that scheme has gone awry. We still don't know if this woman in custody was a smuggler who would have delivered the children to their parents, or a trafficker who would have then sold the children once out of Moldova.

Do you work closely with local police and the border guards?

Alina: Yes. In addition to providing services for victims, we help with rescue and repatriation. We also search for people who are missing and presumed victims of trafficking. Many parents call the hotline looking for their children. Legally, the parents are supposed to take the passport, pictures, or any documents of the child to the police and submit a request for the police to search for a missing person. But because of our high level of corruption in some police departments, what usually happens is that the police, in essence, demand a bribe. It is quite typical that if the police have to go to Russia, for example, to search for this child, they will tell the parents that they need so much money in order to go there. It is usually an inflated sum, and the parents certainly will not have the money to pay. Even if it is a modest sum, they won't be able to pay—we are talking about poor villagers here. And this is not the proper procedure anyway, but who are the parents going to complain to?

It's the same with the victims. If they go to the police and say they want to press charges against their traffickers, the police most often will refuse to do anything. The police will say, "You were there for three years and couldn't manage to escape? Come on. Besides, you knew what was going to happen before you left." So, the police will not go after the traffickers.

Once a woman gets sold and trapped, how long does it usually take for her to get out?

Alina: In the past, trafficked women were typically enslaved for several years. But beginning in 2006 or 2007, it is usually between one to three months. I think the reason for that is because now, the police in the destination countries are doing a much better job of looking for trafficking situations. They are taking it much more seriously and are doing a great job of finding and busting illegal brothels. So now women are usually freed by the police in brothel raids, or they manage to escape and are taken into police custody. In the past, very often even if a woman managed to escape, the police would just return her to the trafficker. That is happening less and less now.

Also, many of our women are helped by the johns, so we need to have a little compassion and understanding for them. For example, we have had several girls trafficked to Cyprus, many of whom were helped by johns from Britain. These guys were in Cyprus to relax or just have a good time, thinking the women were paid sex workers. But when they found out the real situation, many of these johns would let the girls use their cell phones to call for help. In Turkey some of our girls were helped by johns who fell in love with them. These Turkish johns would form a relationship with the girl in the brothel and then try to buy her from the owner. We had quite a few cases like that. In Russia, too, we have had a few cases where the girl was helped by her john.

4. Alina Budeci

I know there has been a lot of effort to educate the public about the risks of human trafficking and migration. Do you feel these efforts have had any effect?

Alina: In order to create a public information campaign, you need to first talk to the victims. You need to find out how they were recruited, what methods the traffickers used. And then you create the campaign. But this takes time, so the campaign is based on information that was pertinent a year or two ago. But the traffickers always stay one step ahead of the police and the NGOs, so you never know how they are changing their behavior. By the time you launch your campaign, the traffickers have already changed their tactics. So, you try somehow to guess what the traffickers might do next, but you never really know.

I will show you a very good advertisement which we found two days ago. It's the website of a massage salon in Romania—very well made. It is written across the top in very large lettering, "Earn €1000 salary per month." And then the website states that prostitution is illegal in Romania and in the Republic of Moldova: "We do not provide sexual services to our clients," it says. "You will have a legal working permit, a contract, and you will be working legally in the territory of Romania. If you work more than thirty-six hours a week, you will receive up to €5000 per month." Well, I'm sorry, but this is not the salary of a masseuse anywhere. The website says they need good-looking girls, and that they need to have a good working knowledge of the country of Romania. However, they don't need to speak or understand Romanian, or be trained in massage. The website states that they will provide the training. They include very glamorous pictures of girls in a beautiful salon. So, it looks professional, and seems legal, with no risks. It might entice several people.

Do you go out on hotline calls? For example, if you get a call from a woman in Romania who is being exploited, but she doesn't know where she is, what do you do?

Alina: Svetlana and I work together as a mobile team, which means we are available 24 hours a day [*grinning*]. That is why we look tired and bedraggled. At any time of the day or night, a social worker, a parent, or a police officer can call us and tell us that this person is here or there, and please go talk to her. So, we pick up a police officer to go with us, and we go to talk to that person, no matter what time it is as long as she is in Moldova. If the person is abroad, what we do depends upon the country and if we know who to contact. This is a bit more complicated. First, we go to the Human Trafficking Center under the Ministry of the Interior. They then write a complaint to the minister of foreign affairs of the country where the victim is located. It sometimes can take up to a month before they get a reply.

And by that time the girl can be dead, or moved, or resold—anything can happen.

Sometimes we contact the police or an NGO directly in that country, especially if it's a country in the European Union. If it is Turkey ... well, it is very hard to work with Turkey. In the past all we needed to do was give the Turkish police a street name and the city and they would start looking for the person. Now we must know the street name, the house number, and even the apartment number where she is. Otherwise, the police will not go look for her because now there are so many domestic procedures they must follow. So, when we work in Turkey we go through the IOM. In Russia, too, this process takes a tremendous amount of time, and we would rather use an NGO than the police. We have tried countless times to contact the Russian police but have never succeeded in doing so. If we get a call from someone in Cyprus ... well, we've had so many cases from Cyprus. The country is divided between the north and the south.[6] In the southern part we have an NGO we can call to go and look for a person for us. In the northern part, the Turkish part, there is no such NGO. So, if we get a call from Turkish Cyprus, we must call the U.S. Embassy, who then calls the trafficking police task force in the northern part of Cyprus, who then may rescue the person. Each country is different.

How did you get interested in this work? What's your story?

Alina: In 2001 I had just graduated from Chisinau University. A colleague of mine told me that she had found an advertisement for a job for trafficking hotline counselors. We both applied, got the jobs, and got sent to training. Back then I knew nothing about trafficking. Our trainers were from La Strada in Ukraine, and I left the training thinking, "Oh my God, I don't know how I can do this." You must know so many ministries, embassies, procedures, laws.... It was so scary! And the first emergency call to the hotline was mine! I remember the phone rang—we all worked in the same office together—and it became deadly silent. Everyone looked at me. There was so much tension in just picking up the phone and starting to talk. It was so stressful because I knew it may literally be a matter of life and death! When I picked up the phone, it was the mother of a girl who had been trafficked. It was a complicated case, and it took us several months to solve it. The girl didn't know where she was. It turns out she was in Turkey. Each time you get a call, it is like a roller coaster ride. But when you succeed in bringing someone back, it is so rewarding.

With each case, we go through a sort of emotional crisis until we can bring the person home. Well, it's part of the burnout service providers get. I had a case with a girl who called from northern Cyprus. It took us two weeks to find out where she was. She kept calling the hotline and saying only, "I am somewhere in Cyprus," then turning off the phone. I had no idea what to do, how to help her. I was worried that her owner would find out that she called for help and hurt her, or move her, or worse. It took us several weeks because every night she would provide us with just a little bit of information and then hang up terrified. Every day we called the U.S. Embassy and gave them what little new information we got from her.

Each case gives us more understanding of what to do and how to do it better. Sometimes victims die after we get them back, or before we can rescue them. That is really stressful.

Does that happen often?
Alina: It happens. We had one case where a woman was killed by her traffickers. But more often they come back with a lot of medical problems, such as AIDS, and die from disease or issues related to drug and alcohol abuse.[7] Or they are so traumatized they just give up and die. A lot of repatriated victims commit suicide.

I imagine it requires a lot of rehabilitation for a survivor to be able to integrate back into his or her life. What kinds of rehabilitation services does La Strada provide?
Alina: We have shelters in Moldova. Reintegration into society can take several years. It requires psychologists, psychotherapists, social workers, and medical staff. We try not only to help victims, but to give them the tools needed to recover and take care of themselves. Victims are allowed to stay in a rehabilitation center for up to three months. That is not reintegration, it is crisis intervention and that's all. After that, survivors need to be able to find work as well as manage their own problems. In the rehabilitation centers we can deal with the worst of the physical and psychological traumas, but we don't really fix any problems. So, La Strada has rehabilitation programs, but not reintegration. All we are equipped to do is to find victims, bring them back, and give them referrals for assistance. It is not enough.

We know it is not enough because people keep getting retrafficked. Why? Because when we bring them back, their situation is worse than it was before they got trafficked. Before they left, they probably had some debts—that's why they got trafficked in the first place, to earn money. When they come back, those debts are even higher, only now they have no place to live. Their parents often do not accept them back. Even their kids don't want them back because they have heard so many stories about prostitutes abroad. Many people try to commit suicide *after* getting home.

It is even more delicate with children. We have started working with children who are victims of foreign pedophiles who come here specifically to buy children for sex. I assume you heard about the Bianchi case?[8] He abused a lot of Moldovan children. He was tried and convicted. This is something that other countries need to know—it is not all right to come here and abuse children just because it is a poor and vulnerable country.

I just testified in court against some traffickers in a case involving a minor, just before you got here today—just now. It was very stressful. The victim was from Balti, the second largest city in Moldova.[9] This case involved a seventeen-year-old girl who was bought by one trafficker and sold to another to work in a day spa. The plan was to sell her to the Emirates [UAE] for sexual slavery, but she didn't know it. She was working in the spa and forced to have sex with clients there. She was free to go home after work. But her family situation was horrible, and nobody would advocate for her. The police couldn't provide enough evidence to prove that she had been trafficked, other than the fact that she was underage and providing sexual services at the spa. So, when the case went to court, the prosecution depended upon her testimony. I was working with her—I was always with her when she spoke with the police. The traffickers claimed in court that she was abused by the police—that the cops forced her to fabricate a story against her traffickers. I had to testify in court that this was not true, that I was always present when she spoke to the police, and that nobody forced her to say anything.

The traffickers were two brothers. Their lawyer argued that the brothers did not know she was seventeen, which was a lie. She was all set to testify in court against them. She had read all the documents and she had made and signed her own statement. But then, on the day she was to appear in court, these two guys stopped her on her way from Balti to Chisinau. They told her what she had to say. When we got into the courtroom, she asked to change her testimony. She said the police beat her and forced her testimony. It was clear that she had been threatened or intimidated by the traffickers to give this testimony and that she was lying. But there was nothing we could do. Without her testimony, the two brothers were convicted of pimping a minor, not trafficking, and they got off with just a small fine.

When we got out of court, the brothers and the lawyer were waiting for me in the parking lot. I was very afraid because they looked very menacing. So, I went back in the courthouse and out the back door, but I do not know if they followed me or not. I don't know if they now know where I work. This *just* happened, just today.

Who are the traffickers? Mafia?
Alina: Our prime minister says that we have no organized crime. We are

the only country in the world with no organized crime! We are so lucky [*laughing*].

Traffickers can absolutely be any kind, and all kinds, of people: small-time criminals who take advantage of a situation; members of large, organized crime networks; Russians, Albanians, Moldovans, Cypriots, Turks—you name it.

Daria Fane at the U.S. Embassy said that La Strada and the IOM are so effective at alerting the public to the dangers of trafficking that traffickers are spending less time in the villages of Moldova. Instead, they try to recruit people in bus and train stations as they arrive in Europe or Turkey, or Russia. Are you working on that end of things?

Alina: Of course, we work with police from numerous countries. But this is something that the NGOs in those countries must do, because we don't have a big international mandate. We do inform people how recruitment here has changed. Now, people who are looking for work just leave, especially men who want to work in construction in Russia. They hear there is a big construction boom right now. So, they get on trains and head for Russia. And yes, they are recruited in bus and train stations, and then they are transported somewhere else.

I will tell you a story about recruitment that happened several years ago. I was not working at La Strada yet. My mother's friend had a daughter who was supposedly working as a dancer in Lebanon. Lebanon is a prime destination country for Moldovan girls. The friend said her daughter was looking for a team of girls to dance with her. She asked my mom, "Can you, or maybe Alina, find some of Alina's friends or colleagues who want to be part of a dance troupe in Lebanon? For each girl you recruit, I will give you €50." At that time, fifty Euros was a huge sum for us. My mom said we couldn't help her. But it was very interesting to find out how someone could easily trick you into being a recruiter.

We are now seeing advertisements seeking Moldovan girls to work in clothes shops abroad. Now, why would they have to pay thousands of Euros to bring over Moldovan girls to work in shops? They don't have their own girls? Moldovan girls don't even know the language. We had a lot of girls who applied for these jobs and left Moldova. Some of them have called home but they say everything is okay, even though their passports have been confiscated and they have no ticket home. They would rather say that everything is okay than to say that they were being forced into sexual slavery. They don't want people at home to think of them as prostitutes, or to find out they worked as a prostitute, forced or not.

* * * *

At that moment the phone rang. Alina had to go to the airport to meet a young Moldovan woman and her nine-month-old baby who had just been rescued from a brothel in Turkey. We abruptly ended the interview so she could go meet her latest charges.

5

Stella Rotaru

Repatriation expert
NGO: International Organization for Migration (IOM)
Chisinau, Moldova
November 15, 2008, and October 19, 2010

Chisinau, the capital city of Moldova, feels tired and looks dilapidated. The broad, tree-lined Stefan cel Mare Boulevard, which is the heart of the city center, offers bright storefronts full of international fashions, cafes, European food stores, and computer shops, belying the despair and poverty that is ubiquitous just two or three streets away. Much of the city of 700,000 was destroyed in World War II and rebuilt by the Soviets following the war. Typical Soviet style *khrushchevky*, nondescript grey blocks of apartments, are everywhere throughout the city.[1] As I made my way from Stefan cel Mare to the IOM building, it was apparent that while independence from the Soviet Union in 1991 might have brought a modicum of freedom and commerce, it certainly did not bring economic prosperity. I wondered how long it would take for a former Soviet republic to recover from totalitarian control. Maybe as long as it takes a survivor to fully recover from enslavement—a lifetime or two.

I arrived at the IOM building and was buzzed through the sheet-metal security gate. Because the IOM deals in migrants, refugees, and trafficking victims, they take security very seriously. Once inside the building, I was motioned past the security guard and up to the fourth-floor interview room. Since I had arranged to interview several members of the IOM staff at the same time, I had a few minutes to look around while waiting for them to finish what they were doing. All at once Martin Wyss, chief of the Moldova IOM mission, entered the room, followed by several of his staff. We made introductions and got right to it. While Martin's intensity and hyperactive energy dominated the meeting, my attention was drawn to Stella Rotaru, who sat quietly looking at her hands for the first few moments of the meeting. She then calmly and quietly left the room, not to return.

When the meeting was over, I went to Stella's office to ask if she had time for an interview. She agreed and I immediately found her to be enchanting, engaging, and authentic. It was clear that she was a fierce advocate for victims' rights, and it was easy to see why she was a main figure in an Al Jazeera documentary on sex slaves, and the focus of a *New Yorker* article on human trafficking.[2]

Stella is fluent in four languages, and at the time of our first interview she had enforcement contacts in numerous countries. Having orchestrated dozens of brothel raids, Stella had helped rescue untold numbers of trafficking victims. On a typical day she would receive calls from cops, detainees, and consulates, or from worried families and friends, and even sometimes from johns. Her most important, most urgent, and hence most stressful calls came from women needing to be rescued from sexual slavery. Often these women had no idea where they were or even what country they were in. Stella had to act quickly and efficiently to get critical information and to communicate it to the local law enforcement partners. She would tell such women to look out the window for any kinds of signs, or to look for addresses on matchbook covers and shopping bags—anything that might be a clue to their location.

Stella's job as a repatriation expert was made more difficult by public attitudes around human trafficking in Moldova. Public skepticism about the vulnerability and intentions of women who get forced into sexual slavery is a huge challenge. Young women who return home from being trafficked are stigmatized at best, victimized and terrorized by their communities at worst. In this interview, Stella discusses public attitudes and how they make it difficult for women to recover from being trafficked, and especially to testify in court against their traffickers.

Despite, or perhaps because of, the human tragedies she deals with every day, there is a strength and a determination to her, tempered by compassion. During our interview there were a lot of distractions, with Martin speaking loudly on his telephone down the hall ("No, I *won't* meet with her—she is too stupid") and with others walking by, or standing in the hallway talking. Stella had no qualms about telling them, even her boss, to "pipe down." One of her colleagues later told me, "No one argues with Stella because they know they will never win." But it is precisely this tenacity that made her effective at saving people's lives. When I mentioned this, she just shrugged and sighed, "I just wish they wouldn't take risky jobs."

How long have you worked for the IOM on human trafficking?

Stella: I have been with the IOM since 2003, but I joined the countertrafficking program in 2005. The repatriation of trafficked Moldovan women and children started in 2000. At that time, Save the Children was doing the repatriation. So, our statistics begin in 2000. But the IOM opened its Moldova office in 2001. That same year, the IOM opened a rehabilitation center for victims of trafficking in Chisinau.

Before 2000 the major destination countries for Moldovan women and children were the Balkans. Most of the recruiting was done by newspaper advertisements, especially in *Makler*, which is quite popular.[3] Typically, offers for work abroad were for low-risk positions such as babysitters, nannies, cooks, house cleaners, that sort of thing. At that time, the recruiters would supply all the necessary documents for "work" abroad. Of course, they were falsified documents, and most of the border crossings were done illegally.

Our clients tell us horrific stories of crossing borders, like being forced to swim across rivers, or hiking all night through forests, or riding through deserts on camels or in trucks in terrible conditions. If they were trafficked to Israel, they would have to cross the desert. If it was the Balkans, they would have to climb through the mountains. Not all the women made it—many died along the way. Sometimes the traffickers would not wait for them or help them if they got sick or injured. The women were usually between [the] ages of eighteen and twenty-four.

Once they arrived in the destination country, the women faced terrible conditions. Their owners confiscated their passports and locked them up in rooms without windows. They were fed very poorly, if at all. They would have to share clothes and would have to sleep in beds in shifts because there were not enough beds for everyone. If they disobeyed their traffickers or the brothel owners, they were viciously beaten. They were not allowed to use condoms, and if they got pregnant, their owners forced them to have abortions, or beat them until they miscarried. They were not allowed to call home, nor were they allowed to keep any of the money their johns might have given them. The only thing they were allowed to keep was gold jewelry. When the johns found out that the women were not allowed to keep any money, they would buy gold for their "favorites." For some reason, the pimps did not take this away. But some women report that when they managed to escape or get rescued, they had a problem with border guards because they had so much gold jewelry on them.

Women were often sold from one trafficker to another to another. Most women in the early days would spend two to three years in slavelike conditions under the control of several different traffickers. If they managed to come home, they arrived in terrible physical and mental condition. They all had intestinal ailments and sexually transmitted diseases. Some of them were left sterile from bad abortions, and most had some kind of sleep disorder and severe psychological trauma. Some women came back pregnant or with small children. In most cases the child was a constant reminder of the horrible conditions that they went through. Our psychologist had to work very carefully with these survivors so that they wouldn't abandon the child. Nonetheless, some women did abandon their children once they returned home. In the early years, victims generally were single women or single mothers from rural areas with a low level of education. Most of these women were identified by La Strada and sent to us for repatriation from the Balkans.

After 2004 the destination countries changed. Turkey became a primary destination country, followed by Russia, the European Union countries, United Arab Emirates, Cyprus, then Ukraine. Also, the ages of the victims changed, depending upon where they were trafficked. For example, women trafficked to Russia and Turkey were between the ages of nineteen and twenty-one years old, but those coming back from the Balkans were a bit older—from ages twenty-two to twenty-nine. For Central Europe, the victims ranged in age between sixteen to twenty-one, because many children were trafficked to Poland for begging. Since 2007 the ages of victims are even more varied. Now they can be anywhere from the early teens to over fifty because we have more cases of labor exploitation.

It is sad and tragic, but most of the trafficking in recent years is done through personal contact, not newspaper ads. The recruiters are friends or relatives of the victim. There is also a trend from Turkey where trafficked girls are allowed to go home, but only on the condition that they recruit a couple of girls to take their place. So, victims become recruiters and traffickers. It's a conditioned choice, because they can only go home if they recruit others.[4] Sometimes the victims are given some money, because they have children or sick parents at home. The traffickers do this to keep them from getting too desperate. In many countries the assumption is that these women knew what they were getting into. But when you talk to them, they say that even if they knew the job was risky, or even if they knew they were going abroad for prostitution, they had no idea that the conditions would be so horrific and abusive. Plus, they went because they were told that they would make money.

Earlier, victims were uneducated, typically having only completed grammar school. However, in recent years the number of trafficked persons with vocational training has increased. We think this is because many young people get vocational training, but employers don't hire them because they are young and unskilled. They are very poor young men and women, so employers "hire" them for a trial period, like an internship without pay, ostensibly to train them. However, at the end of the trial period, they are let go. Many of them want to go abroad to find jobs that actually pay something. Most of the victims still come from rural areas, but there is a decline in victims from the capital. We believe this is because of the amount of public information on human trafficking that is now available in Chisinau.

Recently, the number of male victims coming into our program has increased. For example, in 2007 we had 218 women, 24 girls, 23 men, and 8 boys. That's a 6 percent increase in men since 2005, which is significant. Men are exploited mostly for labor.

Most of our female clients are single mothers. They don't go abroad because they want to be raped by groups of men, or to provide sexual services for eighteen to forty men per day. They go abroad out of despair. They would like to work in Moldova, but they can't make enough money to feed their children. There was one woman who came back from the United Arab Emirates. While she was in jail there, a policeman from Moldova visited her. He asked if she wasn't afraid [to] go to the Emirates to look for a job in the first place. She told him that what she was really afraid of was watching her child starve. Even if these women get a high-risk job as a dancer or a prostitute, they see it as a temporary situation. Their main goal is to get to the destination country. They think that once they get there, they will find other work, or they will escape, or somebody will help them. They think that somehow, they will manage something. They have no options in Moldova. They believe that they must go abroad in order to earn money to support a sick child or family member, or to pay for their child's schooling, etc. It is important to always keep in mind that 90 percent of our female clients were victims of domestic violence before they ever got trafficked. After having gone through rape, beatings, incest, and humiliation and manipulation at home, they think that going abroad can't possibly be any worse than what happens in their own homes.

In 2004 we began aiding kids who are at risk of being trafficked. These are children from very large, poor families, or where the father and mother are working abroad—so-called social orphans. We also focused on children from boarding schools who age out at fourteen and have nowhere to go.[5] Also since 2004 we have been assisting with police cases targeting traffickers as part of our prevention program. It is easier to prevent trafficking than to try to heal traumatized victims. Such extreme trauma stays with survivors their whole lives. Psychologists can only help them learn to live with it.

Debt bondage is still the most pervasive form of manipulation.[6] The traffickers impose a system of additional penalties to drive up the debt and keep people in perpetual bondage. For example, if you open a door or window, you receive a fine, which increases your debt. If you smoke a cigarette, you may get a penalty. If you show yourself at the window, you'll get one. So, this is a terrible system that increases what people owe to the traffickers and keeps victims permanently enslaved. Traffickers use lots of ways to manipulate potential victims into debt bondage.

In Cyprus, for example, many trafficked women enter the country as dancers. They enter on a six-month artist visa.[7] Most of these women are "artists" from Moldova and Ukraine. The violation of these women's human rights begins at the border. Upon orders of the owners of the casino, or dance club, or whatever institution promised them a job, the women are taken directly from the border to a clinic for a gynecological exam, without any discussion or choice. If they are clean, they are then taken to the immigration office, where their passports are confiscated for "security reasons." Finally, the women arrive at the bar or casino, where the owners force them into prostitution. We had one case where a woman arrived in Cyprus and her boss asked, "Do you know what you will be doing here?" And she said, "Yes, I will be dancing." And her boss said, "Not *only* dancing." She said that she did not want to provide sexual services. He told her that was fine, but now she must pay him the US$6,000 she owes him for travel expenses, the medical exam, visa services, etc. He told her, "Just pay this money back and you'll be free to go." Of course, she had no money, which is why she went to Cyprus in the first place.

As for destination countries, I believe Russia has the worst conditions. Women there are generally forced into street prostitution. There are stories about pimps taking victims to construction sites where they are gang-raped, and even raped several days in a row. If it's a big trafficking organization, victims are given drugs and alcohol to foster addiction. They are not allowed to use condoms, so many women come back with HIV.

Why do you think conditions are so bad in Russia?
Stella: In Russia, prostitution is illegal. That, plus Russia only very recently adopted a law on human trafficking.[8] We have an IOM mission in Moscow, and a countertrafficking program started there only two years ago after the adoption of the law. Since then, Russia's official cooperation with us has been very good. Recently we've had many rescue operations. Working together with the Russian police, we've been able to rescue several groups of women.[9]

Of course, we need to remember that many of these women who get rescued have already had their spirits broken. The traffickers give them drugs and alcohol, and they become addicted. They don't want to be repatriated because they're afraid of the situation at home, afraid of being stigmatized or rejected by their families or communities. And what are they going to do when they return? They are addicted and have been forced into prostitution. How will they survive back home? In cases where several women are rescued, there are always some women who do not want to be freed. In the case I was telling you about earlier in Cyprus, the lady was rescued during a regular medical check. Remember, they are given medical checkups upon arrival, and then one day each week the casinos and bars take the whole group of female "artists" to the medical center for a checkup. We rescued her when she was at the clinic. She was afraid because we had to take extra precautions with her—we took her into a special room which was guarded by police. All the other women were very angry with her. Some of these women had become drug-addicted and they didn't want to go home.

Did you rescue them anyway?

Stella: No, the police only rescued the woman from Moldova. We organized this with help from our IOM office in Ankara, Turkey, because this woman was on the Turkish side of Cyprus. So, we gave the information we had to Turkey's human trafficking hotline. The hotline got in touch with Turkish law enforcement partners. And the Turkish police got in touch with the Turkish Cypriot police. We did this rescue relatively quickly, and our victim was home before the end of the year. It was very stressful before the rescue because she would call me every night saying, "I will wear an ivory head band so the police can recognize me." We planned this for a long time.

All the other women with her were legally there on artist visas, so they were not determined to be victims of human trafficking. And they did not claim to be victims of trafficking. They were there legally, so they couldn't be arrested. If they don't ask for help, we can't rescue them. In every country—Emirates, Turkey, Russia—there are trafficked women who accept their situation. Because they are in despair and they see no future at home, or they have become alcoholics or drug addicts, they have no desire to leave.

I would imagine many victims become psychologically dependent upon the captors. Do you see that as well?

Stella: Of course, we see the Stockholm syndrome in many girls.[10] Recently, one girl who refused to be rescued wrote us, "He [the trafficker] has treated me well. He bought me clothes and food, and even gave me some money to send home to the children." They just don't understand that their human rights are being violated. It is very difficult for them to see themselves as victims of trafficking. They blame themselves for what happened. They think they deserve it, or whatever.

We also have many cases where johns have helped the victims escape.

Typically, the woman and the john live together for about six months after he helps her. He goes from being a client to her savior, and then to being her boyfriend, until he gets tired of her. Because she entered the country illegally, she has nowhere to go when he kicks her out. It becomes a real tragedy when a child is involved. In most countries, if the child is born in a hospital, the woman cannot register it as hers because she is in the country illegally. She must register the child under the father's name, and then of course the father will never give the child back to her. Often, when the "boyfriends" want to get rid of these women, they simply turn them in to the police. She gets deported without understanding that it is the "boyfriend" who turned her in. When such women get back home, they wait for the "boyfriend" to call them from Turkey, or wherever. It is heartbreaking to watch them slowly understand that no one is going to call, and that they will never see their children again.

One time when I was in Cyprus, I was told that there are many johns who sell their cars, or their jewelry and possessions, to buy their favorite woman from the pimps. But then the woman must go back to Moldova because the artist visa expires. Once home, they have no desire to return to Cyprus, and the poor men suffer a broken heart. So that is the other side of the coin.

I don't think there are many studies on the demand side, which is unfortunate. We need to understand the demand side in order to effectively fight human trafficking. If there is a demand, there will always be a supply. We need to know why these men go to the brothels. When and why do they help women escape? Why do they live with them afterwards? And why do they keep the children? We have a lot of women who can never see their children because they can never return to the destination country. And even if they could, they have no legal claim to the children.

But there are a few cases that don't end in tragedy, I must say. For example, in the Emirates where one john—oh, I get goosebumps thinking about it—one john helped a woman escape and helped her come back home. He then helped her return to the Emirates legally. Now they are married, she has a good job, and it is working well for them. But this is rare. Yet, her trauma never goes away.

And here is a contradiction that I don't understand. So many people in Moldova are religious, but they are not merciful. When they learn of the experiences of these trafficked victims, they shun and exclude these poor women from society. They even rape them. Some men think, "Well, she was trafficked, and she was a prostitute. If she did it with him and him, why can't she do it with us?" I have heard some horrific stories about trafficked victims getting gang-raped in their village once they return home. We had one case where a woman returned home with HIV and everyone in the village found out. Our regulations require that HIV test results come back to the place of origin. Somebody at the post office opened the results and told everybody in the village about it. It was a complete tragedy because even her family turned away from her. They were afraid to eat from the same dishes. It's awful!

We also have had cases where the victims have agreed to testify in court against their traffickers. When the summons to go to court comes in the mail, however, the parents find it, and then the questions start, as do the problems. We just recently talked to a girl that this happened to. Her father opened the summons and found out that she had been trafficked. He told her that if he ever saw her again, he would kill her, because she brings shame to the family. So, she ended up living in the forest. She could only see her mother by looking at her through the window from a distance. Now she is sleeping in an old lady's home, so at least she has a bit of shelter.

Do you get many social orphans as clients?

Stella: Yes, a percentage of our beneficiaries are social orphans. I will have to look in my files to know how many, but yes. There are many boarding-school graduates that the traffickers are after, and it's easy to explain why. When they leave the boarding schools, they have nobody looking after them and no place to live. The state offers them vocational training in the boarding schools, but after graduating, what do they do?

I believe the IOM was the first NGO to start targeting social orphans and boarding schools to protect vulnerable kids. Right?

Stella: Yes. I fought for it, and Martin [Wyss] did too. We adopted two instruments this year that help us in our job: regulations on repatriation and transportation that were implemented, and a memorandum of understanding [MOU] between state agencies on one side and the IOM and La Strada on the other.[11] This greatly improves cooperation through a normative framework.

Do you find many survivors willing to testify against their traffickers?

Stella: No. Testifying retraumatizes them because they must face their pimp or trafficker every day in court. Usually, the pimp gets a very good lawyer who brutalizes the survivor during testimony. So, every time she is interrogated by the pimp's lawyer, she needs more therapy, tranquilizers, and sleeping pills. Plus, the trials take a lot of time. It is a long, painful experience, and sometimes victims change their testimony. That is why now, assistance through the national referral system is not dependent upon cooperation with law enforcement.

Do you get many victims with serious health issues?

Stella: Yes. We have many unaccompanied minors, especially in Odessa, with some very sad stories. We had one case where both a minor and her mother were trafficked and forced into sexual slavery. By the time we found them, the mother had a very advanced stage of AIDS. We did not try to move her, and she died in the hospital. But we thought it was better for her to die abroad in a hospital than during the repatriation process. She was very young, but she looked like she just came out of a concentration camp. She was so abused, malnourished, and sick. It was terrible.

We also have helped a lot of young boys who were trafficked for begging, for work in construction, or for picking up scrap metal. Many of them become addicted to the drugs that their traffickers give them, so their health deteriorates to the point where they cannot work. Then they are forced to beg. Of course, all the boys use the same needles, and they all get HIV. Also, their muscles atrophy because they are forced to sit all day in the street, begging. One boy from Tiraspol[12] we found in the hospital with severely atrophied muscles from begging. We brought him back home, but at first his family didn't want him back. He refused to go to rehabilitation and physical therapy because he feared that if he tried to recover and failed, he would never walk again, and no one would help him. We had to work very intensely with him. But now he is finally recovered and back home with his family.

When people come back addicted to drugs or alcohol, are there programs, like twelve-step programs, to help them?

Stella: There are programs for those that want to recover from addiction, but they are entirely voluntary. Only people who express a desire to get clean or sober are entered into a detox program [*she looks at some statistics on her computer*]. Out of 295 persons repatriated in 2005 and 2006, twenty-two had substance abuse problems. If they want help, we help them.

We also help the families of our beneficiaries. So, if a survivor's husband is an alcoholic and wants help, we provide him with what he needs to recover, too. We take a holistic approach to the family. If we do not alleviate the situation that led to the trafficking, then the victim ends up back in the same bad situation—the same violent husband or father, the same hungry children, or sick parents.

* * * *

At that point the phone rang, and Stella had to go meet someone at the airport. We ended the interview with a promise to meet for another interview. However, it was not until I returned in 2010 that I was able to arrange that second interview with her. This second interview took place on October 19, 2010, at my rented apartment in Chisinau.

I would like you to talk about how human trafficking has changed, if it has. Has it gotten worse as a result of the economic crisis? I know that some researchers are working on that question right now, but I would like to hear your thoughts.

Stella: Well, in Moldova, trafficking is a consequence of migration, first and foremost. The women, men, and teenagers who got trafficked had planned to go abroad to find better opportunities. They sought a better job, or a better salary, or a way to support their family, or to help their sick parents or children. So, if you think about the last two years, nothing has really changed that much. Also, the profiles of victims have not changed much, either. It is still people from poor families with a high level of domestic violence, single mothers or fathers, or people who have a low level of education.

But if we compare now to 2004 or 2005, the countries of destination have changed, trafficking methods have changed, routes have changed, and exploitation methods have changed. But recruitment is essentially the same. Victims are recruited by someone close to them from [the] same community, school, neighborhood, or village. In most cases the recruiters or traffickers pay for the victim's train or plane ticket, and passport. Upon arrival, the passports are confiscated. What we now see compared to 2004 or 2005 is less violence and more manipulation. So basically, the traffickers still earn a lot of money. However, they now give victims small sums of money to send home. And the manipulation is when the victims start thinking, "Okay, here I have US$200 to send back to my family. Okay, I am exploited, but if I go back home, I won't even have this kind of money." Many of them don't even realize that they have been exploited, that they are trafficking victims, or that they have been sold.

Most of the victims are still identified at a local level. Local multidisciplinary teams identify victims in their communities. These teams have specialists from different fields, like doctors, psychologists, social workers, policemen, and teachers. Moldova is not such a big country, communities are not so big, so it is fairly easy to identify a trafficking victim. All of Moldova is like a small town—we all watch each other. This is how most of the victims are identified now, at the local level. If someone goes away for work and comes back with little or nothing, then people notice.

Has the experience of dealing with people who have been trafficked changed the way you think about life or the way you think about people? Or even the way you think about yourself?

Stella: Umm, this is a good question. I think that I would not have been able to work within trafficking if I did not feel compassion for other people. Of course, before I came to the IOM, I was not even aware of trafficking. To work in this field you must really believe the people who are in this situation are telling the truth. That the people who say they are victims of trafficking really are victims. It is important to understand the push factors—where victims came from, and what happened to them—in order to help them.

It's easy to judge a person, but we are not in a position to judge anyone. People abroad who are identified as Moldovans, no matter what their situation is—whether victims of trafficking, or stranded migrants, or unaccompanied children—they are citizens of our country. And if they need assistance, and we can help them, then we *must* help them. There is absolutely no reason to withhold help from any human being.

What can be done to change people's perceptions and attitudes towards victims? Most of the people in Moldova are Christians. They are believers. They go to church, follow their religious holidays. You would think that one aspect of their religion and belief would be compassion. But when it comes to women, they have none.

When we look at men who have been trafficked and come back home, no one sees them as victims. Even they themselves treat this as a failed migration experience, not a trafficking situation. They don't accept assistance, and they don't hurry back to their homes and their families. Their communities do not think of them as victims because they are men. They do not blame and hate him, like they do the women. So, this is a difficult question, with deep roots, I think.

How do you take care of yourself day after day, hearing all of this?

Stella: When I first got this job, I had to do research and read hundreds of victims' stories. Every story is a personal tragedy, but you must try to keep some emotional distance. Sometimes when a mother calls me crying, I also have tears in my eyes. Or when I read a story about how some parents sold their little girl to get some wine, it hurts me. She was being raped and used for sex from the time she was ten years old. But I realize that I must keep my focus because I must work on many cases as horrible as this every day. At the end of the day when I am feeling very, very tired, I go to the gym, work out, and begin to feel more energy. I practice yoga. And I also like reading, I like music, and seeing friends. Although we don't have so much time for friends [*laughs*]. This is how I take care of myself. It is important to be aware of what you're working with, of the risks inherent in this kind of work, and what can be done to protect yourself.

Has your life ever been threatened doing this work? Have you ever felt that you were in any kind of danger?

Stella: Only once. It was around ten at night and I was still at work. That night there was a call, and I answered the phone. It was a man saying, "Stop digging into the story of this girl's life, if you want to be safe." It was something like a threat. So, I said, "Excuse me, but you must have the wrong number." The man said, "I know this is not the wrong number; it is the right number. I will find you if I must." So, I hung up the phone. Later, I called for a taxi to come get me and take me home. I saw a man downstairs who was walking back and forth. And then I thought, "Oh my gosh, what if somebody is really after me for something?" So of course, I was thinking, "What if?" but I didn't actually encounter any danger. It is the victims that get threatened.

There are many cases where victims change their testimonies after they are back home and have already agreed to testify. Many later confess that the recruiters or traffickers offered them money for silence. Because the court procedures take such a long time, they understand that they are still vulnerable because the recruiters and traffickers know where they live and where their family lives. And I think most survivors just want to forget it all and move on.

But of course, they can't forget. On average I think it takes about one and a half years to prosecute a trafficking case. But there are some cases that take much more time—as much as eight, ten years. It depends on the evidence, but this a question for someone in law enforcement.

What personal challenges have you experienced as a result of this work?

Stella: Because I work during the day with all these sad stories of people's problems, I get burnt out. After a day of work, I often don't have enough energy to meet other people, or even talk with other people. I just need time to be with myself. These are my personal challenges. But after six years of working with all these trafficking victims, I still think they deserve assistance, even if they are partly responsible for their problems.

If you look back in history, slaves and rich people have always been around. Modern-day slavery is still here. It's just in a different shape, different colors. But it's a global challenge, and not just a social challenge. It is a problem of people's mentality. In some countries, it's okay for a father and son to go for a weekend to some brothel, it's a tradition in this culture. How do you change that mentality?

Do you think it's possible to change these ideas? And do you think it's possible to end slavery? Or to at least minimize it?

Stella: I believe that if enough people were aware of this phenomenon, they would want to change something—they would want to be kinder, to make the world a better place. Therefore, I do think it's possible to end slavery. We're all human, and what we do is determined by how we think. So, it all goes back to our parents, to our childhoods, to our surroundings, to people who influenced us. We all have the capacity to make choices, to think, to analyze. When a man buys a woman for his sexual pleasure, it's a choice. Maybe she doesn't have a choice and she's held there by force. But he has a choice. So, it's all about who people are, what they want to be, and what they want the world to be for their children and their grandchildren.

I think that what we do here at the IOM is good. It is certainly better than doing nothing, but it's not enough. It's like pouring water into the desert—it has little or no effect. Why is slavery happening? It's because of the way we treat each other. I've been thinking about the men that buy sex. We know from the stories most johns are violent to some degree. Why do they take pleasure in hurting these women? Because they were abused in their childhood? Because they cannot express themselves in normal ways with their friends or their wives? I think it gets down to how parents educate their children. How parents have been educated in their turn. How men treat women in child-parent relationships, husband-and-wife relationships. It's all a circle. Nothing disappears. All anger, all happiness, goes somewhere and comes back.

Since you work in repatriation, I know that you do some follow-up once people get back. You asked me just a couple of days ago if any of my interviewees had stories that ended well. Now that's my question to you. What happens to people when they come back? One of my interviewees said to me, in a very clear way, that something happens to your humanity when you realize that you're only worth $40. That your life can be sold. And I am just wondering if some of the people that you repatriate can come back from that experience. Or if it damages them permanently. Do you know of any success stories?

Stella: Happy stories ... ummmm, there are some stories that turn out okay. There are relatively good endings when women don't tell their friends and families what happened to them. There are happy stories of women who get married or come back to their families and give birth to children that they accept and love. Or they come back to their children and find a job which at least provides them with some income. Sometimes IOM has small-business trainings and income support for setting up a business. There are a few success stories through these programs.

I don't want to sound negative about Moldova, or about its current situation, but this is real. If you look at the profile of the victims, most of them have little education. They come back home, and we offer them vocational training courses, in partnership with the national employment agency. They learn a profession and then they must look for a job. If they're lucky, they find one. But then, what kind of salary do they get? Is it enough to feed their children? Are they able to meet their basic needs? Many victims we know are not able to earn a decent paycheck, so they go abroad again.

If they go abroad again, it doesn't necessarily mean that they will get retrafficked. But again, why do people go abroad? They are looking for better opportunities. So, let's imagine that someday people could receive better salaries. They would just be content living here in Moldova, not going anywhere. There will still be people who want to see other countries, who will want to try new avenues, and why not? Why should a person not be able to travel?

I think when governments of different countries begin to work together to facilitate better immigration, to facilitate a dignified migration, it will give people more rights and more security, and we'll have fewer problems with trafficking and slavery.

If you were going to say anything about all your experiences, something that you think I might need to understand, or that people reading this book would need to understand about trafficking, what would that be?

Stella: I think people need to understand that it is not okay to buy and sell other people, under any circumstances. It is not okay to take advantage of people's vulnerabilities. I think…. I don't even know if I can formulate this…. I think people must learn to be kinder to each other, to help each other. Maybe this sounds too utopian. To help doesn't necessarily mean to share what you have. To help means not to be indifferent. This is a difficult question. People need to know that slavery in its modern incarnation is still going on. They need to understand that no one wants to be raped, used, or sold several times per night. I think people need to know that children are not commodities to be sold and abused by other people.

* * * *

Stella ended the interview on this note. I have remained in contact with Stella over the years. She got married, moved to New York, and left anti-trafficking work far behind. In the last conversation that we had about slavery, Stella indicated that she no longer was able to remain optimistic about ending trafficking and all the misery that causes it and is caused by it. I can't blame her. She spent eight years in the trenches, trying to patch people back together who had endured unspeakable degradations. Just like one of my informants commented that something happens to you when you realize your life is worth only US$40, something happens to you when you see what one human being can do to another.

6

OKSANA, LENA, YULIA, AND NATASHA

Various NGO positions
NGOs: Interaction, IOM
Tiraspol, Transnistria, and Chisinau, Moldova
November 16, 2008, and September 20, 2010

I first met Oksana in October 2008 in Chisinau, Moldova, at an international conference on human trafficking jointly sponsored by La Strada and the International Organization for Migration (IOM). Oksana is the director of the NGO Interaction, in Tiraspol, Transnistria. She is passionate about her work and will stop at nothing to help trafficking victims. When I met her, I immediately thought that if I had been trafficked, I would want *her* in my corner. In our brief conversation at the conference, she invited me to come to Tiraspol to interview her. I told her I would think about it. Numerous people had warned me against going into Transnistria, due to the fact that it was under the control of a separatist regime and could be quite dangerous. Since it was not formally recognized as a country, the U.S. has no embassy there, and my husband and I would be quite on our own if we got into trouble. (Because their work in Transnistria is so dangerous, all the women interviewed in this chapter asked that I not use their last names.)

Transnistria (or, in Russian, *Pridnestrovie*—literally meaning "along the Dniester River") is wedged between Moldova and Ukraine. This tiny strip of land became an outpost for the Russian Empire in 1792, following the Russo–Turkish War. In the twentieth century, Transnistria became a strategically important Soviet military base and home to the Russian 14th Army. During World War II, the Soviets industrialized the area to produce armaments and ammunition. After the war, Moldova absorbed Transnistria as part of the Moldavian Soviet Socialist Republic—one of the fifteen republics of the former Soviet Union. From 1949 to 1952, Leonid Brezhnev, later to become the Soviet leader, personally supervised the "Sovietization" of the Moldavian SSR, deporting some 275,000 Moldovans to Siberia and Kazakhstan. In order to further dilute the Moldovan population, he encouraged ethnic Russians to settle in the region.

Today, Transnistria is officially part of Moldova, although both the Russians and Transnistrians dispute this. On September 2, 1990, as the Soviet Bloc was breaking apart, the Second Congress of the Peoples' Representatives of Transnistria unilaterally proclaimed Transnistria's separation from Moldova. Within three months, Mikhail Gorbachev, then leader of the Soviet Union, declared all decisions taken by the Transnistrian Congress legally void. However, Transnistrians rejected Gorbachev's declaration and fought to break away from Moldova. A civil war ensued, killing more than 700 people. The Russians sent in "peacekeeping" forces, driving the Moldovan army back across the Dniester River. Despite a cease-fire agreement in 1992, the region remains one of several post–Soviet frozen conflicts overseen by Russia, which maintains a strong military presence there.

Transnistria's unilateral declaration of independence isolated it from most of the world and placed it in a legal limbo that paved the way for corruption, poverty, and vastly unequal economic development. Immediately after declaring independence from Moldova, the Transnistrian government privatized most of the industry in the region. Russian and Ukrainian oligarchs immediately took over most of the area's enterprises. The remaining industries became properties of the Russian state.

As a disputed and relatively lawless territory, Transnistria has become a hideout for a variety of criminals, including various neo–Stalinists who took part in purges and human rights abuses in the Soviet era, as well as notorious mafia chiefs and arms smugglers who are avoiding prosecution. Russian and Ukrainian organized crime syndicates operate with impunity in this little strip of land. Hence, the territory has also become a major source area for human trafficking, especially sex trafficking. It is also a major transit country for persons being trafficked east from Europe and west from Russia. At the same time, because of the high level of government corruption, the concentration of crime syndicates in the area, and the retarded development of civic society, most NGOs refuse to work in Transnistria or are refused permission to do so by Transnistrian authorities. I was surprised when Oksana told me Interaction had been operating there for over five years.

Because of the persistence of Soviet–era mentalities and the attendant bureaucracy, it has been extremely difficult for Interaction to function. In this interview, Oksana talks about finding ways around Transnistrian law in order to secure funds to help repatriate and rehabilitate victims of slavery. To the Western reader, this may seem somewhat unethical. However, the legacies of the Soviet period persist and "business as usual" in this part of the world is anything but usual to a typical Westerner. Oksana is determined and unstoppable in her efforts to fight slavery, help trafficked persons, and foster civil society. And under her guidance, Interaction has been quite successful in doing just that.

Consequently, I decided I couldn't pass up the opportunity to visit the last bastion of Soviet life. So, I boarded a stuffy minibus bound for the Transnistrian capital city, Tiraspol, about one and a half hours east of Chisinau. My new friends at the IOM in Chisinau warned me to be wary—the border guards in Transnistria will often arbitrarily turn buses back or pull foreigners off and shake them down for bribes. As fate, luck, and irony might have it, I arrived there on November 7, the anniversary of the Great October (Bolshevik) Revolution.[1] Transnistria, probably the only area left in the world to celebrate the revolution, was decked out in full Soviet regalia.

The first thing I noticed about Tiraspol, a city of a little over 100,000, was that the streets were all but deserted, despite it being an important holiday on the Transnistrian calendar. There was absolutely no litter or graffiti, and there was a general silence among the citizens, who were carefully keeping to themselves. The giant, military statues and monuments of Transnistria mirrored those that represented Soviet splendor in the USSR. There was even an imposing statue of V.I. Lenin standing in front of the Soviet-style presidential palace. An eternal flame flickered weakly above the Tomb of the Unknown Soldier. Old men sat fishing along the sandy banks of the Dniester River as a barge struggled to make its way upstream. On this holiday afternoon, two girls raced horses up and down the main thoroughfare, presumably after taking part in the morning parade.

Having gotten across the unofficial border without incident, the minibus trundled to a stop at the downtown bus station. I met the driver that Oksana had arranged for me on the street. Driving a circuitous route through several neighborhoods, he finally brought me to my destination. As we pulled up to a dreary, nondescript apartment building, I noticed a small sign that said, "Social Development Center." The center is hidden in plain sight in a working-class neighborhood. I asked the driver about it, and he explained that since the anti-trafficking work here is quite dangerous, it is best not to be too obvious. He indicated that I should go down the stairs, into the basement. I gingerly picked my way down a long, dark corridor with rooms on either side in various stages of disrepair. The whole scene felt a little sinister and I was wondering what I had gotten myself into. At the end of the corridor, I opened a heavy metal door and entered the office of Interaction, housed within the Center for Social Development. In contrast to its surroundings, the office was light and warm, with bright posters on the walls and a plant in the window. Oksana was waiting for me, so we launched right into the interview.

When did you start working here and what is it you do?
Oksana: I started here in 2002. Ten of us founded this organization, but we only have three full-time people working here. The rest of our founders are teachers, counselors, and people from other fields who work with our clients on an as-needed basis. We started anti-trafficking work in 2003.

Initially, we offered seminars on human trafficking awareness. I and an acquaintance from another organization taught the seminars. The following year we launched an extensive public information campaign against human trafficking. I already had some experience because I had been helping La Strada in Chisinau reintegrate a group of victims here in Transnistria. La Strada could not work here directly owing to the cold war between Moldova and Transnistria—the local authorities would not permit it. To work with clients in Transnistria, La Strada had to register a separate office here and have a Transnistrian staff. Even as we were setting it all up, we didn't know if the local authorities would actually let us operate here. The Transnistrian government claims that human trafficking is *not* a problem here, and that illegal migration does not happen in Transnistria.

In the end, the government did not allow La Strada to work here. Therefore, when I did any kind of victim assistance, I had to be very discreet because it was basically illegal. La Strada in Chisinau would give me money for victims in Moldovan *lei* [the country's currency] and I had to smuggle it in cash across the border. It was extremely stressful, but I managed to help every client that needed help. It was the same story with the International Organization for Migration. We started working with the IOM in 2004, but we could not accept any humanitarian aid from them because of Transnistrian law. Also, by law, I could only give a maximum of one hundred dollars a year to any one person. But our clients needed everything—food, clothes, shoes. They needed to feed their children. Because we were very limited by how much we could legally help our clients, we had to have two separate bank accounts—one in Chisinau and one in Tiraspol. Donors would give us money in *lei* that we would deposit into our Chisinau account. Some of that money we transferred into our account in Transnistria so we could pay for the electricity, heating, telephone, and office products. We couldn't smuggle all that money over the border—we would get stopped for sure if we tried. Because the laws are so crazy, the money that we use to assist clients we have to smuggle into

Transnistria, and money that we use to run the office, we transfer from one account to another in order to pay the fees and taxes.

Are the majority of your clients female?
Oksana: Yes. We have very few men because men are not yet ready to accept the idea that they have been trafficked and need assistance. Our culture is so patriarchal that our men cannot admit that they may need someone to protect them or save them. They think they must do it themselves.

Does human trafficking in Transnistria differ at all from trafficking in Moldova?
Oksana: No. It is pretty much identical. Well, maybe the destination countries are a bit different. Most victims from Transnistria are trafficked to Turkey, Dubai, Russia, and Ukraine. Moldovans are trafficked to those places too, but they are also taken to Italy, Spain, and Portugal.

Is there as much poverty here as in Moldova?
Oksana: Poverty levels are about the same, except people here get larger pensions because the pensions are paid by Russia. The Transnistrian government pays a small proportion of the pensions but most of the money comes from Russia. We have a lot of Russian citizens who live here but are registered as if they live in Russia.[2] In Moldova, most people are Moldovan or Romanian citizens, while here we have a lot of people not only from Moldova, but also a lot from Ukraine, Russia, and Bulgaria.[3]

Do people here understand the concept of human rights? And do they understand the connection between the violation of those rights and exploitation?
Oksana: Not at all. First, people look at NGOs as if these organizations are all front organizations set up to spy on the population for some state entity like the internal police. People here don't believe an organization can exist without being controlled by the government for some sinister purpose. When I tell potential clients that we are a fully independent nongovernmental organization, they don't believe it. They think we are controlled by the government in Chisinau. People here do not trust the government and they do not believe that anyone would spend time and money to help them. When we help, they say, "Who *are* you? Why are you doing this? What do you want?" And if we stop helping them, they say, "We are going to report you to the president or call the police on you." No matter what we do, people don't believe that we can operate independently from the government.

As for human rights, that is something the people here understand very poorly—very poorly.[4] However, people in positions of power, especially those in the Supreme Council and the president's office, are well educated and understand very well how a civil society is supposed to work and what human rights are. Yet, if someone starts exercising their rights *too much*, those in power will try to put up so many obstacles that one cannot function. For example, our organization put together some informational anti-trafficking seminars. We were all set up to run them. We had all the legal permissions we needed, we had already advertised them, everything. But then at the last minute the local authorities said we couldn't hold those seminars and they tried to shut us down. First, they gave us permission to work, and then they took it away. Again and again, they give us permission, and then take it away. Even though we have a license to engage in educational activities, the authorities try to stop us and make it impossible for us to do our work.

Do the traffickers operate differently here than in Moldova? Can they operate more easily owing to the different legal system?

Oksana: No, it is pretty much the same here as in Moldova. Our local authorities have the legal right to detain someone who is suspected of trafficking. We have an article in our criminal code dealing with trafficking. But the traffickers study the law and find ways around it. In previous years traffickers would take their victims across borders themselves to make sure their "cargo" arrived at its destination. However, Eastern European border guards began to question the girls if several were traveling with one man. Now, the victims travel alone on documents provided by the traffickers. The victims think they are going to a job and voluntarily leave the country, only to be met at the other end by slavers or pimps.

The traffickers create fake job contracts and work agreements for their victims. Before sending their victims out of the country, the traffickers make them sign an agreement stating, "I am voluntarily leaving the borders of Moldova. I am a citizen of such and such a country, am free and understand where I am going. I know that I am traveling on a tourist visa and realize that I do not have a right to work there or to practice prostitution." So, if it ever goes to court for prosecution, it is impossible to convict the traffickers. But, as you know, when she arrives at her destination the traffickers are there waiting for her, and she gets sold and taken to a brothel or locked up in some apartment.

But it is not always prostitution, there is labor exploitation as well. Trafficking for slave labor doesn't get enough attention and needs to be talked about more. People are sold to factories and various other enterprises for forced labor, including begging on the street. When the victims arrive in a different country, the traffickers immediately take them to another city so that the victims do not know where they are. They don't know the name of the city they are in. They might not recognize the language, they don't know when they might be moved again, or what circumstances they may be facing. This is a very common problem in Dubai—a lot of Moldovans are trafficked to Dubai.

What happens if you get a call from Dubai? What steps do you take?

Oksana: Typically, it is the victim's relatives that call our hotline. If given the chance to make a phone call, the victim usually calls a spouse or parent, who then calls our hotline. The hotline collects all the information that the relatives have but sometimes it is not much. If we can figure out where the victim is, even if we can discern what country they are in, then our hotline operators call the IOM. The IOM then gets in touch with their partners in the region—Dubai, for example. Once the victim is found and able to be repatriated, the process is straightforward. The most important thing is that the victim wants to return home and puts a lot of his or her own effort into getting back home.

However, we get some calls from people who have no information about where the victim is—nothing whatsoever that will clue us in to where we might start looking for her. In that case, there is not much we can do until we get more information.

How do you handle a call from someone who doesn't know where he or she is?

Oksana: It is more difficult, but we can find them a lot of the time. You see, when a person leaves the country, they must have some kind of passport or legal document. They don't use the Transnistria passport because no country recognizes Transnistria as a country. Usually, they use a Moldovan passport, but sometimes they have a Russian or Ukrainian passport. Moldovan passports are very easy and fast to process—you can get one within one day. So, when someone crosses the border out of Moldova, that person goes into a database. When the victim enters a country and goes through customs, it is also noted in the database. In other words, we can usually trace a person's movements every time they cross an international border because the passport is scanned at customs. So, we can at least often figure out what country a victim might be in.

However, it is nearly impossible to find people who cross borders illegally. A lot of people from here cross into Ukraine illegally, and from there into Poland illegally, and on into the European Union. This is easy to do. But finding someone in the EU is very difficult. It is a large territory and there are no internal borders. People can move freely between countries without a trace.

Once you do find them and bring them home, what happens after someone is repatriated?

Oksana: We have a whole assistance package including medical help, legal support, and educational assistance. We also provide vocational training as well as small grants and loans for survivors to start businesses. Transnistria has no money to finance these programs. We get the lion's share of our money from the IOM. We also have several donors from European NGOs, and we get some money from the European Union. There are quite a few international programs aimed at helping victims of trafficking.

In the beginning, none of these organizations wanted to give money to Transnistria since we are a so-called breakaway region. Their focus was on Moldova. But then more and more persons were getting trafficked from Transnistria, so they decided it would be better if they could help us, too. I consider it a violation of human rights *not* to help someone in crisis. I thought it was horrible when the organizations designed to help trafficked persons didn't want to help people here in Transnistria. If they know people are in crisis, despite the politics, why not help? They have a moral obligation to help us!

In Chisinau, Moldova, there are several international NGOs working on human trafficking. Are there any international missions here in Tiraspol?

Oksana: No, Interaction is the only organization working against human trafficking here in Transnistria. In Moldova, of course, there are more organizations because the state has declared an intention to stop human trafficking. But here, unfortunately, the government is only beginning to understand that we have a problem with human trafficking. The government is only now preparing to pass a law regarding trafficking. But I think it is practically impossible because trafficking legislation is not a priority for them. Someone needs to shake them and scream, "Ratify it now!" Every time I call our legislative representative, I say, "Please ratify this law; please ratify it now!"

I am afraid that is all the time I have now. I got a call yesterday from a victim and I must go now to meet her. Lena and Yulia can answer any more questions you might have.

* * * *

While I had been interviewing Oksana in the Interaction office, Lena and Yulia were busy at the desk. The office has only one desk and all three service providers must share it while answering phones and writing reports. Yulia is the head of public relations and public outreach for

Interaction. Lena helps with reintegrating victims. As the interview wore on, I discovered that Lena and Yulia also ran the hotline. They had one cell phone between them, which was the Transnistria hotline for human trafficking. They took turns taking it home with them at the end of the day in case a distress call came in after working hours. The two complement each other very well and interviewing them was delightful.

Lena, do you get many calls from relatives who think their family member was trafficked, when in fact she was not? How do you handle that?

Lena: Well, for example in one recent case we got a call from a man who introduced himself as the father of a girl who left the country eight years ago [in 2000] for Cyprus. She initially was there to visit a girlfriend and have a little vacation. While there, her girlfriend arranged for her to get a job as a waitress, so she stayed and worked in Cyprus for four years. In 2004, she returned home because her mother was sick. She stayed only a short time and returned to Cyprus.

The father said that it had been four years since anyone has heard anything from her. He said it was very unlike her not to call. According to the father, his daughter quarreled with her girlfriend and after that she went missing. He said that his daughter left behind two children—one an underage boy and the other a twenty-year-old girl. Both siblings were living with their grandparents, who were pensioners. Since they have very small pensions, it is quite difficult for them to provide for their two grandchildren.

He did not ask for any social or financial assistance. He just wanted us to help him find his daughter or to find out what happened to her. Of course, we set the case in motion, asking the father for all the information he had. He had a copy of his daughter's passport, which helped a lot. However, just two days ago he called us to apologize and asked us to close the case. He said his wife was gravely ill and did not want him to be looking for his daughter. She has no desire to find out what happened to her daughter. Sometimes there is this kind of conflict within a family. Naturally, we closed the case.

We have had other cases where a friend calls the family and says, "She is fine, she is just really busy, and it is very expensive to call. But do not worry, she is working and doing well." But the friend was working for the traffickers as a recruiter, and everything was *not* all right. So, we must be very careful. Frequently, relatives themselves are the recruiters. Uncles, aunts, friends, relatives can all be recruiters. Even parents. Sometimes parents will sell their children, thinking the child will have more opportunities abroad, not understanding what happens to these children under the control of a trafficker.

Most Transnistrians who get trafficked from here are from small villages. Most of them don't even know that you need a passport to go abroad, they are *that* naïve. They only know life in the village—cows, goats, fields, and farm work. They can't even imagine what might happen to them or their children abroad. They think everyone who lives abroad lives like a millionaire. Many people think that going abroad will give them a splendid life.

Can you say how common it is that friends or relatives act as recruiters?
Lena: Well, we don't keep track of this type of statistic but in most cases that is exactly what happens. The victim almost always has some kind of a relationship with the recruiter, either as a friend or a relative. There are even cases where husbands sell their wives.

In a recent case, a man whose wife got trafficked to Lebanon called us. He said that she had gone there before, but always on a work visa to do temporary contract work. In the past she always came back with money. She worked as a waitress in Lebanon, and everything was legal and decent. She was not a sex worker of any kind. But now he hasn't heard anything from her.

This last time, she decided to use an agent or a middleman to find work in Lebanon. This agent called the wife's mother and gave her a mobile phone number that she could use to call her daughter. When the mother called that number, her daughter said that her passport and documents had been taken from her and that she was locked up with some other girls and forced into prostitution. The husband found the "agent." It turns out the employment "agent" was a recruiter. The husband tried to persuade this recruiter to free his wife. The recruiter said that if he wanted his wife back, he had to first pay two thousand dollars for the medical exams, travel documents, and other expenses associated with taking his wife to Lebanon. This is a huge sum of money for us. We ended up turning the case over to the IOM just this week, so I don't know what is happening with it now.

[At this point, Yulia finished her task and joined in the interview.]

***Does it often happen that the police or government officials are working with the traffickers, getting bribes or payoffs?*[5]**
Yulia: Well, we know that the traffickers are getting fake documents made through the embassy. So, there must be someone helping them from the inside. Recently we had two cases like that. In one case, a woman was taking a minor girl across the border, and they got stopped. One customs official noticed something was wrong, that the woman was wearing a wig and

glasses to disguise herself. The girl was only fifteen years old, even though her passport said she was three years older. So, some official helped her get that fake passport. In another case a travel agency was sending people abroad and arranging legal visas and work permits. However, the agency was working with some traffickers who would meet the clients at their destination and then force them into prostitution or slave labor. Some of the victims are pressing charges against that travel agency now. The case has been going on for over a year already.

How did you come to work in trafficking?

Lena: I didn't really. Before I started working here, I had no idea that such a thing existed. But it is everywhere. I will tell you a story about myself, about the recruiting process.

Yulia: Tell them how you almost got trafficked.

Lena: I have a very good friend—my best friend, in fact. One day, I got an e-mail from him that said, "Lena, I have some good friends who are in the business of finding people work abroad—in Israel and other places. It is contract work that pays really well. They arrange work visas for people to leave the country. If you have a desire to work abroad and make good money, write me back." He doesn't know where I am working now, or what I do here. We are not supposed to tell anyone where we work or what we are doing because it is very dangerous. So, my best friend, either knowingly or not, was trying to recruit me for trafficking.

Yulia: Yes, it's a very typical case of recruitment.

Lena: Naturally, I did not reply to the message. I did absolutely nothing. So, this is how easily people get trafficked through acquaintances.

Of course, sometimes no matter how careful you are, you can still get trafficked. We have cases where women go on vacation and get sold. One woman bought a packaged tour to Turkey that was legal and legitimate. She got in a taxi in Istanbul and the taxi driver just stole her. He kidnapped her and sold her to some pimps. She was just on vacation, and she got trafficked. That is why it is so scary.

Yulia: They will sell anyone, even their relatives. That's the power of greed.

You've said it and Oksana mentioned it too—that the work you do here is dangerous. Can you expand on that a bit?

Lena: Yes, it is very dangerous. Even before I started working here Oksana was getting death threats from someone. To this day, when she goes out on a call, she is not sure if it is real, or if someone is waiting there to kill her. Have you seen our door here? [*The door is a very thick steel security door with an alarm and a very secure lock.*] That door says it all. When I come in on the weekend and work by myself, I lock myself in and shut the windows and curtains because it is very dangerous. We have gotten a lot of threats on the telephone.

The recruiters do not like our work because we are rescuing people while they are trying to sell them. That is why we do not publicize the address of our office. We also do not tell even our friends where we work or what we do. Only the very closest family members may know anything about our work. And even then, it is best if they don't know too much. We never give our names on radio or in newspapers, and never show our faces on TV, because it is a very small town. If one person finds out, soon the whole town will know. And then we would have to have bodyguards, and no one wants that.

Yulia: Yes, it's a very dangerous field. We often get death threats.

You said it was a small town—do you know the recruiters?

Lena: Not personally, but we know their names and phone numbers because our clients often tell us who recruited them.

* * * *

It was time to end the interview. I needed to catch a minivan back to Chisinau. As I left the building, I couldn't help but wonder if someone was watching us, if Oksana, Lena, and Yulia would remain safe, and how long they could keep working under such difficult conditions.

When I returned to Moldova two years later, in 2010, I arranged to interview Oksana again, but this time in the offices of the IOM in Chisinau. I was very interested to learn what had changed over the intervening two years and how her work was going. Natasha, a public outreach expert with the IOM, joined us for the interview. Oksana herself had not changed—she still had the seriousness of purpose that I had noticed before. I wondered how she did not get cynical, with so many victims and so little government help.

Oksana, are you still the hotline coordinator for Transnistria?

Oksana: Yes. But now we coordinate with the hotline for domestic violence. Interaction is still working in public outreach in Transnistria and for the IOM. We have started to identify potential victims through the domestic violence hotline. Most trafficking victims were previously victims of domestic violence.[6] Of course, women can also be victims of domestic violence after having been trafficked. Imagine the incredible stress in a family when the husband or wife is so severely traumatized. When a slave is returned home, it is very difficult for all members of the family and can often lead to some form of domestic violence. We now have two hotlines, one for domestic violence and one for human trafficking.

We provide information about legal migration and about the risks it entails, as well as new rules for labor migration in other countries. As we expected, people are returning home now because of the financial crisis. Demand for labor is down everywhere, so many Moldovans working abroad have lost their jobs and are returning home. They do so not only because the financial crisis makes it harder to find work abroad, but because they miss their homes and their families.

As for the domestic violence hotline, we receive at least one hundred calls a month depending upon the time of the year. The number of calls to the hotline is increasing every month. Because of good advertising and outreach, people are getting used to the idea of NGOs helping with various social services. In our country, social services are a new thing and not everybody knows how to find or get help from these services.

Do you think they are still afraid of asking for help from an NGO?

Oksana: Oh yes, they're afraid. Additionally, Transnistria is not very big, and most people live in Tiraspol, a city of only about 100,000 people. These people know each other and are afraid to call to ask for help. They are afraid someone will find out that they have been forced into prostitution or beaten by their spouse.

We have other obstacles as well. For example, last week we had a call from La Strada in Chisinau. Their trafficking hotline received a call from a woman who was trafficked from Moldova to Transnistria. The traffickers planned to take her from Transnistria to Russia and then to the Emirates. Moldovan police are not allowed to enter Transnistria, even to collect a trafficking victim. So, they called me. I called the Ministry of Internal Affairs in Transnistria to see if someone could transport her to Chisinau. But the Ministry is not well equipped or trained in how to handle trafficked persons. The policemen in Tiraspol sat in the house with this girl and waited for someone to take her to Chisinau. Meanwhile, the trafficker showed up and the Transnistrian police were able to take him into custody while another one of our cops took her to a shelter. This took two and a half hours. Our policemen are ready to help, but they need training—they don't know what to do with victims.

In Bender there are two authorities, Moldovan and Transnistrian.[7] Transnistria controls the area, but Moldova has a police force there for border security. The Transnistrian and Moldovan border police cooperate unofficially. They're friends and probably have beers after work together. It's so strange. Politically they can't be friends. The law states that the Moldovan police cannot operate there. But Transnistria and Moldova have a mutual agreement through their Ministries of Internal Affairs to exchange criminals. So, if the Moldovan police take somebody from Bender, the local government will not stop them.

We also work in partnership with a different NGO who received a grant from UNIFEM [United Nations Development Fund for Women] to lobby for a law against domestic violence. I don't know the results. Domestic violence is a huge problem here.

Natasha: I haven't seen any information yet.

What about the human trafficking hotline? Do you get many calls on it?

Oksana: Over the last two years we have been getting between sixty and seventy emergency calls per year from people who have been trafficked abroad. Some of the cases are still open and we are still in contact with the victims, collecting as much information as we can so that we might be able to get them out. Usually, they are girls calling from the Emirates, or Russia, or Turkey. We send all the information to the IOM because they have working agreements with a lot of different countries. Once we have enough information, usually within two or three days, we can help rescue them.

What percentage of the calls result in an actual escape or rescue?

Oksana: Our success rate is around 80 percent. We consider success as knowing what happens to the girls. Not all of them want to come home. For example, we sometimes will get a call from the mother of a girl who says, "I cannot find my daughter." Then, when we find the daughter, it turns out that she is not trafficked and is not interested in coming back home. This happens rarely. Sometimes a parent just wants to find out where his or her daughter is.

Natasha: If I remember statistics correctly, we had more calls about domestic violence on the trafficking hotline than on the domestic violence hotline. There is more trust for the trafficking hotline, maybe because it has been around longer and is better advertised.

Two years ago [2008] it was still not known what kind of impact the global financial crisis would have on immigration and trafficking. People working in NGOs said that they expected waves of immigrants coming home because there were fewer jobs in Europe. At that time the IOM estimated that about one-third of Moldova's workforce was working outside of Moldova, so there were a lot of social orphans. Has that changed in the last two years?

Natasha: It was initially expected that there would be a wave of migrants coming back. That did not happen. People preferred to stay abroad even without work. Those who migrate illegally still must pay people to help them. We don't know exactly how much people are paying to go abroad illegally now. Two years ago, people paid about US$2,000 to arrange for a job in Europe illegally. Now it might be as high as US$4,000. If it is for a professional job, or highly skilled labor, it might cost even more.

As for the children left behind, there are about 100,000 Moldovan children with both parents abroad, according to the Ministry of Education. But their statistics are not the most trustworthy. Moldova really needs to see what the real situation is.

Would you be willing to talk about yourselves personally? How did you get into this kind of work? What is your educational background? Why trafficking, and how do you sustain your work in trafficking? What kinds of challenges do you have in your personal lives?

Natasha: My university degree is in software programming. [*Everyone laughs—it seems a strange degree for working in anti-trafficking.*] My second degree was in foreign languages, English. I worked as a freelance translator for a time. When I came to IOM, I actually started as a field coordinator working with Holocaust survivors. About three years later, that program ended and I transferred to the countertrafficking unit. I do not work directly with victims of trafficking, but sometimes I go to interview the families of victims. Mainly my job is to supervise contractors and contracts. So, I don't have the emotional burden of dealing directly with trafficked victims.

Of course, when you meet the families together with the victims, it still affects you emotionally. I know that the people who are on the front lines get severe burnout. My burnout is just from workload. People who hear the stories, like those in social assistance, psychologists, etc., their burnout is much worse.

Oksana: There was one situation in my own life where I could have been trafficked. But because of God maybe, the minibus I was on was stopped by the military police, and we were not taken by the traffickers but were sent home. I lived in Tiraspol, but that experience took place in Macedonia. At the time, I didn't see the significance in the fact that the bus was full of young, nice-looking women. It's strange. I didn't understand what was happening at the time—I thought we were going for employment abroad. Thank God the military police stopped the bus before we got to our destination! A policeman investigated the situation and said it was trafficking. The traffickers denied it. No one took any money from us, but they did take our passports. None of it seemed strange to me at the time because I did not know what trafficking was. And the person who was taking us abroad seemed normal. I believed what he said.

When I started working in countertrafficking, I understood how young women could be so naïve. This work in human rights in general, and especially in countertrafficking and civil society development, these are my specialties. I had to study it on my own. I try to learn more about children's rights and women's rights—gender equality. These areas are also related to my topics. I have a love of culture, especially music, and I am an organizer for the theater. That helps with the burnout, working with music and the theater. But sometimes I get so very tired. Sometimes I send someone else out on calls, like Natasha, when I am too tired or burned out. Or I can call Natasha and ask her to listen to me and tell me if I am all right.

Natasha: In my opinion, after working in countertrafficking a person becomes more critical, maybe even cynical. When I look at news stories about certain people and situations in another country, I think to myself, "This is probably trafficking." You know, you become much more aware of it. Oksana mentioned how young girls can be so naïve. But I must tell you that during perestroika, which were very difficult times without any possibilities for work and without access to the basic necessities, I went through periods when I was looking for any kind of job. Twice I read announcements in the newspapers and went, here in Chisinau, where they were gathering girls for Cyprus. I went to one "job interview" where there was a man and a couple of teenage girls. I was seeking an office position. But he said, "No, we have nothing here. But in Cyprus it would be so much better: better work and more money." But I simply didn't want to leave Chisinau for Cyprus.

I was not so desperate, because my relatives worked and we survived by helping each other. So, I didn't go for that job. A couple of months later, I answered another ad. I went to a different address and met the same man! He and his network rented old one-story buildings with small offices in the same area of the city center to set up phony employment agencies. They moved from building to building to give the appearance of a new and different "employment agency." This was early in 2000. I had absolutely no idea what human trafficking was.

Then within a year and a half I got a job with the IOM. Because I wanted to stay with my family, I refused to leave Chisinau for jobs in Cyprus and escaped getting trafficked. Now when I look back on those interviews, it absolutely looks like recruitment to me. And the second time it seemed to me that the guy recognized me.

Happily, I found a job, but even a person with a university degree, like me, has limited opportunities here. That is why migration is so high in Moldova. Because of my experience of almost getting trafficked, I now realize that when a person is led by circumstances, they cannot judge clearly or make good decisions even when they are being very careful.

Has this work affected your personal lives?

Oksana: My husband doesn't believe that my work has any value. He thinks it's not as important as construction, for example. He is an electrician, which he thinks makes him secure. He also thinks that NGOs do not need to help people or educate them. It's up to families to educate their own.

My life is affected by the political situation in Transnistria. Sometimes local authorities try to stop NGOs from working. For example, a local politician will call me and invite me to come talk to him about our work. When I get to his office, he starts asking questions like, "Why do donors give you money? What do you tell them? How much do they give you and other NGOs?" Then at the end of the discussion he will say, "You know, I dreamed about you." And I think either he needs a psychiatrist, or I do. You never know what will happen. It is strange and scary.

Or some policeman will call me on a Saturday evening and say, "Hi. I have some information for you, and I will come to your home." I tell him, "No, please don't come, it's Saturday." One time my husband was home, so he went with me to meet the policeman. But there was no information, it was just some phony excuse to harass me. I live by the law, by moral values. I don't do anything wrong, but I get threatened a lot by the police and local politicians. So now, when anyone calls me and asks to meet me, I send an e-mail to all my friends to let them know that I was asked to go somewhere and tell them where. When I get home, I send them a note letting them know that I am back, and everything is okay.

It seems like I am nervous all the time. When I can leave Transnistria, I sleep better, and I can think about things other than work. In general, every day when I first open my eyes, I really don't think about my children. I think about my security, about my work, and about what is going to happen next. That is not normal, but it is for me, you know. These threats and my anxiety are also not very good for my husband. He doesn't like my work.

Do you ever get to rest?

Oksana: Actually, sometimes I say that I would like to have a holiday for a year. And my staff say, "Please don't go away for a long time!" If I leave the office for a week, or sit with my small child at home, I call them to ask how they are and they say, "Come back!"

You know, we bought [the] office space that we are in [in Tiraspol] two years ago. I don't exactly know how this happened, but I worked on this idea to invite volunteers from the U.S.A. to come and help our organization. And two volunteers came! A lot of foreign delegations came to look at our work here. They described our work and our needs and circulated it among donors. And those donors gave us the money. This is really good therapy for me, you know? To get this kind of support and be able to help more people. We will renovate the building with a new entrance, so one part can be more secure for hotline workers. We are growing, but it is not easy. Sometimes I just need to rest.

For three years now we have had volunteers come from the U.S.A. They come to our office and make our lives more colorful. We share ideas and they help us with resource management. They also help us with fundraising. Because life in the States is so comfortable, sometimes our American volunteers don't understand what we need. Even when they become members of an international organization, they don't understand. That's why I invite anybody who wants work in trafficking to come here in order to better understand the situation. The Peace Corps cannot come because Transnistria is not a recognized country. But other people can come—your students, for example. It will only cost them US$100 per month for an apartment, and US$100 for food and transport. I will send you my e-mail address, and you can send me volunteers [*laughing*].

Well, that sounds like a fair exchange. Oksana, thank you for your time. And good luck with your work here.

* * * *

I did not stay in touch with Oksana once I left Europe. However, I have been following her through her NGO's website. Interaction has broadened its focus since I was there. Their stated purpose is now to "promote gender equality and fight trafficking in human beings, to encourage individuality, creativity and development of critical thinking skills of children, and to build civic society by facilitating cooperation between non-governmental organizations, initiative groups and other sectors of the society."

Since Russia's 2022 invasion of Ukraine, Interaction has offered summer camps in Moldova for Ukrainian children between the ages of 14 and 17. The programs are intended to support Ukrainian children living abroad, helping them build self-confidence, gain life skills, and forge friendships with other Ukrainian children living abroad.

Oksana is now the executive director. I wonder if she ever got that rest she so badly wanted. I suspect not.

7

Ion Vizdoga

Director
NGO: Center for the Prevention of Trafficking in Women
Chisinau, Moldova
October 18, 2008, and September 23, 2010

Ion Vizdoga agreed to meet me in his office at the Center for the Prevention of Trafficking in Women in downtown Chisinau, Moldova. As I waited for him to arrive, I wondered who, exactly, Ion might be. I heard of him from various anti-trafficking professionals, and everyone seemed to have a great deal of respect for him. He litigates trafficking cases. In Moldova, it requires a tremendous amount of courage and an even greater amount of integrity to withstand bribes and threats in order to pursue justice. Ion was a federal prosecutor in Chisinau, Moldova, from 1993 to 2002. He then served as the director of the Center for the Prevention of Trafficking in Women beginning in 2003. That he had not been corrupted, harassed out of anti-trafficking work, or been killed spoke volumes about him.

One of Ion's main tasks at the Center was to convince victims not to withdraw their criminal cases against their traffickers. Between 2003 and 2008, the Center represented more than a thousand trafficking victims and Ion personally represented well over 200 of them. Most trafficking cases in Moldova never get to court, and those that do often drag on for years. There are endless frustrations and dangers for prosecutors and witnesses associated with human trafficking trials in Moldova. Indeed, in 2006 the Organization for Security and Co-operation in Europe (OSCE) began monitoring such trials in Chisinau. The resulting report documented witnesses receiving poor treatment by the court and by law enforcement, abuse, and even threats from both the defendants and the judges. One judge even told the OSCE monitors, "These young ladies are prostitutes. They go abroad and prostitute themselves but are not happy with the money they get. So, upon their return they complain that they were trafficked."[1]

That same year, the American Embassy in Chisinau also conducted a study of trafficking trials in Moldova. It revealed an utter failure to protect victims who agreed to testify against their traffickers. It also uncovered in the courts a pattern of downgrading trafficking charges to pimping, thereby reducing many sentences to small fines. The courts also often released defendants from jail before their trials had even been concluded.[2]

In 2005, under pressure from the U.S. government, Moldova passed a strong anti-trafficking law. Since then, despite all the problems, Ion and the Center have helped to convict hundreds of recruiters from Turkey, Russia, Ukraine, Albania, Romania, Israel, and Serbia. However, more and more recruiters are from Moldova since they are less conspicuous and better protected by their networks. So now, typically, foreign traffickers will buy a woman from a Moldovan recruiter and sell her abroad for five times the original purchase price. Most often it is the recruiters who are arrested and tried in trafficking cases, yet they don't figure significantly in the trafficking chain. They typically are women, and often themselves are the victims of trafficking or some kind of coercion.

Making the fight against human trafficking more difficult is the high level of corruption among the police and government officials. I wanted to meet Ion because I knew that he spoke openly about the complicity of the police and high-ranking officials in sex trafficking from Moldova. Further, as Moldova was trying to create some kind of legal system following the collapse of the Soviet Union in 1991–1992, people like Ion came face to face with the crime of human trafficking before it had even been identified as such, before there were any legal definitions of human trafficking, and before there were any laws prohibiting it. In this interview Ion discusses his early attempts to create legislation that would prevent the selling of children abroad, as well as his encounters with government corruption.[3]

Finally, Ion strode into the office. He was very tall and very large, and his energy filled the room. He was a youthful thirty-eight-year-old, with a keen intelligence and an inquisitive nature. He immediately took control of the interview, as if he had been dying to tell his story for a long, long time and now was dumping the information as fast as he could. He spoke amazingly fast and with great emphasis and inflection. By the end of the interview, I was exhausted from trying to keep up with his rapid-fire information, his quick mind, and his deep compassion.

Can you talk about when human trafficking first appeared in Moldova and how it has developed?

Ion: Yes. Under the Soviet Union all the international borders were closed but there were no borders between Soviet republics. You couldn't leave the Soviet Union, but you could travel anywhere *within* the Soviet Union. For example, if you wanted to leave Moldova and go to, say, Vladivostok, Russia, to do some work, there was no problem. That would have been entirely legitimate. The only problem would be the issue of residency registration.[4] Consequently, when the Soviet Union collapsed, the newly independent countries were not prepared to monitor movement across borders. That is one reason why human trafficking appeared almost immediately after the collapse of the Soviet Union in 1992—because the borders were so open.

I started working in the Prosecutor's Office in 1993 and worked there until 2002. The first cases of human trafficking that I investigated were as early as 1994–95. These were cases of children who had been trafficked largely for adoption. At that time, former Soviet states had no legislation regulating the international adoption of children because all these newly emergent countries were just starting to build their legislatures and legal codes. They were only just beginning to pass legislation. So, in 1994–95 we began to see cases of children, even newborn babies, that were stolen from Romania and trafficked through Moldova. It was easy to cross the Romanian border with a child if you had the child's birth certificate. Nothing else was required. You didn't need proof of parenthood, or guardianship, not even a photo ID—nothing.

Traffickers, usually unmarried women, would travel to Romania, pick up a stolen child, and transport it back to Moldova. Once in Moldova, fake documents were made for the child and the "mother." This was before we had wide use of computers in this part of the world. All legal documents were handwritten. The "mother" would marry a foreign citizen interested in "adopting" the child for a handsome price. The foreign citizen would automatically get legal paternal rights over the child. And so, the new "dad" would then leave the country with the child, never to be heard from again.

I had not heard of this before.

Ion: Yes, if you didn't work in law enforcement at the time you would not have heard of this. Most people started working in anti-trafficking after 2002, but these cases were even earlier than that—in 1994–95.

Because we were investigating criminal cases involving trafficked children, we found another type of trafficking network involving pregnant women, especially students or unemployed women. This was still in the mid-1990s. At that time Moldovans struggled with abject poverty. A lot of people had absolutely no money to buy milk, bread, or anything. So, this network would find unmarried pregnant women who went to state clinics to have abortions. The traffickers would pay these girls not to have the abortions but to carry their pregnancies to term. They would rent apartments for these women, so that there would be five or six pregnant women living in each apartment. There was always a nurse with them that gave them food and vitamins. Every week the girls would be taken to a clinic for prenatal checkups. Right before they gave birth, the girls would marry a foreign citizen that the traffickers had arranged to be here in Moldova at the time of the birth. As soon as the child was born, the "dad" took the baby out of the country. We found over thirty women who had basically sold their children to foreigners through this large trafficking ring that included attorneys, judges, and even people who worked at ZAGS, where marriages are registered.[5] It was a huge network.

However, because there was no legislation regarding taking children abroad, and because the ZAGS documents claimed that the man was the natural father, we could do nothing about it. After we identified this criminal network, the Prosecutor's Office worked to change the legislation so that foreign nationals would be prohibited from taking children abroad. Ultimately, we enacted European-style laws regarding adoption. But at that time, there were no laws against trafficking persons or exporting children outside the country.

Also, in the mid-1990s, traffickers would run want ads for young women in our newspaper *Makler*.[6] Typically the ad would say something like, "Looking for young, good-looking women without complexes to work abroad ... for US$500 a month." At that time, five hundred dollars was a lot of money.[7] The *Makler* was full of these kinds of ads put out by *registered* employment firms. These ads caught my attention because at the Prosecutor's Office I was responsible for recent cases of exporting people.[8] These firms were really front organizations for human traffickers. They would gather a group of women—singers or dancers, for example—and send them abroad to work. The traffickers arranged visas for the women and obtained all the necessary documents from the Ministry of Culture. Then the whole group would leave Moldova, ostensibly to work abroad. However, these "women without complexes" would actually be enslaved and forced into prostitution.

We categorized all those actions as illegal enterprises. The officials helping to arrange these trips abroad were getting payoffs from the traffickers and not declaring that money as income. Remember, at that time we did not know what human trafficking was. There was no European Convention against trafficking, no laws against it—nothing![9] So, in 1995 we proposed new legislation to address the issue of selling human beings. Consequently, in Article 105 of our criminal code we added a provision against selling people—pimping.[10] And all those cases involving women forced into prostitution came under this new law against pimping. Those charges carried only fines, not prison sentences.

The first article that directly addressed human trafficking came into our criminal code in 2001, Article 113.2. But this article only addressed the trafficking of children, because those were the first trafficking cases we had. The penalties were very light because we really didn't know what the trafficking of children really meant. At that time, we at the Prosecutor's Office worked closely with Parliament. We would see some type of activity, like trafficking, that had no existing laws prohibiting it. Then we would propose a new law to Parliament and usually within six months or so Parliament would sign it into law. It was an interesting time, and there was a good level of collaboration between the Prosecutor's Office and Parliament because we were getting such new types of crimes. So, in 2001 we adopted a new article on human trafficking that was informed by the Palermo Protocol. Also in 2001 we opened the Department to Combat Human Trafficking under our existing Department for Combatting Organized Crime.

Then in 2003, we got an entirely new legislative system to meet international standards. Article 165 of the new criminal code dealt with human trafficking. We had to make some amendments right away to the new code. For example, we made a provision so that trafficking victims could not be charged with crimes that they were forced to commit while under the control of a pimp or trafficker. For example, a woman forced into sexual slavery by a trafficker could not be charged with prostitution. These types of legal protections had to be implemented because often trafficked victims are forced into committing crimes such as stealing or selling drugs.

I had a difficult case from Dubai where charges were brought against victims for crossing the border illegally with fake passports. A group of Moldovan women were trafficked to Dubai. The traffickers took their passports as soon as they cleared passport control. The traffickers then altered those passports and gave them to some trafficked women from Ukraine, with the Ukrainians' pictures in them. They gave the Moldovan women passports taken from other trafficked women with the Moldovans' pictures in them. That way the women had "official" IDs, but they could not use them to go home because they had no passport for their home country.

In Dubai, Turkey, and elsewhere, one cannot check into a hotel without a passport. Also, visitors must leave their passports at the reception desk of any hotel. So, the traffickers could put the women up in hotels with fake IDs in order to service johns, but the women would not run away because they could not go home, since they actually held passports from some other country. Three of our girls ran away anyway. They got arrested trying to cross the border into Moldova with fake documents and were charged with falsifying state documents. But since we changed the criminal code, all three women won their criminal cases.

There were many cases in which victims were charged with crimes. That is because law enforcement in the former Soviet Bloc is the opposite of how law enforcement is supposed to operate. Our system operates solely to report to the Parliament. It is not concerned with protecting society or an individual's rights. The ultimate goal, of course, is to report that everything is okay. And that kind of orientation violates the rights of the accused, the indicted, and the victim. Law enforcement doesn't care about human rights or civil rights. The only thing that is important is the quota[11]—how many cases they closed this month.

In Moldova, each police officer must sift through hundreds of crimes, but the planned quota calls for closing 151 cases a month—not 149, not 152, but 151. No more, no less. They always hold back on prosecuting numerous cases so that they can always hit the planned target. That way it looks like crime is always under control, at least statistically. But crime was not under control. Between 1995 and 2000, armed gangsters basically controlled the city of Chisinau. At night they would drive around, and no one would mess with them. Even the police were afraid of them.

Why do you think law enforcement wanted to simply say that crime was under control and not to actually deal with crime on the streets?

Ion: Largely because it was not possible to control crime. The problems were huge, so the authorities wanted to at least give the impression that things were okay, even though they weren't. And I can't really say that things have changed that much. Now the largest criminal network operating in Moldova—the main organized crime syndicate—is the Ministry of Internal Affairs itself.[12] After the Communists came back into power, they liquidated the organized crime networks.[13] The Communists had some very effective methods for wiping out organized crime—they used all sorts of extralegal methods, including beatings. They would arrest and imprison people without an investigation or a trial back then. So, most of the criminals simply left Moldova. They ran away. This all happened during Petru Lucinschi's time.[14]

One of the biggest organized crime bosses was a guy by the name of Grigory Karamalak. He was by far the most powerful syndicate crime boss in Moldova. I was at the Prosecutor's Office when he got arrested, but the court let him go free.[15] He paid big money bribes to be released. The authorities illegally confiscated all his property, so he left Moldova. This was in the authorities' best interests, because if he was here, sitting in jail, he would have a phone and he would still be running his operations from his prison cell.

As it was, numerous authorities confiscated all his businesses, especially his gas stations—Karamalak owned all the gas stations in Moldova—and transferred them into their own names as their personal property. They made his illegal businesses legal under their names. Corrupt authorities and policemen got their hands on his businesses, and he ran away. They left him with nothing here in Moldova, so he went to Russia. He is still living as a free man in Moscow, and we cannot extradite him because he became a Russian citizen.[16] Also, we can't really convict him of anything because we can't find anyone to testify against him. He was the kingpin of organized crime here in Moldova, but no one will testify to that. Everyone is still afraid of him.

Since Karamalak left Moldova, we don't have such high levels of organized crime here as we used to. That is because many corrupt police officers stole businesses from organized crime bosses and now run them as legitimate businesses. Many authorities retired as millionaires from the money they made entirely illegally. Today, people are not afraid of organized crime because there is not so much of it in Moldova. Instead, they are afraid of the police and the lawlessness that the Communists are creating by working in cahoots with corrupt police.

Now we have the Center for Fighting Economic Crimes that the Communists created. Usually that's who people are afraid of. They drive out competition, so we only have large businesses, usually run by high-ranking officials. The authorities are making themselves rich at the expense of small businesses. We have almost no small or midsized businesses here in Moldova anymore, because those in power only protect the large businesses. As soon as someone opens a small shop or business, the police start coming around every day for "control inspections," which just means they expect a bribe or payoff of some kind. Sometimes up to ten authorities a day may come in for an "inspection." Not just the police, but tax authorities, all kinds of authorities from the Center for Fighting Economic Crimes. We have over a hundred different bureaus that conduct "inspections." No little enterprises can afford all these "inspections" and "fees." Until the state starts supporting midsize businesses, the country will not flourish.

Same is true of agriculture. All the state ministers have been buying up huge tracts of agricultural land. Even the president's son, the minister of the economy, has tens of thousands of hectares of land.[17] He has been buying up all the land in Moldova because the price is low right now. The average price of a hectare is approximately US$500 [about US$200 an acre]. And these bureaucrats can easily export their own agricultural products since they give themselves all the licenses and permissions they need, or they create joint ventures for processing their products. No one else has a chance.

Does this lack of economic opportunity contribute to human trafficking?

Ion: Of course, yes. The police are also making huge money off trafficking. The most powerful pimps in Moldova are former cops who are protected by high-ranking friends in the police force and in the Ministry of Internal Affairs. Like this guy Ion Bejan.[18] He was convicted on criminal charges of corruption. But he controlled all the big traffickers—not the little pimps, but the really big traffickers. They were all paying him and a few other policemen protection money. A lot of that money got funneled up to the current minister of internal affairs. It was a really well-organized racket.

Now, official criminal cases of trafficking have declined a little. They are lower than they were in 2005–07. That is why the police came up with a new initiative. They created a new article for the criminal code—Article 362.1 on "Organization of Illegal Migration." People were leaving Moldova voluntarily for work abroad and were not getting exploited. The police made this initiative so that they could get more money from people arranging illegal work visas for Moldovans.

People continue to leave Moldova because the average salary here is around US$200 a month, and no one can live on that. So, they go abroad and send money home. But most people cannot legally leave Moldova and work in Europe. It is nearly impossible to get a work visa for Europe from Moldova. That is why a lot of Moldovans tried to change their citizenship to Romanian.[19] However, since 2002 Romania stopped giving citizenship to Moldovans. Now the only way for Moldovans to leave the country to find work is to do so illegally. They usually leave under a tourist visa or some falsified document so that they can get out of the country. Then, when they come back to Moldova, they get caught by the police: "Where have you been? Who helped you leave?" The police can confiscate all the money and property from the person who helped them. In addition, the prison sentence for helping someone obtain illegal documents to leave the country is from seven years up to life. So, the police also receive a lot of bribes, not from traffickers but from people who arrange illegal visas. The police themselves wrote this article in the criminal code for the sole purpose of getting bribes and payoffs. People will pay anything if they are facing a life sentence in prison. This goes all the way to the top—the president of Moldova supports it.

You can see it yourself in the case of our minister of internal affairs, Gheorghe Papuc.[20] He was removed as head of the Ministry of Internal Affairs in March 2008, because he was mixed up in a lot of corruption cases, including one case involving the smuggling of two hundred kilos of heroin. His "brother" was also involved.[21] But in October, they reinstated Papuc as the minister of internal affairs largely because he holds the whole corrupt structure together. Illegal trafficking of persons, running guns, smuggling drugs—it is all run all by and through the Ministry of Internal Affairs. And it is a very large, well-armed, and organized syndicate that feeds the state.

Police officers also receive salaries of US$200 a month. Like everyone else, they cannot live on this amount, so they create special laws that will help them get bribes and payoffs. Officially they make US$200 a month, but a lot of them are driving cars that cost five to ten thousand Euros. So, the structure feeds itself. If a revolution happens in our country, it will happen between the police and society. And it will be very bloody because the police are well-armed, and they keep close control over civilians. They know that if they ever lose control of the masses, they are out of a job. And the Prosecutor's Office is not armed like the police. We cannot protect society from the illegal activity of the police, because the police protect the interests of those in power.

How do the courts work? If a trafficker gets caught, is it possible to prosecute the case? Or is the system of bribes and payoffs so widespread that no one gets convicted?

Ion: Well, the courts … it is not like in the U.S. with an independent judiciary. It is a dependent court system that is not objective. When the Communists came to power, they carried out a complete administrative reform, eliminating the regional court system [and] leaving us with only district courts.[22] The Communists then filled the district court system with their own judges and administrators. This happened under the direction of Artur Reshetnikov, who decided the fate of the judicial system here. He is now director of the Security and Information Service.[23] But he is the one who decided to liquidate nearly all the courts. Before, we had ordinary courts at the local and district level, tribunals, the Court of Appeals, and the Supreme Court of Justice. Now the only ordinary courts are the district courts, and they were the most corrupt of all our previous courts. So, we went from two branches of power down to one.

What that means for trafficking cases is that the court does not look at the evidence that is presented against the traffickers. I am an attorney, so I represent both the criminals and the victims. My main interest is for the court to be just. But what I see is that criminal trafficking cases are prosecuted in the court without evidence. Penalties for human trafficking range from ten years and higher in prison. When a person is convicted and sentenced to ten years in prison without evidence, for me this is a problem.

Because at any time, me, or you, or any innocent person can be caught in this system and wrongly convicted.

How is that possible—that the court doesn't look at the evidence, or prosecutes a case with no evidence?

Ion: You must understand that we have a two-stage process for criminal cases. We have the official investigation before the criminal case is opened, and then we have the criminal proceedings. For example, if some policemen "catch" a "trafficker," for them it is very profitable. In the investigatory phase, they do not say, "We have this, and this, and this as evidence." No, they just need to make the accusation. With penalties of ten years and higher, the policemen can demand huge payments to drop the investigation or to reduce the charges to pimping instead of trafficking. So even if a person is innocent, he will pay because the system is so corrupt the court may very well find him guilty. And if he is guilty, he will also pay so that he gets off or gets a much lighter charge.

Our judicial system is not objective. It is all a rigged game with bribes and payoffs. I am always thinking about the poor, simple person who has no assurance that if he follows all the laws, he will not get sentenced for some crime. Today he is free, but tomorrow he might get sentenced to ten or fifteen years in jail for no reason.

And we can't really change it. Who is left here in Moldova to create a stable state? Most people between the ages of 25 and 45 have left the country to find work abroad.[24] And their children are left behind with the old people. So, who is here to work or to build a good state? And now the government is trying to control all the money that these people are sending back to their families from working abroad.

What about your job here? Are you at risk?

Ion: Our Center has been operating here since 2001. Between 2001 and 2003, we were trying to find ways to combat human trafficking, especially because we still did not have any criminal laws against it yet. We got our first law against human trafficking in 2003 while I was still working at the Prosecutor's Office. At that time, a woman from the U.S. Embassy offered to help us create an NGO called the Association for Female Lawyers. This association organized a team of female attorneys to make sure trafficking victims had access to justice. It worked very closely with our project, the Center for the Prevention of Trafficking in Women. Together these two organizations defended the interests of trafficking victims through the judicial system.

In 2003, I left the Prosecutor's Office to become director of the Center for the Prevention of Trafficking in Women. I brought with me a team of attorneys, all of whom had worked as state prosecutors in the Chief Prosecutor's Office. When the Communists came to power in 2001, these prosecutors all resigned because they didn't want to work for the Communist government. Now they work at the Center as attorneys for victims and gather information from all over Moldova about trafficking crimes. We also have over one hundred volunteers who investigate possible cases of trafficking in schools, colleges, and communities. We also investigate missing persons by looking for them abroad. When we find them, we bring them back home with the help of the IOM. We file complaints against the traffickers and help file police reports. We remain advocates for the victim from the moment the complaint is filed until a final verdict is reached in the courts.

Until 2006, this project was funded by the U.S. Department of State, but as of July 2006 the funding has ended. We received some financial help from the Danish Ministry of Foreign Affairs, but we have been getting less and less money. I think we will soon have to close because there is no longer enough money to pay people for their work.

Also, all our lawyers have tremendous problems with police harassment. The police are very corrupt. In fact, one of our attorneys is in prison right now on trumped-up charges. She was doing specialized work in trafficking of human organs for transplant. She found a lot of victims, filed the complaints, and was making sure these cases got prosecuted. She was getting some very good results. Several very important people in the government were involved in this trafficking ring and she helped get them convicted. These authorities were protecting Moldovan doctors who examined the victims and sent them abroad to have their organs harvested. This attorney stepped on the toes of some very powerful judges and officials, and they set her up. A couple of traffickers ended up dead, probably because of turf wars. But the government found "witnesses" to testify that she had ordered the killing of these traffickers. She has been in prison already a year and a half with no real investigation. Her case is scheduled to be heard on November 27 [2008].

Have other attorneys at the Center faced harassment by the authorities?
Ion: Yes, all the time. We get a lot of phone calls that basically say that if we continue our activities, we are going to pay dearly for it. We also get people coming in pretending to be trafficking victims and offering us money. We provide free services, free legal defense, so if we take money the authorities can shut us down. We frequently get people coming in and trying very persistently to give us money. They want to discredit us any way they can. The previous director, Benjan, was quite corrupt, probably in cahoots

with corrupt officials or traffickers. The entire time he was director, he was trying to discredit the Center. For example, once I defended one trafficking victim who was always trying to give me money. It turns out she was wearing microphones that Benjan had given her in order to entrap me! When I found out, I threw her out. I told her that when she stops conspiring with Benjan she can come back and receive free legal advice. After that, she came back and confessed that she had been wearing two microphones every time she came to the Center. She said that there were always policemen on the street listening to what we were talking about, just waiting for me to do something wrong so they could come in and arrest me and shut the Center down.

Why would she do that? Why would she try to set you up?

Ion: It is complicated. I was defending her in court. She was trafficked to Israel through Moscow. She managed to run away from her first trafficker and moved in with another victim, one of our former clients. These two needed monies to come back to Moldova from Israel, so they decided to engage in prostitution in order to earn enough money to get back home. When the two of them arrived back in Moldova, they were arrested for leaving the country illegally and for prostitution. They told the police about being trafficked to Israel. It turns out the person who sold them to Moscow, and then to Israel, was a Moldovan policeman. He was a major in the police force. She was from Transnistria. He brought her from Transnistria to Chisinau and arranged to get travel documents for her. He then took her to Balti, and from Balti he put her on a train to Moscow.[25] The people in Moscow sold her to Israel. All the while, she thought she was going for a job in Israel. Anyway, the police refused to investigate it as a criminal case of trafficking. Instead, they insisted that she willingly left the country and that the major might be guilty of pimping, but not trafficking.

They started to threaten and harass her, telling her that I was cheating her and that she would never get any material damages from the case. Ultimately, I was able to get her US$5,000 in material damages from the court. Nonetheless, after she tried to set me up, she got scared and left Moldova. She went back to Transnistria. She divorced her husband because the police were threatening him, too. She took her US$5,000 and opened a small shop. But she is still scared. She dropped all criminal charges against the major because she is still being threatened. She told me that she cannot testify in a criminal case because she cannot come to Chisinau. The police told her if she entered Moldova, terrible things would happen to her.

So, that is our system. Every day I am in court, every day at the

Prosecutor's Office, and every day working with the police, [and] I see the trouble victims have. The system is corrupt all the way through.

* * * *

I could have talked to Ion all day, but he had a lot of other things to attend to. I have had a little contact with him since 2010. He left the Center for the Prevention of Trafficking in Women and now works as an attorney. I follow him on Facebook and miraculously, through all these years, he is still fighting corruption and human trafficking, and he has not been arrested or murdered by the police. He is an unstoppable force in the anti-trafficking world in Moldova.

PART II

Interviews with Survivors of Slavery

> *They would not call it slavery, but some other name. Slavery has been fruitful in giving itself names. It has been called "the peculiar institution," "the social system," and the "impediment,"…. It has been called by a great many names, and it will call itself by yet another name; and you and I and all of us had better wait and see what new form this old monster will assume, in what new skin this old snake will come forth.*
> —Frederick Douglass, speech to the American Anti-Slavery Society, May 1865

Lena and the hundreds of thousands of Eastern Europeans who are trafficked, sold, and enslaved are part of a much larger international trend. In order to understand the events that so profoundly and deeply affected my interviewees' lives, it is necessary to discuss the particulars of the current trade in human beings. This introduction offers a general overview of the modern international slave trade and is intended for people who know little about this dreadful crime.

A little over two hundred years ago, Europe and the United States adopted laws to ban slavery. Most of the world followed suit over the course of the nineteenth century. However, as one abolitionist remarked at the time, the laws may have gotten rid of the slaves, but they did nothing to get rid of the slavers. Indeed, since the middle of the twentieth century, international slavery has returned with a vengeance. Today, hundreds of thousands of persons are trafficked across international borders and enslaved each year for the purpose of exploitation for economic gain. Many millions more are enslaved within their own countries. Recent studies suggest that there are more slaves now than at any time in history. Recent estimates range from 40 million to 45.8 million individuals enslaved in the world today. Of these, 25 percent are children, 71 percent are female, and 29 percent are male.[1]

Generating in excess of US$150 billion in illegal profits each year, trafficking in human beings is the second fastest-growing illegal activity in the world today, surpassed only by the global trade in drugs.[2] Several years ago it outpaced the international trade in illegal arms, estimated at $100 billion a year.[3] According to the International Labour Organization (ILO), 22 percent of enslaved persons are victims of forced sexual exploitation. Sixty-eight percent are victims of forced labor exploitation, in fields such as agriculture, construction, domestic work, and manufacturing.

Some of the people whose stories you are about to read fell victim to large, organized criminal networks working with the aid of corrupt state and local officials. Most, however, were the victims of small criminal networks that are fluid and opportunistic. In all cases, the trade in flesh depends upon a network of recruiters, pimps (for sex trafficking), traffickers, and, of course, consumers. Recruiters are typically female and someone the victim knows and trusts. In some cases, victims are recruited through official-looking employment agencies or other organizations that appear legitimate and trustworthy. Consequently, the fate of most victims is already sealed before he or she even knows that they have been sold. Often, and especially in the case of sex trafficking, the recruiter herself is a victim of trafficking whose "owner" promises her release if she can recruit more women for him.

One element that distinguishes trafficking from human smuggling is the use of fraud, coercion, or threat. Some of the women I interviewed thought they were going abroad to be exotic dancers and understood that there was an element of risk involved. One even knew that she would be expected to engage in prostitution. However, none of them knew the brutal conditions they would face, nor the violent and dangerous sexual behaviors they would be forced to engage in, nor that the pimp and the trafficker would keep all the money, leaving them with nothing.

At its core, human trafficking is an economic crime that is fueled by producers' demands for easy profits, consumers' demands for cheap products, and the johns' demands for illicit sex. In *Disposable People*, author Kevin Bales details the economics of modern slavery. Discussing the myriad forms of slavery and human trafficking in the world today, Bales differentiates between the old slavery and the new. One of the primary differences is that today the value of a human being is practically nil. He argues that today slaves are so easy and cheap to obtain that they are literally disposable.[4] The experiences of my interviewees confirm this argument—all of them were treated by their captors as if they were cheap commodities to be used up and discarded.

But the men and women whose stories you are about to read are not disposable, nor are they commodities to be bought and sold. Yet their stories belie the notion that slavery no longer exists, and that one human cannot own another. Some of my interviewees agreed to tell their stories in order to warn others of what can happen when one leaves home. Others recognized that in the telling, the pain diminishes and a little more healing takes place. All of them were explicit in wanting to effect change. In telling their stories, these courageous men and women gain back ownership of their lives and become subjects of their own stories and not objects to be bought and sold. They reclaim their humanity.

8

IGOR AND ANATOLI

*Victims of organ trafficking
with their lawyer, Neli Babcinci
Village of Hancauti, Moldova
October 6, 2010*

I heard about Neli Babcinci long before I met her. In my 2008 interview with Ion Vizdoga, he mentioned that a colleague of his had been arrested on trumped-up charges and was serving an eighteen-year sentence in prison. That colleague was Neli Babcinci. When she began representing victims of human trafficking and encouraging her clients to testify against their traffickers, she came up against a corrupt judicial system and complicit government officials. Two of her clients were murdered before they could testify, and a high-ranking judge, working in conjunction with some traffickers, cooked up a scheme to frame Neli for conspiracy to commit murder. When I returned to Chisinau in 2010, Ion told me that Neli was out of prison and offered to set up an interview with her for me. Ion had managed to take advantage of a unique historical moment, the 2009 so-called "Twitter Revolution" in Moldova, to press an appeal of Neli's case and secure her release from prison.[1]

Prior to the "Twitter Revolution," the Party of Communists of Moldova (PCM), under the leadership of Vladimir Voronin, was in power. Many of the judges and government officials under the Voronin regime were quite corrupt.[2] Some officials engaged in human trafficking themselves, others took bribes or collaborated with traffickers in other ways. It was within this system that Neli tried to prosecute trafficking cases and ran afoul of the Voronin government. Many of her clients were trafficked for sexual or labor exploitation, but she also began to hear stories of people being defrauded while selling their kidneys. In the first decade of the twenty-first century, scant attention was being given to organ trafficking.[3] Neli was the first person in Moldova to bring attention to the illegal trafficking of human organs and, more importantly, to call it human trafficking.[4]

There remains some debate over whether organ trafficking qualifies as human trafficking given that, in most cases, the victims agree to sell their organs and then get cheated. However, in the United Nations Convention Against Transnational Organized Crime, in particular the supplemental Protocol I, commonly known as the Palermo Protocol, organ trafficking is placed under the definition of human trafficking. The Protocol states that human trafficking is

> the recruitment, transportation, transfer, harboring or receipt of persons, by means of the threat or use of force or other forms of coercion, of abduction, of fraud, of deception, of the abuse of power or of a position of vulnerability or of the giving or receiving of payments or benefits to achieve the consent of a person having control over another person, for the purpose of exploitation. Exploitation shall include, at a minimum ... the removal of organs.[5]

The UN Global Initiative to Fight Human Trafficking identifies three categories of human trafficking for organ removal. In one type, the victim has no foreknowledge that an organ is going to be removed. Traffickers kidnap, drug, force, deceive, or even kill people to harvest their organs. More typical is the second category, where people agree to sell an organ but are either not paid at all or are paid significantly less than the agreed-upon amount. In the third category, vulnerable persons, typically the poor and homeless, are treated for an ailment, which may or may not exist. During that treatment their organs are removed without the person's knowledge.[6] Any of these three categories requires a host of people involved in the trade, from recruiters to organ donors, corrupt medical professionals, and recipients. It would be impossible to trace all those involved, which makes it a perfect, and very lucrative, crime from which high-ranking government officials may profit.

Because the demand for kidneys and other organs far outpaces the supply, it is easy to find wealthy people from developed nations willing to pay upwards of US$200,000 for a black-market kidney and sometimes more for other organs. In 2010, the World Health Organization estimated that 10 percent of all transplanted kidneys worldwide were obtained illegally, and that approximately 10,000 black-market organ transplants take place annually.[7] Poor Moldovan villages are the perfect places for organ traffickers to find people desperate enough, and naïve enough, to sell their organs. Neli's advocacy on their behalf nearly cost her life.

I met Neli shortly after her release in 2010. She offered to take me north to interview two of her clients who had been victims of human trafficking for organ removal. They lived in the little village of Hancauti, located in the Edinet region of Moldova. It is about 212 km [131 miles] from the capital city of Chisinau, but it might as well have been on a different planet. Most inhabitants have never been to Chisinau, and many have never even been to the closest city, Edinet, a mere 17 kilometers away [a little over 10 miles]. The village has about 1,122 inhabitants. Most villagers have very small subsistence farms or small sheep or goat herds. The village has no industry to speak of.

During Soviet times, the village had a larger population, with more farms and herds. However, after the collapse of the USSR in 1991, and the subsequent economic crises, more and more people left their villages. Now, there are few left in Hancauti, and those that remain are desperately poor. Unfortunately, Hancauti is like many villages in Moldova—abandoned, and forgotten.[8] It is for this reason that Moldovan villages are one of the main sources of illegal organs for international trafficking in the world. According to the World Health Organization, every six minutes an organ is removed from a Moldovan villager to be sold on the black market.

Human trafficking for organ removal is more shrouded in secrecy than any other type of human trafficking. It is nearly impossible to avoid bumping into dangerous organized crime syndicates in researching it. The reasons for this are complex. The very nature of the crime demands a large, organized network and complex trafficking routes since victims are very poor, from small villages, and recipients are quite wealthy, typically from urban areas with advanced medical technologies. Organ traffickers must bring together recruiters, victim donors, doctors, hospitals, medical staffs, and recipients. Since globally the demand for organs has outstripped the legal supply, the stakes are very high for the recipients, as are the profits for the traffickers. All of which means that the trade in organs is extremely clandestine and dominated by organized transnational crime networks. Consequently, little academic attention has been given to this global phenomenon.[9]

Further, the United Nations Office on Drugs and Crime (UNODC) notes the harmful physical, psychological, and emotional effects on "donors" who sell their organs on the black market to alleviate their poverty. Recruiters often coerce, deceive, or otherwise exploit vulnerable persons into selling their organs, which contributes, directly or indirectly, to their victimization, including damage to their health, stigmatization, and further impoverishment.[10] As anti-trafficking activist and author Siddharth Kara points out, the "poor, vulnerable, disadvantaged, and outcast people of the world are chewed up and sold for parts by those with power, rights, and resources with little consequence."[11]

According to the UNODC, the vast majority of victims are male. At the same time, they also note there is a scarcity of evidence-based data on human trafficking for the purpose of organ removal. Therefore, there is little information on how organ trafficking networks operate, the experiences of the organ sellers, buyers, and doctors, the criminal involvement of transplant professionals, the collusion and corruption of hospitals, the defrauding of health insurance companies, and the like.[12]

Consequently, I was quite interested when Neli invited me to meet her clients. As we rode through the Moldovan countryside, Neli took the opportunity to give me some background information about the two men we were going to meet.

Neli: This man's name is Igor R. He is now about thirty years old. His mother abandoned the family when Igor was very little. He has no recollections of her. He was raised entirely by his disabled father, a shepherd in the little village of Hancauti. Igor grew up helping his father tend the animals and making sheep's milk cheese. He never received any formal education.

He met his wife, Angela, in this village. She is eight years older than he and was a widow with two small kids when they met. After they got married, they had a child of their own. In 2002, around the time they got married, Angela's brother, Anatoli B., sold his kidney for money so that his wife could go to Italy to look for work. At that time, it was very expensive to get to Italy. Either you went legally, but then you could not work, or you went illegally, and you had to pay for someone to get you into the country. Either way, it cost up to US$3,500–$4,000. Since Angela's brother Anatoli sold his kidney and was not feeling poorly, Angela decided Igor should sell his so that she could go to Italy to look for work too.

After about a year of being pressured by Angela, Igor decided to sell his kidney. When he returned to the village after the operation, the traffickers, of course, did not pay him the agreed-upon sum of US$7,000. They cheated him out of US$3,000, leaving Igor with US$4,000. Igor gave all the money to his wife because she decides everything in that household. If she had not given Igor permission to talk to us today, he would not have met with us. She controls him.

With that money, Angela went to Italy to find work. Yesterday, when I was asking her if we could meet Igor, I asked her if she was able to earn some money in Italy. She said that she had worked for a while but spent everything there that she had earned. Now she is back with no money and three kids. Igor still works as a shepherd. Angela will let him live in the house only in the worst of winter. The rest of the time, he lives with the sheep. You will see.

Today we will see the conditions he lives in and where he spends his nights. He is very skinny and in poor health after the operation. Igor doesn't drink. He can't read or write. He is typical of someone in Moldova's lowest social level—an illiterate peasant, extremely poor, and with no possibilities for improving his life.

Some people might ask why we should feel sorry for him. Many people would not consider him a victim of trafficking since he agreed to sell his kidney of his own free will. But I argue that he *does* qualify as a trafficking victim. First, he was cheated out of a lot of money. So that is fraud. Second, he had no idea what the consequences of the operation might be. He did not understand how the operation would impact his health. He did not know what his life would be like with only one kidney. He lives a very difficult life, with hard physical labor, extremely poor conditions, and insufficient food. He walks the fields all day, every day. So, if it is cold, his feet freeze. He sleeps in an open shed. His living and working conditions are not good for someone who is weak or sick. You will see.

But first we are going to meet Anatoli, Angela's brother. He agreed to talk with you as well. However, he does not want us to come to his house. I am to call him when we get to the village, and he will come meet us.

* * * *

As we approached the village, Neli called Anatoli. We met him at his car, which was parked on the side of the road that led to the village. Anatoli did not want us to take pictures, and he seemed a bit uncomfortable talking to me. I explained the purpose of the interview and asked him again if he wanted to talk with me. He said yes again. I do not know if his discomfort was because I was a foreign woman (he had never met an American before), or if the Russian we were speaking was not his first language, or if we were simply too many worlds apart. Nonetheless, about halfway into the interview he relaxed a little and became more open and animated. Neli later told me that the recipient who had bought his kidney had died on the operating table. She said he was deeply troubled by the man's death.

Anatoli is a large man with close-cropped blond hair and dark, suntanned skin. He looked like he had spent his life tending fields. Indeed, he was born in the village and grew up there. He had gone to school and received a secondary education. In his younger years he had gotten manual labor jobs in Russia, Belarus, and Ukraine. Now he lived alone in the village and worked as a day laborer in the fields. He never knows when he will have work or when he won't. Each day is a new struggle for survival.

He sold his kidney in Germany in 2002. He was thirty-nine years old at the time and relatively healthy. He has three children and two grandchildren. All of them, including his wife, have left Moldova. His children and grandchildren are living and working in Ukraine. Only Anatoli remains in the village.

We stood leaning against the trunk of his car for the interview. The day was mild and sunny, but a strong wind blew out of the south. It was an odd place for an interview—surrounded by nothing but fields, standing on the side of a dirt road, with no buildings in sight. Neli introduced us, and then she and my husband, Dee, stood some distance away so that Anatoli and I could talk "in private."

Anatoli is a very proud man. It was clear that he did not want to appear to complain or to show any sign of weakness. I have edited this interview quite a lot, since most of his answers were monosyllabic. I had to ask numerous follow-up questions to prompt him to explain his thoughts.

I understand that you sold a kidney a few years ago. How do you feel now? How is your health?

Anatoli: There is nothing wrong worth mentioning. As usual, it is sometimes good, sometimes bad. It is up and down.

Are you able to work?

Anatoli: No, they just laid me off. I don't work now.

Do you want to tell me about what happened with the operation?

Anatoli: Of course. Nothing happened, really. I sold my kidney in Germany and then, when I returned to Moldova, I went to Chisinau because I needed help with my health. My health was poor because of the operation, so I eventually went to a rehabilitation center in Chisinau for a month—maybe a little longer. This was in 2004, in November, nearly two years after I got back to Moldova.

Where did they take you to remove your kidney?

Anatoli: To Germany, somewhere. I don't know where. They bought me the airplane ticket. I don't know exactly who paid for it, but someone did. They just gave me the airline ticket. I have no idea how much it cost, no one ever told me. Someone met me at the airport there in Germany and took me to some type of hospital.

How did you hear about selling a kidney? Was it easy to arrange?

Anatoli: I found out through hearsay, rumor. Everyone in the village knows about this. It is nothing terrible. Someone said, "Do you want to make some money?" and I said, "Yes." But it wasn't really all that easy to arrange. It was actually a little complicated. First, they [a woman claiming to be a nurse and her male assistant] gave me a medical analysis and took my blood. And then they had to find a recipient that would work with my blood type. All this took a long time ... from March until ... well, it was nearly a year. I expected it to be easier.

Were you afraid?

Anatoli: Yes, I was afraid. For a long time afterward, I couldn't lay down on a bed because it reminded me of the operation. I was that afraid. But after I talked to the psychologist [at Neli's rehabilitation center in Chisinau], the fear quickly subsided.

And did they pay you for your kidney?

Anatoli: Yes, but not as much as they said they would. It is in Turkey where they have all the really bad problems with treating people badly and cheating them. There, they do the operation one day, and the next day you are on your way home. There is no interview with the doctors, nothing. No recovery time, no medication for pain or infection, nothing.

But you went to Germany. They usually pay closer attention to the law in Germany. How was it you were able to sell your kidney?

Anatoli: Well, I lied a little bit. I said that he [the recipient] was a relative—that he was my uncle.[13] He knew a little Romanian, so we communicated in Romanian. As far as the doctors could tell, we knew each other. But we did not. I never met him before that day. He was born in Romania but lived in Israel, and I am from Moldova.

How many people went with you?

Anatoli: I went by myself; it was no big deal. But I wouldn't do it again. Once is enough. After the operation, I had a really hard time. I couldn't work. But there were no complications—no infection or anything. Everything was pretty clean. It was not like in Turkey where they do the operation in a dirty basement. I was in a normal clinic. After the operation, they kept me in that hospital for ... [*long pause*] about two weeks until they were sure I had recovered. That was some years ago. I still have a bit of pain, but I don't whine about it. There could have been many more complications. My side and back aches sometimes, especially when I try to do hard physical labor. And in this village, there is no easy labor. But I got the pain only after I started working. For a time, I didn't have to go to work because I had money from the operation. But now all that money is gone, and I must work. It was hard at first, but now I am used to it.

Do you have any medication for the pain?

Anatoli: Medicine? What medicine? I can stand the pain, and it usually passes in two days or so. Sometimes it is bad, but it changes a lot. I can stand it. I just can't do much when the pain is here.

Do your neighbors know you sold a kidney?

Anatoli: Everyone knows. Probably everyone in Moldova knows. I think all of Russia knows, too [*snorts ironically*].

Well, at least we haven't heard about your kidney yet in America.

Anatoli: [*Laughing*] Give it time. Maybe you'll tell them.

Do you know if others in this village have sold their kidneys?

Anatoli: I only know of Igor, and you are going to meet with him soon, yes? He is the only one I know personally who sold a kidney. And you will see, he is in very rough shape. Really difficult conditions. I have heard of others selling kidneys, but I don't know them personally. I have heard of a lot of other people who sold kidneys, but who they are and where they come from, I couldn't tell you. I won't deny that Igor and I did it, but I will not talk about others.

How is your life now?

Anatoli: Work. My life is work when I can find it. I have enough money day by day because I live alone. I only need to feed myself. But I never know if I will get work for a day and then nothing for two weeks. Or I can work for a month. It is enough for me to buy food. I do not have anyone else that I must provide for, so it's okay.

Thank you so much, Anatoli. It was good to meet you. I am grateful that you agreed to talk to us. Take care of yourself.

Anatoli: Be well.

We drove a few more miles down that same road through gently rolling hills. Neli told the driver to stop, and we got out of the car. I saw nothing but an empty sheep pen in the distance and a rough, three-sided lean-to made of corrugated metal next to it. Was this our destination? I didn't have time to ask because Neli was already out of the car and heading across the field toward the sheep pen. Just as I caught up to her, Igor flew over the hill in a horse-drawn flat-bed cart at a very fast pace. Since the cart had no bench seat, he was standing up, legs widespread to keep his balance as the rickety cart bounced over the rough ground. He pulled up next to us, set the horse to graze still attached to the cart, and walked the rest of the way with us to the sheep pen. Even though there were no sheep in the pen, the stench of animal feces and urine was overwhelming. I could not help but imagine what it would be like on a hot summer's day.

Right next to the pen was the lean-to. The side facing the sheep pen was entirely open. Its original purpose must have been to provide the sheep shade in the summer and shelter in the winter. However, it is now where Igor lives. It has corrugated metal on three sides held up by an assortment of tree limbs and rough wood planks. The roof is lashed on. The walls are "insulated" with cardboard and rags. A piece of plywood separates the shack into two halves. One half is where Igor sleeps. It has a dilapidated wooden table with an assortment of tools and a kerosene lantern on it. Next to the table is Igor's bed—a wooden plank-style bed piled with filthy blankets and rags. The floor is bare earth.

The second room is where two homeless boys sleep on a similar bed. They help Igor with the sheep and help him make cheese. Next to the bed hang four five-gallon sacks of sheep's milk cheeses dripping into buckets. It is not clear if these boys themselves had been trafficked, or if Igor is protecting them from being trafficked. They are social orphans. I did not meet them, and Igor was unwilling to talk about them. The three of them live here until the snow stays on the ground. They manage to find shelter in the village during the worst of the winter months—Igor moves into his wife's house, but I do not know where the boys go.

Igor is tall and very thin. It is obvious that he is in poor health. He holds himself in a way that suggests he is in great pain—both physical and mental. He wears tattered sweatpants, a wool sweater, tennis shoes, and a wool cap. All are filthy and ragged. I was embarrassed by my new Sara coat and nice leather boots. I wanted to give him something, but I also did not want to demean him or hurt his pride. So, I just stood there, awkward in my discomfort.

Igor was extremely shy and seemed very hesitant to talk to us, even though he gave me permission to talk with him for this book. He very rarely made eye contact. Most of the time he looked at his shoes and mumbled answers to my questions in as few words as possible. It makes sense—we were foreigners asking very personal questions. I asked him if he wanted Neli present during the interview and he said yes.

Neli translated for us since Igor only knows Romanian, so the whole situation was a little awkward. Neli made the introductions, and we began the interview.

8. Igor and Anatoli

Hi Igor, thank you for agreeing to talk with us. How is your health?

Igor: Well ... good and bad—sometimes I feel good, sometimes bad—usually I feel pretty bad. I have physical weakness and a lot of pain. My other kidney is weakened so it often hurts. My missing kidney hurts, too. They tell me this is called phantom pain.

Did you receive any medical assistance after the operation?

Igor: No. The operation was done in Turkey, in a clinic. It seemed like a pretty good clinic—clean and all, and they had good equipment.

Neli: Yes, recently the police found that clinic and closed it down. It did have excellent equipment.

And after the operation, were you able to stay there and recover?

Igor: No, in exactly three days I was home.

Neli: His case is the first I had heard of that. Usually, even in Turkey, they keep donors five to six days. But Igor was home in three days. The trafficker, a guy named Zis, drove Igor to the airport in Istanbul after the operation.

How did you decide to sell a kidney, and how did you know who would help you arrange it?

Igor: Everyone in this village knows how to sell a kidney.

Neli: People knew that he had very difficult living conditions and was very poor. He had heard that others had gone abroad and sold a kidney. Since they were okay, he decided to do it. His only thought was to get enough money to buy a house.

So, you flew to Turkey and landed at the airport. Then what?

Igor: I was with three other guys. And we had a "boss" with us—a guy who made sure we did what we were supposed to and to make sure everything went smoothly. This guy Zis met us at the airport. He took us to a restaurant. I don't know where or what it was. I had never been in a restaurant before. But he fed us there. Then they took us to a medical clinic. Early on the second morning they did all these medical tests. And then they came and got me and took me to go have the operation. When I woke up, all four of us were lying next to each other in the post-op room. We all had a kidney removed.

Neli: I asked him if any of them met the recipient and he said "no."

Igor: No, I never met the guy who got my kidney. Then on the third day we all were returned to Moldova.

How did you get from Chisinau to Hancauti?

Igor: Anatoli, whom you just met. He met me at the airport in Chisinau. Later that very evening they brought me my money. Marin brought it.[14]

And did they pay you what they promised?

Igor: Well…. While I was still in Chisinau, they called me and said that I had to pay for the documents that were necessary for me to travel. And I had to pay to have the operation. They said it cost US$2,000 and that I had to pay for it. They didn't tell me about that before we left for Turkey. Then Marin called me and said he will bring me my money, which he did. Marin is the bridge between those who want to sell their kidneys, and those who make it possible. He brought me US$8,000, but it was fake money.

Fake money? What do you mean? Counterfeit?

Igor: No, a lot of the bills were old—from 1972, 1975.

Yes, but that is still money—at least in the U.S. it is.

Neli: Not here. No bank and no money exchange will take dollar bills, or any bills, that old. In this part of the world, our currency has gone through so many "reforms" and changes that no one trusts *any* bills that are more than five or ten years old.[15]

Igor: Yes. So, I got cheated out of US$400 more because it was old money. Of the $10,000 they promised me, I got only $7,600. But I didn't complain because I started getting threats. They threatened to hurt me and my family if I said anything to anyone. So, now I am really afraid.

Neli: You can see it in the way he holds himself, yes? He is intimidated and terrified. Because of this, he is now developing some psychological problems.

On the fourth day after the operation, you finally returned to the village. How did you feel?

Igor: Yes. It was horrible. I couldn't stand up straight, I hunched over to the side. The pain was very severe, and I felt really sick. I was very, very uncomfortable. I felt like an old man, but I was only twenty years old. That was eight years ago. But what was worse was that they took advantage of me. I immediately understood that they lied to me and had always intended to cheat me. I was very upset.

Did you want to get back at them in some way?

Igor: No. I didn't think anything like that. I didn't think about anything at all. I just wanted to get back to the village as fast as possible and stay there.

[*He exhaled a very loud sigh and was becoming agitated. I understood that he had said enough and that I should end the interview.*]

Well, those are all my questions. Thank you very much, Igor. I am grateful you agreed to talk to us.

** * * *

Neli had a brief conversation with Igor in Romanian as Dee and I walked slowly across the field to the car. I looked back once, and Igor was standing by the sheep pen, with his shoulders slumped, looking at us. As we got in the car and turned down the road that would take us to the highway, I noticed that it was starting to lightly snow. For the next several months, every time the weather turned cold, I was haunted by visions of Igor and the two boys huddled under filthy blankets in that shack.

9

ANYA

Victim of sexual exploitation
NGO: La Strada
A small village near Chisinau, Moldova
November 23, 2008

If I were to draw a profile of the typical trafficked person from Moldova in the early twenty-first century, it would be Anya. According to statistics compiled by La Strada International in 2005, 99 percent of trafficked persons from Moldova are women, and 90 percent of them were victims of domestic violence before being trafficked. Eighty percent of female victims were under the age of twenty-five, and between 70 and 80 percent came from rural regions of Moldova.[1] The vast majority of trafficked women have a low level of education, making them noncompetitive in the labor market, and 80 percent had an average monthly income well below the poverty level.[2] Consequently, the overwhelming majority of women who were trafficked from Moldova were trying to escape poverty or violence at home.[3] At the same time, only 9 percent suspected that they might be expected to provide sexual services abroad, and 86 percent did not know what their future work would be.[4] Anya touches on all these themes in discussing her life. She also recounts the horrifying moment she learned that she had been sold.

That human trafficking happens in the margins of migration is a theme that repeats throughout all these interviews. People's motivations for risking illicit migration—the so-called "push" factors—are also similar in nearly every case.[5] This interview provides insight into some of the traffickers' methods of recruitment and how they transport and sell persons. Anya, along with several other women, was transported to Turkey from Moldova. Ultimately, she was taken to a hotel where several slave owners gathered to bid on young women in a modern version of a slave auction. Until the moment that she was ordered to remove her top for inspection, Anya had no clue she had been trafficked. She escaped being sold to a brothel owner by jumping out of the sixth-floor window of the hotel, breaking both of her arms and legs in the process.

The essential component of Anya's decision to migrate, and indeed the essential component of all slavery, is work. Lack of sustainable employment is the main reason people risk migration. The promise of work is the lure that traffickers use to enslave people. And forced labor—sexual or otherwise—is what generates huge profits for slave owners. So work, or lack of it, drives the trade in humans. In order to understand the desperate conditions that led Anya to leave her home and look for work, one must understand economic conditions in rural Moldova. Consequently, I was very grateful when the psychologist at La Strada called and said that a survivor of trafficking, Anya, had invited me to her home in the Moldovan countryside so that I could interview her.

Marek, the driver from La Strada, picked me up in downtown Chisinau at eight o'clock sharp on a crisp November morning. He said little as he deftly dodged the potholes in the main road leading away from Chisinau. We were headed to a small agricultural village about 40 kilometers [25 miles] northeast of Chisinau, affording me a first look at the Moldovan countryside. The soil is rich, black earth, but we pass only defunct farms.

Moldova is the poorest country in Europe since gaining independence from the USSR in 1991. It has had to face some nearly insurmountable obstacles in trying to establish a viable state and economy following the collapse of the Soviet Union.[6] Under Soviet rule, Moldova's economy was largely agricultural, based on state-owned and collective farms. After independence, the state initiated a program of privatization, breaking up many of these collective farms and transferring them to private ownership. These efforts were hindered by considerable dislocation of the rural population, a dramatic loss of productivity, and corruption. Further, Moldova lost a large part of its manufacturing sector when Transnistria declared independence from Moldova in 1992. Moldova's industrial hub was located in the breakaway region of Transnistria.[7] The loss of Transnistria made the Moldovan economy primarily agricultural, depending heavily on wine exports to Russia. The wine industry accounted for nearly 25 percent of Moldova's gross national product, with an estimated 60 percent of that wine going to Russia.[8]

However, in March 2006 Russia placed a ban on the importation of Moldovan wine. By all accounts, the ban was politically motivated. Russia was punishing Moldova for seeking closer ties to the European Union and the West. The effects of the ban were devastating. Moldova lost hundreds of millions of dollars in foreign trade, and wine production dropped by over 63 percent.[9] Numerous other industries that depended on the wine trade were also hard-hit, devastating the Moldovan economy and forcing tens of thousands of people off their farms and out of their jobs.[10] The impact of all these crises on ordinary people was clearly apparent as we drove past an endless array of abandoned farms. It became clear that Moldova was a land of rich resources and poor people.

Anya lives in a typical Moldovan village, one of hundreds that have been emptied by the cascade of economic crises since 1991. With no jobs to be had, hundreds of thousands of Moldovans left to find work in Russia, or Italy, or Cyprus, or any of a myriad of places willing to hire cheap labor. By 2008, at least one-third of the working-age population of Moldova had left and was working outside Moldova.[11] In the villages, up to 60 percent of the inhabitants had left, leaving behind an estimated 230,000 children without a mother or a father.[12] Indeed, all the villages we visited seemed totally devoid of people between the ages of eighteen and fifty. I began to understand why so many people from Moldova fall prey to trafficking. Desperate to feed their families or make a better life for themselves, they risk legal or illegal immigration, leaving themselves and their children vulnerable to being trafficked.

We arrive in Anya's little village in less than hour. It is only 40 kilometers from the capital, but for the villagers Chisinau might as well be across the ocean. The village is poor, and few inhabitants have ever been as far as Chisinau. Our car attracts the attention of some villagers as we slowly navigate the rough dirt alleys that separate the buildings in the village. It is the only car that I can see in the village. Finally, we find Anya's apartment building, one of two three-storied whitewashed housing blocks. The water source for the buildings is a community well, decorated in typical Moldovan style with an ornate tin-stamped roof adorned with flowers and stars. A white goat is chained to a stake in front of the buildings while others wander, freely munching the sparse grass on the front lawn.

Anya was educated in the little school in this same village. After completing eighth grade, she went for three years to a local high school in a nearby small town. She then attended a professional trade school for a year to learn how to be a tailor. Ultimately, she became an apprentice at a shoe factory in the neighboring village of Bengara, spending the next three years learning how to make shoes. Her job was to make the details on the shoes like tassels, stitching, laces, etc. For a brief time, she worked in a shoe factory in Chisinau until she met and married her husband.

They returned to the village soon after they got married. It was only then that she discovered that her husband was an alcoholic. When he drank, he often beat her. It was while trying to get away from him that she ended up getting trafficked. After a few minutes of small talk and pleasantries, we got down to the interview.

What happened after you got married?

Anya: I continued to work but he took all the money and spent it drinking with his friends. Then he would beat me. We lived in this very apartment, and I endured his abuse for seven years. Then I decided to leave. First, I went to Odessa, Ukraine. I bought goods from a discount warehouse called Seventh Kilometer and resold them in Odessa. I sold a product to wash glass. I also sold chemicals to clean rugs. I made a little money and returned home.[13]

Did you return to the village?

Anya: Yes. I came back to this apartment. While I was gone, my husband had run up a lot of debt, drinking. I mean *a lot* of debt. All the money that I made went to pay off his debts. I thought, "What am I going to do?" I decided that I'd leave again, thinking maybe I would go back to Odessa, but it didn't work out.

Why didn't it work out?

Anya: I don't remember why I didn't go to Odessa—it just didn't happen. This was in 1998. My sister had already left for Greece, and everything was going well for her. She had a job and an apartment. One day she called and said, "Why don't you come here? I can give you a job. You can stay with us. You need to get away from him." I thought about it and decided to go. She sent me the money for a ticket, but I could not get a visa, so I decided to go to Greece illegally. I didn't say anything to my husband. I didn't tell my parents. I said nothing to no one. I just left.

How did you get to Greece without a visa?

Anya: I found someone to take me there with a group of women. There were nine of us and the four men who were going to smuggle us into Greece illegally. I was the youngest in the group. We each had to give these guys US$2,500.

That is a lot of money. Did you trust these people?

Anya: I didn't know what to do. It didn't really matter if I could trust them or not, I was desperate. I could no longer live like I had been living.

From Moldova we crossed into Romania. Once in Romania these guys took us into some woods and set us up in a camp. It was a camp that is used by hunters. This was in the spring. They told us we had to wait a little while for one of their guys who would come and take us across the border [from Romania into Serbia and then into Greece]. So, we waited. And waited. We waited for a week. And we all asked, "We gave you our money. We don't have any more money. What is going on?"

Why did you wait so long? Why didn't you just leave?

Anya: They had taken our passports, our money, everything. One night they said, "Okay, that's it. We're going. Our guy is at the border." So, we took off that very night in a minibus. They drove us through the woods to the Yugoslav border.[14] We drove for hours. We should have already crossed the border. But then they said they had made a mistake, and their guy wasn't at the border. They said we would have to wait one more night. So we returned to the camp and waited there in the woods for three or four more days without food or water. Without anything. We ate mushrooms that grew in the forest. We made a fire, cooked and ate the mushrooms without anything else. No bread. Nothing.

While we were waiting at this hunter's camp, these four guys left to go see if their man was there at the border. They left in the minibus and never returned. We had no idea where we were. We had no idea where to go, which direction we came from. How do we find the road back? We didn't know anything. We were in the woods in the middle of nowhere.

What happened? What did you do?

Anya: Well, the authorities found us. They chased us through the woods with dogs, and caught us, and took us back to Romania. They asked us a few questions and wrote everything down. First one policeman came and asked questions, then another. They asked, "Who was your guide? Who brought you here? What road did you take through the forest?" But all we knew was that the guys in the minibus drove us around and then dumped us in the forest. We didn't know their names or anything about them.

In the end, I stayed in Romania.[15] I didn't want to go home with no money. The guys who were supposed to take us to Greece had already taken all our money, our passports, and everything. So, I stayed in Romania.

What did you do there?

Anya: I found work in a restaurant. It was a Turkish restaurant in Timisoara.[16] I worked there for six or seven months and was able to get a "white" passport.[17] I saved a little money and decided to return home, hoping that maybe things might be okay. But again, my husband had accumulated debts. He had sold all our furnishings to pay his debts. I had a different wall unit there—that one's new. He sold the old one. He sold all the furniture—everything [*her voice shook as she tried to hold back tears*]. He sold absolutely everything! I had a home phone. He ran up a huge bill, around 2,000 *lei*.[18]

What happened after you returned home?
Anya: Again, when I got back I paid the bills, or at least all that I was able to. I was already thinking, "What am I doing…. He drinks and I give him money? He spends all my money without paying his debts!" I understood that this would never end, so I left him and moved in with my mother. But I still didn't have any money. She kept asking me, "When are you going to get a job? Your daughter is growing up. She needs food, clothes, money for school. It all takes money."

Could you find a job in Moldova at that time?
Anya: No. There were no jobs, so I decided to leave again to find work. One of my acquaintances had left and then returned back here to the village. Well, not even an acquaintance but a friend of a friend. We had met once before, and then we bumped into each other in the village. She was very sympathetic. She told me she had a sister living abroad with this rich guy. She said her sister had a really good job and everything was wonderful for them. She told me she was getting ready to go there to work. She said, "Why don't you come with me? You can relax and forget about your husband." I believed her. I thought, in any event I have no money, no work, nothing. So why not? There's no reason to stay here.

I told her that I had no money and no passport. She said, "No problem—we can fix that. I have some money I can give you. You can pay me back later." And I believed her. I knew people who knew her. She was from my village; it wasn't like she was some stranger. I had no idea people could sell other people. I was so stupid. I could not even imagine that anyone could sell me. I knew nothing about human trafficking. I had never heard of such a thing. [*Her voice drops to a near whisper*] Selling women….

So, what happened next?
Anya: I went with her to Chisinau. She got me a passport—one of our internal passports first, then an international one. It only took a couple of days.

Was it a fake passport?
Anya: No. It was a normal passport. Normal. Then she…. Then she … [*long pause as she struggles for composure*] sold me to another woman, but I didn't know it at the time. She said, "I want to introduce you to my really good friend—my best friend." Her "friend" was a huge Russian lady. She

was this big [*spreads her arms wide*]. And Russian. I looked at her and thought to myself, "She's going to eat me!" Such a fat woman. That was my first impression. But the Russian lady befriended me. She was very sweet to me and said very kind things. She said everything is going to be fine and that she would help me go abroad and find work. I believed her.

In a couple of days, we boarded a plane and left Moldova, the fat Russian lady and me. I didn't even know where I was going. I thought I was going to my sister in Greece. I had told the fat Russian that I had a sister in Greece, and I wanted to go there, and she had said, "Yes. We will take you to your sister. Yes, we will take you there."

Did you go to Greece?

Anya: I thought so, but I actually ended up in Turkey. I didn't know the language or anything. I didn't understand anything. They asked me a few questions at the airport, but I didn't understand anything.

Then we took a bus from the airport. It turns out I was not in Greece but in Istanbul. Istanbul! I thought I was in Greece! I didn't find out I was in Turkey until much later.

Were you the only one who traveled to "Greece" with this Russian woman?

Anya: No. There were other girls—not just girls but a couple of families. That's why I did not have a clue. I could never have guessed what was going to happen to me. The Russian told us in Chisinau that we should not talk to anybody and that we must not ask any questions since we were going to enter "Greece" illegally. They said even though we were traveling illegally there wouldn't be any problems with the authorities if we stayed silent. So, I did. I kept my mouth shut.

When we arrived, the fat Russian lady herded us onto a city bus. On the way from the airport, we stopped numerous times at various bus stops. At every stop there was a taxi driver waiting who would come take some of the girls off the bus.[19] But no one came to get me. So, I rode to the last stop at the end of the line with one other girl. I wanted to get off the bus and ask someone, "Where am I?" But there were two bus drivers. One of them was [a] big black guy who pointed to me and said, "Stay seated, we're going back." So, I sat down and asked the other girl, who was sitting beside me, "Where are we?" She threw her hands up in the air and said, "I don't know anything! I don't know." So, we just sat on the bus waiting.

Then I noticed a woman walking toward the bus. She was wearing some kind of a headscarf. She came up to the bus and started talking to the two drivers. They gave her our passports and she gave them some money.

9. Anya

They pointed at us and said, "Get off." I looked at the lady. She snapped her purse shut [and] motioned for us to get off the bus. She said, "Come on, let's go. Hurry." And like a robot, I followed. I was pretty numb and confused.

Did you know what was happening to you? What were you thinking?

Anya: I didn't know anything. Clearly something was wrong with the situation, but I didn't know what. Nor did I know what to do. I could run away, but where would I go? I had no money, no passport, I didn't even know where I was or who this lady was. Every time I thought that maybe I could run away [*she laughs bitterly*], then I would think, "Where would I run to?"

The lady with the headscarf took the two of us to a hotel. A big red hotel. We went inside and up to the second floor. I remember that there was a long corridor and lots of rooms. I also remember that there were a lot of girls there. At the time, it got my curiosity—where am I now? What is this? Who are these people? But I was too afraid to say anything.

A guy on the second floor of the hotel told us to go into a room. He pointed to one, and the lady with the scarf came with us. She said, "There's a shower, go wash. Then you'll eat something. Rest a bit and then we'll talk." So, we did, we took showers. They brought us some chicken to eat. We ate, we washed up, and I fell deeply asleep. I slept nearly twenty-four hours.

What happened when you woke up? Were you alone or was the other girl with you?

Anya: On the second day—I slept straight through the morning—the woman with the scarf came and got the girl who had been with me on the bus. She said, "Now we have to get to work." She told the girl who was with me to dress up pretty and then she left. I looked at the girl and said, "Where are you going?" She said, "Don't worry—I'll go and come back."

"When will you return?" She didn't answer. She left and I stayed. I looked around. There were magazines on a little table in the room. I read, "Turkey" this, "Turkey" that—I understood the word "Turkey." It was all about Turkey in these magazines.

And you still thought you were in Greece?

Anya: Yes. When the girl returned, I asked her, "Am I in Turkey?" She said, "Yes. What? You didn't know?"

"No. I didn't know."

"Where did you think you were going?"

"To my sister in Greece."

"What sister?"

"In Greece."

And she started laughing. To her it was really funny that I was so terrified and stupid. That's the thing about those people [*long pause*]. They were all so strange. I asked, "Where's the woman with the head scarf?"

"What woman?" She laughed again. "What's up with you? Did you just fall out of the sky? Where did you come from? The moon?"

I said, "I'm going to my sister's. TO MY SISTER. Not here with you. I'm waiting for that woman to take me to my sister."

She said, "No. You are going to work." And I said, "What kind of work?"

"These girls—everyone here goes to work."

I asked, "What kind of work? Tell me so I will know."

So, she explained to me that a man will come. I will go with him to a room.... Or to a restaurant.... Or wherever. Or maybe to a hotel. I said, "I will not go. I didn't come here to work like that." She said, "If you want to eat, you'll work. If not, then.... Well, when *I* didn't want to go with them, they beat me unconscious." I got hysterical. Crying.

They brought in a telephone and called the fat Russian woman who took me from Chisinau. Remember, she had been very nice to me—like a friend. She talked real softly and sweetly on the telephone. She said, "I'll come get you. Look, the guy will come with the taxi, and he will bring you to me. So go with him. He will bring you to me."

How long had you been in Turkey by now?

Anya: It was already my third day there. I arrived on November 22, 1999, in [*long pause*] Istanbul. On the 25th they sent me back to that woman, the fat Russian woman. They sent another girl with me. Once we were in the taxi and going down the road, I asked this girl where she was from. She said she was from Transnistria. When I heard she was from Transnistria, I told her that my village was really close to Transnistria. She said she was from Tiraspol and we chatted a little bit.[20] She spoke Russian. We were sitting together in the back seat of the taxi.

There was a driver and another guy in the front seat. Once we were underway, the guy up front started asking us all kinds of questions in Turkish. I didn't understand anything. She answered all his questions in Turkish. They were all speaking Turkish, so I didn't understand a word. Then they all looked at me and I got really scared. I asked, "What is he saying?"

"He said you are very pretty."

Again, they started talking in Turkish, he said something, and they all laughed. Again, they all looked at me. So, I asked her again, "What's he saying? What does he want?"

"He wanted to know how old you are, so I told them you were twenty." I asked her who this guy was, and she said he was a client. I knew what a client in a store was, but that didn't make any sense to me. When I asked her what kind of a client he was, she said, "A client. Just a client." So, I asked her what he was buying [*laughs bitterly*]. She laughed so hard. "He's going to buy *you!*"

I said, "What? How can he buy me?" And I got hysterical. "Explain this to me. Tell me what's going on!" She said, "Later. We'll explain later. Later. Later."

We drove for about an hour and a half. It was outside of the center of Istanbul. I don't know which direction we went. I… [*pause*] I don't…. [*pause*] I don't remember. I don't know … [*long pause as she stares off into the distance*] I didn't understand what streets … [*pause*] Where…. I didn't know anything. Then we arrived. She said that we had to get out of the car. There was a guy on the street waiting for us. He was alone and sitting in front of a building. The two men from the car took us into the building and upstairs and the third guy followed us. I paid attention to where we were going. We climbed to the first floor—no exit doors anywhere. We kept going up, to the second, third, fourth, fifth floors. On the sixth floor, we went into a room. In the room was an older guy sitting at a table set for tea. I think he was the owner of the building. We sat down at the table with him. I asked the girl from Tiraspol, "Where's the fat Russian woman?" And she said, "Later, later." She was laughing and talking to them in Turkish. They all looked at me. I said, "What." Then she said, "Stand up." I said, "Why?"

"JUST STAND UP!" So, I stood up and looked at them. "What do they want?" I was wearing pants and a jacket. She said, "Show us." [*Anya indicates that she was to lift up her top.*]

I didn't know—I wasn't going to…. I sat down and looked at them. I wanted to run right out of there. All the men left except the owner and another guy. They sat talking and I sat looking out the window. Looking out and thinking, "Where have I landed? What's going to happen to me? Who are they? What do they want? Why is she helping them?"

Nothing made sense to me. They told me we were waiting for someone, that someone was coming. And then they put us [*Anya and the girl from Tiraspol*] in another room that looked like a bedroom. It was little and the window was open. I sat by the window and looked out. I kept thinking, "What are they going to do to me? What's going to happen?" I was getting hysterical again. Then she said, "Enough! Stop! They are here."

"Who?"

Then she began talking. "Now they are going to sell us." I began crying hysterically again. "I don't want to. I have a daughter. I have a family. I don't want to ... [*long pause*] ... work like you work."

"Don't worry. We'll try to escape. Somehow we'll run away."

Why would she say that? Wasn't she one of them?

Anya: I think she felt sorry for me. I think she didn't want to be sold either. I really don't know. But then she said, "When they take us downstairs, we'll try to run away then." I said, "How?"

When ... we ... had decided how we would escape, that older guy came back and took us into a big room on the sixth floor. On the right was a divan. Next to the divan was a window. A Russian woman from Chisinau, not the same fat one, a different one, sat near the window. There were men sitting on the divan, drinking tea and laughing.

That Russian lady.... She was so.... Her head was ... huge [*voice shakes*]. She was sitting, and two men stood next to her. The same kind.... Turkish. Dark. I got really scared. I looked at them and asked, "Where's the fat Russian lady?" Then the Russian lady began yelling at me, "I am sick of you and your fat Russian lady! Forget about her! Forget it! She SOLD you!"

When she started yelling at me, I finally started to understand a little—what was happening to me. The other girl started crying softly. Then the Russian lady said, "Turn around, take off the jacket and turn slowly." I said, "I won't!"

She said, "You will, or you'll catch hell."

"I won't."

"You will!" Then she looked me over and said in a low menacing voice, "It will be better for you if you do it than if we have to make you do it." So, I took off the jacket and saw that she was motioning for me to turn a bit. I turned once and looked at her. She pointed to my top. "LIFT IT UP!" I started crying. I lifted my top up quickly and immediately pulled it right back down again, very fast. I noticed that the curtains were fluttering in the breeze. I went over to the window and looked down. I looked at my feet, and God, how I wanted to.... I wanted ... if only I were a bird [*Anya cries, struggles to speak, and then continues, her voice shaking*], I would immediately fly away. I said a silent prayer, "God, give me wings. Please God." And I jumped. I don't remember anything else.

Do you remember anything after that?

Anya: When I came to, it was night. I saw a big window, maybe two or three windows. I remember white tablecloths—there were tables with white tablecloths, a window, and white curtains. On the other side of the window there were men in black suits. They were all sitting at a table. It seemed like they were very near to me. I tried to raise my hand. I wanted to knock on the window to get their attention. Maybe they could help me somehow.... That I could... [*She breaks down sobbing for a few minutes.*] I came to in the hospital.

Somehow, I held onto the bedside table and tried to stand up. Only my back was in some kind of brace. My spine really hurt, so I laid back down. Later, some people came and held me by my hands and feet as they put casts on my legs and arms. They were Turks. I think they asked me why I was in Turkey—if I had been sent there to do THAT kind of work. They gave me back my passport and I hid it. I hid it here, like this [*pantomimes hiding it down her pants*]. I was thinking that I would be able to run away from them. That I could take my passport and somehow get back home.

You still had your passport?

Anya: Yes. I still had my international passport—no one had taken it from me. It was in my purse and my purse was on me when I jumped. So, when the ambulance took me to the hospital, the medics found my passport. My last name at that time was K__a. The doctors knew that it was Russian, but they didn't know any Russian language. They only knew "vodka" and "stowaway": *vodka* and *zaika*. They thought that K__a and *vodka* were the same word—the same thing [*laughs*]. Oh! And I was in so much pain! They would pull on my legs and arms.

Like traction?

Anya: Yes, yes. Everything was broken—everything. They would stretch me and say, "Vodka, don't cry. Vodka, don't cry. *Zaika*, don't cry." I was in so much pain. I was crying from pain, and when they would say, "Vodka, don't cry," it was so funny. Everything hurt, but when they said those words, it was funny.

How long were you in the hospital?

Anya: Oh. I laid in that hospital, in the emergency ward in Istanbul, for about fifteen days. I was all in casts. My head was bandaged, I had braces on my spine, both legs had casts, both arms had casts. And I just laid there. I couldn't do anything else. My arms and legs were broken, some of my discs were crushed and vertebrae dislocated. So, I laid there in the emergency ward for fifteen days. No one came to see me, no one asked me anything. The nurse came every morning with the doctor during rounds. Every day they would look at me and the doctor would say, "Give her

Novocain." They gave me one pill a day—Novocain. It is a very, very weak painkiller. I was very worried because the pain was so intense, I couldn't stand or anything. And I had a really high temperature.

After fifteen days they took me to another hospital—not the emergency ward but to the trauma ward of another hospital in a different place.

And your mom? Were you able to call her? Did she know anything?

Anya: No. Nobody at home knew anything. I was in a different hospital, but it was just the same—they didn't give me a shot for pain. I was covered in casts head to toe, so there was no place where they *could* give me a shot. They only gave me pills. I didn't eat anything. I couldn't eat anything. I was only able to eat a few little eyedroppers of soup a couple of times a day, as I remember it.

After I was at the new hospital for a couple of days, someone came to visit me from the embassy.[21] I don't remember who it was. I don't know if he was with the police or if he was there to help me, or who he was. He asked me a bunch of questions that I didn't know how to answer—I still didn't fully understand what had happened to me. I remembered that I had fallen from a very high place. As I was talking to him, I began to remember the situation exactly. I tried to explain to him, but he couldn't understand my heavily accented Russian. So, he left and said he would come back with a translator. But before he could return with a translator, another guy came to see me. He spoke Russian. He said that if I gave anybody any information, I would have big problems back in Moldova. I asked him who he was, and he said, "It doesn't matter who I am. If anyone asks you what happened, you are to tell them that you were in an accident while riding in a taxi. You are not to say anything more. Nothing. Understand?"

So that's what I said when the man from the embassy came back with a translator. I was terrified and afraid that anything could happen to me. I told the authorities that I was in an accident in a taxi. They asked, "Where? What street?" I said I didn't know the street. I said I didn't remember anything—only that I was in a car accident. That seemed to satisfy them, and they left.

Sometime later that older guy, the owner of the hotel, came to see me. He was there when I jumped out the window. I believe he asked someone what had happened to me. He found me and came to see me in the hospital. He talked to the doctors. They told him that my bones were not knitting together—that they had already rebroken my arms and legs and put on new casts. In the first hospital, they had put the casts on wrong. So, in the second hospital they took the casts off and reset my bones. But my bones still were not growing together properly. The doctors said I needed an operation, but that it was very expensive. They were going to send me back to Moldova that way—all broken and in casts. There was a way to transport sick people on a little airplane. But the owner of the hotel said, "She came here on her feet, she will leave here on her feet." He then took me from that hospital to a third hospital.

Why did he do that, do you think?

Anya: I have no idea, maybe he felt sorry for me, or guilty. I don't know. I was in this second hospital three or four days. I kind of came to my senses there. Then the hotel owner told me he was going to have me transferred to a private hospital where they would give me the necessary operations. He said it was a very good hospital and he showed me how they were going to weave my bones together. He said everything was going to be okay.

Was he one of them—the traffickers?

Anya: No, he was not one of them. I understand that now. I don't know why he decided to help me. He had a favorite girl. You know, Turks have wives and girlfriends. He had a young girl. He came with her to see me. She knew a little Russian—just a little. They came together so that she could explain things to me. Sometimes when I didn't understand her— there were some words she didn't know—she would look at me and say, "How can I explain this?" If, for example, she didn't know the word for dog, she would begin to bark, or meow, or whatever. I would lay there, in a full body cast, and watch her and laugh. She was such a good lady.

In the private hospital they gave me a separate room that had a TV in it. They had a very interesting bed there. You could raise the head and raise the feet. The nurse came and she spoke a little Russian. She showed me how to use the control panel for the bed. It was so interesting. I could raise my head to eat and then lower it. I thought, "Maybe I'm in heaven? Where else could I be?" I asked the nurse if I was in heaven and she laughed and said, "No, you are just in a hospital. A very good hospital."

Finally, they took all the casts off me. Without my cast, my legs hurt but I didn't know if I should tell anyone or not. I worried about everything. I laid there and worried. The nurse came and asked if everything was okay, and I said yes. I didn't tell her I hurt.

After seven days the doctors had completed all my tests and analyses and prepared me for an operation. They came to me and they said, "It's time to go." I thought it was time for me to go home, but instead they wheeled me into surgery. I was so scared.

Of course. Was this your first time in a hospital? Your first surgery?

Anya: No, I was in the hospital once in Moldova. But it was just a simple operation to have my appendix out. But what they did to me here, this was major surgery. They put a.... They placed something in me.... I didn't really know what they were doing.... Then they.... It's easier for me to show you. Okay? [*She goes to a cabinet in the living room and pulls out a file of x-rays. She holds one up to the light.*] You see, here they put a metal pin in me. It's easy to see.

It still hurts and you can see my leg is turned out a little. [*She lifts her pant leg and shows where the scars are on her thigh.*] See? You can see all the holes where the stitches were. See all the scars? They still hurt. Sometimes they hurt a lot. I had several operations. It was.... It was horrible. It looked terrible. I had stitches in my head and when they took them out, I looked in a mirror and cried—the scars were thick and red. They actually did a little cosmetic surgery later so that it wouldn't be so obvious. Now you can just barely see them, right?

Well, after they finished ... after the last operation, after they had completed all the operations, the hotel owner took me back to his hotel. I stayed there almost a month while I recovered. I was on crutches at that time and finally they took out all my stitches. I had thirty-six stitches in my right leg alone here. I was getting ready to go home—to go back to Moldova. I went to see the doctor one last time. He wanted to see me take a few steps without the crutches. It was very hard, but I was able to take two steps. He said I was very strong—that I held onto life very tightly. He said he had never met anyone so determined to live.

How did you get home? You had no money, right?

Anya: The hotel owner's girlfriend gave me an airline ticket to Moldova as a present so I could go home. I finally called my mother. I don't remember when exactly that was. She immediately asked where I was and why hadn't I called her earlier. I said, "Mama, I've just had some operations and I'm not able to walk without crutches, and I'm in a brace." I told her a little bit about the operations, and she hung up on me. My mother didn't believe me. She said that I was lying so I wouldn't have to send home any money.

Since my mother didn't believe me, I called my father. I was crying and I told him a little bit. He said, "Don't cry—just get better. When are you coming home? Call and I'll meet you at the airport." Before all of this, life was very difficult. As you know, I went to Odessa and Romania in order to find work. My mom looked after my daughter, so my mom thought I should be buying groceries for them, sending them money, taking care of them the whole time.

How did you find La Strada? Or did they find you?

Anya: No, I found them. When I first returned from Turkey, I lived and worked in Chisinau. One day I heard an advertisement on the radio, something about a hotline. I started listening with more interest, and they were talking about the selling of people. In truth, I thought it was a joke. But then I thought, what kind of joke would this be? The next time I heard the advertisement, I listened more closely and wrote down the telephone number. But I was too afraid to call. I thought about it all day long but just could not make the call. On the second day, I tried to phone them. I didn't know what I would say or what I would ask, but I thought I would at least call. So, I did, and a really sweet, soft voice answered the phone. It was Alina from La Strada. She asked me a couple of questions that I was afraid to answer. She asked me where I lived, and I gave her my address. She asked when I might be able to come to the office to see her.

I was afraid—really, really afraid. For a long time, I didn't call her back. But then, I don't know.... It was fall, late fall. I heard that advertisement again, and I decided to try it again. This time when Alina answered the phone, she said, "We have a present for you." And I said, "A present? Fancy that!" I knew this just couldn't be real, that it had to be some kind of terrible joke. But she said La Strada could help me. Again, she asked me when I might be able to come to the office. I told her I didn't know—that I would have to talk to my husband.

When I told my husband that there was this organization that would help me, and that they had a present for me, he said, "You're some kind of an idiot! You still believe in fairytales!" And I said, "Maybe they're for real. Maybe we should find out." He got angry and said, "Think about it! They might be trying to sell you again. You want to go back to Turkey?"

I thought about it and figured that I should find out if they could help me. So, I called the number again, talked to Alina again, and decided to go to the La Strada office. They immediately started helping me—they gave me groceries that day. They provided me with counseling, and even helped me buy a sewing machine so that now I have my own little tailor shop in my home.

What are your dreams for the future?

Anya: I have no dreams. The only thing I want is to be able to walk without a limp and without pain. That will never happen.

If you could tell the people reading this anything, what would you tell them?

Anya: You can't understand what happens to one's humanity when you discover that you have been sold for US$40—that your life is worth nothing but $40. Tell them we are human! Human! You can't sell human beings. Tell them we are HUMAN!

* * * *

When I interviewed Anya in 2008, she had been back from Turkey for eight years. She and her sixteen-year-old daughter lived together in the little village, where she had a small but profitable tailoring business. She divorced her alcoholic husband, and later met and married a man from the village. He knows her full story and supports her unconditionally. She is still estranged from her mother and has no plans to pursue a reconciliation in that relationship.

Most days, Anya suffers from pain in her legs. She often has severe headaches, likely brought on by emotional trauma. She still has nightmares and will always walk with a limp. She is one of the lucky ones.

10

Alexei

Victim of labor exploitation
NGO: La Strada
Chisinau, Moldova
November 27, 2008

When I first met Alexei in front of the offices of La Strada International in Chisinau, he was loudly singing old Elvis Presley songs. I later found out that he was trying to connect with the "American lady" and show me that he loved American rock 'n' roll. He was thin, tall, and shabbily dressed. One could see a keen intelligence in his eyes and the scars of a very hard life etched upon his face. His nose had the swollen crook of a boxer's nose from being broken several times. The right side of his face bore pronounced scars from deep cuts to his chin, cheek, and brow ridge. With his full brown hair neatly trimmed, it was difficult to guess his age. He later told me that he was fifty-three, although he looked much older. He spent nearly nine years as a slave, being sold a couple of times, before falling into debt bondage slavery while trying to escape. When he finally managed to flee his captors, he ended up in prison outside of Moscow for not having proper documents.

Alexei's story underscores that men, too, are at risk of being trafficked. Most public and media attention is focused on women and sexual slavery, almost to the exclusion of mentioning male slaves. In recent years, however, there has been increasing awareness that not just women and children are vulnerable to trafficking and slavery. Men migrate in large numbers, and an increasing number of studies recognize that adult men are subject to labor exploitation to a much greater degree than previously thought.[1] One reason for the underreporting of trafficked adult males is that they are often treated as irregular migrants and deported without investigation. But the methods used by slavers to control these men are the same as those used to control women for sexual exploitation: confiscation of passports, violence and threats of violence, withholding wages, confinement, fraud, physical abuse, abduction, and the like. In this interview, Alexei discusses the brutality he endured as a slave and the difficulties he faced in escaping and returning home.

Alexei's experiences demonstrate the considerable overlap between categories of servile labor exploitation. In 1930, the International Labour Organization (ILO) provided the first internationally accepted definition of forced labor, which depended upon two key elements: coercion and involuntariness of the labor.[2] This definition differs from that of debt bondage in that the victim must be forced to work involuntarily. In debt bondage, the victim voluntarily agrees to work, free of charge, to pay off a debt. It becomes slavery or exploitative because there often is no termination date. Typically, the lender constantly adds to the debt through accrued interest, fines or fees, or exorbitant charges for living expenses, so that the debt can never be repaid. A third type of slavery, chattel slavery, reduces people to property and entails de facto ownership of the person. Alexei was subjected to all three types of labor exploitation categorically and sometimes simultaneously during his captivity.

Having met on the street, we went into the La Strada office together. The staff offered us tea and led us into a small office, where we settled in for the interview. Alexei spoke of his ordeal of being trafficked with intensity, waving his hands in all directions for emphasis. There were large blisters on the palms of those hands. His glasses, which were provided by La Strada, had a crack running across the length of the left lens. He carried a pair of reading glasses in his vest pocket. These glasses were missing one of their support arms. Alexei told me that he didn't need new glasses, that these were still usable and good enough for him.

Of all my interviewees, Alexei was trafficked the earliest. He was sold in 1994, and trafficked for labor exploitation from Perm, Russia, to Afghanistan. After several years of laboring as a slave in Afghanistan, he managed to escape, only to be trapped again and sold to a trafficker in Tajikistan. One of his owners in Tajikistan allowed him to leave after several years of bonded labor. Alexei managed to make his way to Russia, where he was imprisoned for entering the country illegally since traffickers had long ago confiscated his documents. Besides, all his documents were from the Soviet Union. By the time he managed to escape slavery, the Soviet Union had collapsed, and travel across the borders of the newly established post–Soviet states was complicated and dangerous. He finally made it back to his homeland of Moldova in 2004—ten years after he had first been sold.

10. Alexei

Tell me a little about your life.

Alexei: I was born in Chisinau, Moldova, in 1948 and lived right in the center of town. I got through the tenth grade.³ Then I got a job here in Chisinau at Moldova State University in the Military Department.⁴ However, I didn't wear a uniform—I was a civilian. I had to follow all army rules and regulations, but I was not technically in the army. I worked there from 1970 until 1986. And then my father died.

Not long after he died, I left for Russia, where I was able to get a job in Perm, in the Western Urals. In fact, I traveled all around Russia. It was the Soviet Union back then and it was very easy to travel. All you needed was your Soviet passport. You didn't need visas or permissions, or anything. Everyone used rubles and you could travel freely. I had some relatives in Perm. My uncle worked in the natural gas industry there, building gas lines. I worked with him on the gas line for five or six years. He paid me very well. While working for him, I was able to rent an apartment. Everything was great.

Then I returned to Chisinau in 1991, because my mother became ill. When I returned, nothing was the same. Moldova had a different type of government and economy. Everybody was buying and selling, buying and selling.⁵

*Was this because of perestroika?*⁶

Alexei: Yes, yes. Perestroika was a very difficult time. People didn't understand the changes and you couldn't rely on anything. Everything seemed broken and people were confused, frustrated, bewildered. Nobody knew how to keep going, or what would happen next. The government-owned factories shut down and nothing worked.⁷ In Chisinau the only enterprise left open was one little cooperative that made house slippers [*tabachki*]. One could make a little money sewing slippers—they still paid wages. Primarily, people took the slippers to Poland to sell them. Other people went to Turkey to buy goods there, bring them back, and sell them here.⁸ This was how people managed to live. In 1991, I started going to Moscow to buy things to bring back and sell here in Chisinau.

Then, in 1994, my mother died. She was the last of my family, there was no one left. I lived in her two-bedroom apartment in Chisinau and got along well by myself, except it was hard to make money. With my mother gone, I decided to go back to Russia again to find work. I leased out my apartment for a year and left. I intended to stay for only a year in Russia, but it took me ten years to get back home. That is because I got trafficked. I was working in Perm with the Russian military, and they sold us to some guys in Tajikistan. You know Tajikistan?

Yes, well, there was a military-owned lumber mill in Perm, Russia.[9] I got hired to help deliver lumber to Tajikistan. We drove a Kamaz truck from Perm—just two of us.[10] The military guys in Perm lied to us. They disappeared us in Tajikistan.

Disappeared you?

Alexei: They were ... [*long pause while he struggles for the right words*] This is how it worked. Tajiks drove Kamazes from Tajikistan loaded with watermelons, cantaloupes, all kinds of melons to Perm in order to sell them. These Tajiks had a boss in Perm—a Russian colonel. He would oversee the unloading of the melons into a warehouse. I worked in the warehouse as a stevedore. This colonel is the one who arranged to send me to Tajikistan. He said that he would get all the necessary documents and permissions for me to haul lumber to Tajikistan and that I would make good money. He said that the truck would be a little old, but that it would make it to Tajikistan. I took the bait. I quit work as a stevedore at the warehouse and left to deliver wood to Tajikistan. But this guy, Colonel Stepanov, lied to me and my partner. He sold us.

You mean this Russian colonel Stepanov sold you to the Tajiks?

Alexei: Yes. He sold us. And it even wasn't Tajikistan that we went to, but Afghanistan—240 kilometers [about 150 miles] from the Afghan border, near someplace called Char Dara—that's where we ended up.[11] But we didn't know. It was our first time there. By the time we arrived, he had already sold us and received the money. In Russia he was a colonel in the army—three stars![12] And he sold us, that snake! What do you call that? When a military officer sells some of his own people? He was Russian, *our* colonel! They are all snakes. He sold the truck, sold us, sold everything. He got the money, and we never knew about it. Like fools, we just left for Tajikistan.

When we arrived, there was nothing there, just a cement-block house, some asphalt, and the steppe. We were met by some tough-looking guys. They took everything from us: our documents, possessions, everything. They even confiscated our shirts but left us with our pants and shoes. They took everything else.

They killed my partner, the driver. They shot him and forced me to unload the truck. My partner was thirty-five years old. At that time, I was older—I was forty. But to them, he was a problem. He resisted. He tried to run away, so they shot him with an AKM Russian carbine 10 ... ten cartridges.[13] After killing the driver, they forced me to work for them, tending to the crops, goats, sheep, camels ... it was very difficult.

Did you receive any money or compensation for your work?

Alexei: What? No! After about a month, I started trying to figure out how I could escape. I needed to go back home, but how? I would need to travel through a little piece of Afghanistan, Tajikistan, Uzbekistan, Kazakhstan, Russia, and then Moldova. I would have to travel through all those countries with no documents. They took all my identification. I had no documents, no passport, no copies, nothing.

The only "free" time I had to think about my escape was when I was washing, shaving, or eating. That was the only time I had to myself to plan an escape. Otherwise, it was the goats, or the watermelons, or the cantaloupes.... I worked every day. I did not have one day off. I was a slave for them for four years and three months.

Eventually they sold me to this Muslim guy—I think he was a friend of theirs. All I know is that I was taken to a small village to work for a Muslim guy, Titimar. He had a large family living with him—mother, grandmother, children, dogs, even goats. And I was there one day, two, three … a month. I began to panic: "What am I going to do? How am I going to get home? I must find a way to escape!" But it was in the middle of nowhere. There were no airplanes near there, no trains, nothing. And this guy who bought me was a slave trader, but he kept me for himself. All these guys sold slaves. They could look you right in the eye and sell you. That's what they did there, their business was slavery. Slavery is a horrific thing.

When you got there, did you know where you were?

Alexei: No, they didn't tell me where I was. I found out after I lived there a while. It was a little village, about 10,000 people, I believe. They were all Muslim Afghan Tajiks. There are Tajiks, and Afghan Tajiks—these were Afghan Tajiks, and they spoke a different language. They had a different way of life, too. There, where I was, the war hadn't been there. The war was further south—it was a bit farther away.[14] There was nothing where I was. The whole region was empty—half empty. I was not far from the Tajik border. The border was totally open: there were no border markings, no lines to cross, no border guards like there were during Soviet times.[15] There was a road that one could come and go on, but no one was guarding it. They bring a lot of drugs across the border here.

They use a lot of slaves to harvest drugs in that area, but I didn't harvest drugs. Titimar mainly raised sheep. He also had camels, horses, and cows. I had to feed them and take care of them. I worked all day, every day, and did not get a single penny. Titimar fed me, gave me cigarettes, and sometimes a little wine. Someone gave me some clothes. But that is all I got. I never got any money. Titimar was rich, so the food was pretty good.

But I had to get up early every morning and I finished work very late at night.

Did he beat you?

Alexei: No. I was beaten later, when I got sold to that druggie, Anash.[16] He smoked marijuana. He beat me so much that it damaged my kidneys. One of my kidneys doesn't work. He also broke some of my ribs and cut me with a knife. See all these scars? [*He points to two long, deep scars on his face that run from his brow ridge to his chin.*] He cut me up two times and then he didn't bother me. That is because he needed me to work. If he didn't need me to do work, he would have killed me. I decided that since my life depended upon my working for him, I would work hard. I have that kind of character—I will survive no matter what. I am not afraid. I wasn't afraid then.

But I couldn't escape from Titimar's place, and the women and children kind of got used to me being around all the time. The children followed me around like a little herd. I'm kind of a poet and I know American rock 'n' roll. The kids would say, "Hey, Russian! Come here, come here and sing to us" [*laughs*]. The kids would follow me around and say, "Here, have a cigarette. Have some melon, eat, eat. Come on now, sing for us. Give us a song." And I would sing for them. I figured if I could somehow get closer to them, maybe they would help me escape. The children seemed to love me, and the women were good to me, they never hit me or abused me.

And so, time passed: a month, two, three … summer. A year passed and I was already used to being there. I already kind of understood them and they kind of knew me. I was able to relax a little bit. I just turned around and it seemed like, *opa* [oops]! now it is 1996. Then, *opa!* now it is 1997, now 1998. But I had to get back to Chisinau. I had leased out my apartment only for a year—I was sure I had lost everything. I couldn't send a message to my tenant, couldn't write anyone, nothing.

There were, I think, eight of us slaves there—eight men. They were mostly Russians, but there were also some Chechens. Oh, and there was a Kazakh family—a wife and kids. They had already been there several years by the time I arrived. One of the Russians had fought in the Soviet war. But after the war, he stayed and adopted the Muslim faith. He married a Muslim woman, and they had two kids. Titimar had given him his freedom and a small house to live in. He was afraid to go back to Russia because during the war he fought on the side of the Afghans and killed Russians.

And then, after three years had gone by—three years!—I found this guy, a produce trader. He went from Afghanistan through Tajikistan to Russia, selling produce and tobacco. His tobacco was like gold, it was very good. I begged him, "Help me, please! Help get me out of here." I had no documents, but he agreed that if I would work for him for a year without pay, he would help me. A whole year. I agreed. This was in October 1998.

At this time, the guy and his partners were transporting onions. They had four Kamaz trucks full of onions—about thirty tons. He promised to hide me in a box under the onions. I waited what seemed like forever for him to come for me. I was afraid he wouldn't help me, but he did. He came and got me and hid me in the onions as promised. I crawled in the box in the back of the truck. He gave me some water, a piece of *lavosh* [flatbread], and covered me in onions. It was four in the morning, and we quietly drove off. This was Thursday, October 28, 1998. Within an hour and a half, we had left Afghan territory. When we arrived in Afga, Tajikistan, he said I could ride in the cabin of the truck. There were already two guys in the cab, but three will fit in a Kamaz truck. He said, "You don't need documents here, just money." In Tajikistan the police are like that: if you give them money you can do anything.

So that's how I got out of Afghanistan. Once we were in Tajikistan I sat in the cabin, but I was afraid. What if suddenly they catch me? We traveled for nine days to reach Russia. We only stopped to eat, go to the bathroom, wash, shave, and get underway again. We finally reached Chelyabinsk Oblast in the Southern Urals, on the Russian–Kazakh border. There were such beautiful hills there. When we got there, we stopped. He said to me, "Look there. See those little houses in the distance—that is already Russia. You will soon be there, and you will be freer. You will be able to talk to people easier." It was easy to bribe your way cross the border there. The border guards and customs agents were Russian. My "friend" gave them onions and they let us cross the border, even though I had no documents.

He drove me a bit further, where the former director of a *sovkhoz* [state-run collective farm] lived. They agreed that I would work for him to pay for my escape. In essence, he gave me to the director as a present. I was forced to work there. So again, I was sold into slavery—this time in Russia. Every day I had to tend to the cows, geese, chickens, and again I got nothing. They just fed me. I was a slave again! The director told me I was his indentured servant. We agreed that he would eventually help me get a Russian passport and even some money in exchange for my work. He said he would let me go once I worked off the debt. This was our agreement.

The director was rich. He was a big guy in the mafia, and he owned a lot of land. I knew he likely could be ruthlessly violent, so I always tried to please him. Yet, I was always thinking about when I might be able to get out of there. It was this guy's son who beat me and cut me. He would get drunk and smoke dope and beat me for fun. So, I knew I had to be careful.

I worked there for over a year, without a day off. I was just one of the animals. I would say, "Anatolii Georgivich, it has been over a year. Help me get my documents." And he would say, "I will get you your documents, but I have to go into the city to get them." He didn't want to get me a passport because then I would leave. It wasn't to his advantage to get me a passport. And to him, I was nobody. "What is your name?" "Alexei." But then he would say, "You don't have anything to prove that. Maybe you are Vasya, or Misha, or John. You can't even prove what your name is." He did that to torment me.

But his wife was kind. She fed me well and let me listen to music on her tape player. She often left home and left me alone. She saw that I was trustworthy. So, it was a little better there, except for the son, Anash. The director "gave" me a television set for my room, and a cassette player, and he "gave" me books. What I didn't know is that he was charging me for them, and I was going further in debt. In the end, he got sick of me pestering him and so he let me go. He bought me a bus ticket, gave me some clothes, shoes, and some food. But he never arranged for my documents and never got me a passport like he promised.

When I left his place, I got as far as the outskirts of Moscow, to Sergiev Posad.[17] I worked at the monastery there as a groundskeeper for two years. But again, the issue of my documents came up. This time with the militia. They would arrest me, hold me, then let me go. Arrest me again, then let me go. All because I had no passport or legal documents. It's only paper, yet it's the most important thing. You can't cross borders without it. I somehow had to get a passport, or a temporary passport. All I needed to do was get to an embassy, but nobody would help me. Not the mafia, not the people in Zagorsk, nobody. Ultimately, I got arrested one last time and they sent me to prison.

I was in prison for a whole year. My case was so small and so unimportant that they didn't even bother to set a trial date for me. But it was comfortable enough in there, they fed us good. It was Moscow. We ate good, we drank tea, we read books. The only real problem was we didn't get enough fresh air. While I was in prison my legs started to hurt. My lymph nodes became inflamed with polyarthritis. But at least in prison I no longer had to work.

After a year I finally got a trial. The trial was in June 2001, in Moscow. The judge gave me amnesty. In fact, in 2001 they were giving lots of people amnesty. They released me, but I couldn't walk because my polyarthritis was so bad. They gave me a release paper, one hundred rubles, and let me go free. I decided I needed to get back to Sergiev Posad. Maybe I could get my old job back. I went to the nearest metro station. And there, at the metro, I met some kind of a pastor or preacher. He asked me,

"What's wrong with you?" I told him I couldn't walk. He asked me where I was from, and I told him that I had just been released from prison. He said, "You know, I have a church—Lord Jesus." His name was Hugo van Niekerk, pastor of the Lord Jesus Church. He and his wife, Rika, lived in Moscow. He said that if I came to the church on Sunday, he would help me. So, I came. There were pastors there from the U.S. They prayed. I prayed. Everybody prayed over me, and my legs got a little better.

Honest to God. They prayed for me, fed me, and invited me to stay with them. I slept there in a little room. They were able to help me get a temporary passport so that I could go home to Moldova. They took me to the Moldovan Embassy in central Moscow and arranged for me to get a temporary passport so I could cross the border. This was in April 2001. But my passport was only to get me into Moldova. I had to cross the border with Ukraine before I could get into Moldova. At the Ukrainian border, they didn't accept my document because it was temporary. They deported me back to Russia. They wouldn't let me into Ukraine, even to just pass through. So, I was held in detention again. Again I was in prison, again I lost my freedom, and again I was sleeping on a plank bed. Finally, the Russians deported me back to Moldova.

∗ ∗ ∗ ∗

By the time Alexei finally made it home in 2004, he had lost everything. He had been bought and sold several times, been imprisoned twice, and he had several health issues. The tenant who rented his apartment in 1994 had died, leaving his apartment abandoned. Consequently, his apartment and everything in it was sold. All his friends had either died or emigrated—one to Israel, one to Canada, others to God knows where. So, he arrived back to his hometown of Chisinau physically and psychologically broken, with no place to live, no money, and no prospects for a job. He had been sold outright several times, enslaved, and then trapped in debt bondage. In 2004, over 59 percent of Moldovans in Alexei's age cohort lived below the poverty level due to underfunded social welfare programs, low pensions, and rampant unemployment. Alexei was able to find a job as caretaker of a cemetery. He received a little room to live in that included heat and water, plus the equivalent of US$100 a month.

Just by sheer luck, Alexei heard about La Strada and sought help there. La Strada provided him with psychological counseling, medical care, clothes, and medicines. At the time of the interview, Alexei was slowly getting his health back and was coming to terms with his experiences.

11

NADYA, VIORIKA, AND LIDA

Victims of sex trafficking
with IOM psychologist Lilya Gotshalk
NGO: International Organization for Migration
IOM Offices, Chisinau, Moldova
October 5, 2010

The depiction of young Eastern European women as sex slaves has been sensationalized in the media and in movies. These stories focus on the brutality endured by the enslaved women or the drama of escape or rescue. And to be sure, the contemporary sex-slave industry involves the systematic rape, torture, and killing of millions of women and children worldwide whether through murder, suicide, drug and alcohol addiction, or sexually transmitted diseases like HIV/AIDS.[1] Lurid media coverage and emotional appeals by celebrity fundraisers rarely mention what happens to someone after they have returned home from being trafficked. The intense public attention on the victimization of women and children eclipses the stories of survivors' lives after trafficking. Yet, as most of my interviewees demonstrate, while being a slave was a pivotal moment in their lives, they are much, much more than this thing that happened to them.

How does one survive the ordeal of being raped numerous times a day for months or years? As someone at the IOM office told me, "We can repair their broken bones, we can surgically repair the damage done to them internally, we can even fix their broken jaws and smashed-out teeth, but it is much more difficult to mend the often irreparable psychological effects of trafficking."[2] How do they live with the trauma? How has it changed them? How do they continue on with life? These are questions that haunted me from the time I first learned of sex trafficking.

The answers to those questions depend largely upon what happens to survivors once they are repatriated, and what kind of support they get.

Unfortunately, very large numbers of persons get retrafficked, largely because they are returned home to the same conditions of poverty, domestic violence, lack of economic opportunity, or gender bias that led to their being trafficked the first time. A few of the women I spoke with (who declined to have their stories included in the book) felt that they were now damaged goods and thought they would return to their trafficker, hoping to at least get paid for prostitution this time. Several others got deceived and trafficked a second or third time because they had so few options open to them.

Such was the experience of Vitoria. She thought she was going to Italy to work in a bathing suit factory but instead she was sold to a brothel in Cyprus. Her recruiter was her best friend from high school. Once she was rescued from the brothel and repatriated to her little village in Moldova, she still had two children to feed and no way to do so. When I interviewed her in October 2010, she was preparing to go to Moscow. A friend had arranged for her to work as a seamstress there. I asked her if she was not afraid that this might be another setup. She said, "What can I do? My children are hungry, and I have no food and no money. What other choice do I have?"[3] I do not know what happened to her. I never heard from her again. She might have gotten retrafficked, or she might have gotten a job. In any event, she did not receive sufficient support once she was repatriated to change her circumstances. And I know she took the trauma of her enslavement with her to Moscow.

Unlike Vitoria, the three women interviewed here represent differing levels of success in healing the trauma of sex trafficking. Their stories underscore the importance of psychological counseling and vocational rehabilitation, as well as family and community support in recovering from sexual slavery. Further, each of these women demonstrates that her experience of trafficking does not define her—that once a slave does not mean always a slave. These courageous women are surviving their experiences and have found their own ways to recovery with the help of the IOM.

I arranged the interviews through the psychologist Lilya Gotshalk, who works with the Chisinau Assistance and Protection Center, run by the IOM. Opened in 2001, the Center was the first rehabilitation center in Moldova. It provides safe accommodation for returning victims, as well as medical care, psychological counseling, and vocational training. At the time of the interview, these three women were all in different stages of rehabilitation. All three of them opted to have Lilya, their psychologist, present during the interview.

My first interviewee was Nadya, a twenty-nine-year-old mother of two. She brought her youngest son, Maxim, with her, and clutched him as if he would shield her from me. Maxim was two years old, with beautiful blue eyes and blond hair. He was chubby and happy, chattering nonsensical words and smiling with much pride in his ability to produce such interesting sounds. Nadya held him on her lap throughout the interview.

Nadya was very thin. I noticed that her fingernails had been chewed to practically nothing. Nadya had the bad fortune of meeting what is called a "Romeo pimp"—a man who courts and seduces young women and then sells them. Nadya met and married one of these men, who then took her to Turkey and sold her to a brothel. She was out of Moldova for a total of six years, from 2003 to 2009, with a few brief trips back with her husband/trafficker. She had one child with him and one with a Turkish man who was one of the johns. This Turkish man helped her escape her husband, but he in turn also brutalized her.

She was very traumatized and seemed reluctant to speak, even though she said that she really wanted to talk to me. She said she was motivated by the thought that maybe her experience could warn others of the dangers of trusting men. She comes from Orhei, a small town of 32,000 inhabitants located about 46 kilometers [28 miles] from Chisinau. Her psychologist, Lilya, said that she hoped the interview would encourage Nadya to follow through with professional training at the IOM.

Hello, Nadya, nice to meet you. Can you tell me a little about your trafficking experience?
Nadya: My husband took me to Turkey and sold me. He forced me into prostitution.

How did you meet your husband?
Nadya: We met through some friends of mine. I married him and had no way of knowing that he was selling people abroad. I was still very young—eighteen or nineteen years old. I didn't know much about life, or men, or anything. He courted me and was very sweet. He brought me candies and little gifts. It was nice. I fell in love with him. He told me that I would have a good life with him and that we would have a nice family. So, I married him and went to Turkey with him. He sold me there. Before we left Moldova, we had a son together. Our son was only one year old when we left for Turkey. My husband said I couldn't take him to Turkey with us, so I left him in the care of my mother. I thought we would be right back, but he sold me. My first son is now seven and just starting school.[4]

How were you able to get away from your husband?
Nadya: I met a person ... a john. He was a Turkish guy and I guess he liked me. He bought me from my husband so he could keep me as his own

property. I had a son with him—my younger son, this little guy Maxim [*she bounces him a little on her lap for emphasis*]. That is how I was able to get away from my husband. This Turkish john bought and paid for me and kept me at his house. I lived with him for about four or five years. But he was very cruel. He beat me and treated me very badly. One time he hit me in the face with an electric iron! So, I took my son and ran away from him. I ran to the Moldovan Consulate in Turkey.[5] They helped me get back to Moldova. By this time Maxim was almost a year old. But then, *he* [the Turkish john] came after me. He found me and sweet-talked me into going back to Turkey. He said he was sorry. He told me everything was going to be okay and that he would treat me better. I trusted him.

My mother kept saying, "Don't do this! Don't do this!" but I had no job in Moldova and no possibility of feeding my children, so I went back to Turkey with him. Immediately we started having the same problems, only he was even more cruel. So, I ran away again. This time I went to the Turkish police. They contacted the Moldovan police, who helped me get back home. I have not seen him or talked to him since.

It has been really hard for us. But thanks for the IOM—they are helping us [*long pause*]. So, little by little…. [*deep sigh*].

What kinds of problems have you had since you returned to Moldova?

Nadya: Well, I have a small child, so it is impossible for me to get a job. I can't wait until he is old enough for daycare so I can find some work. But right at first, I had the court hearings and proceedings. I tried to bring a case against my "husband," the man who trafficked me. But he ran away. He is no longer in the country. I heard he was in Italy or Spain. I don't know where he is, but he is not here in Moldova. So, I can't bring charges against him.

From what I understand, there are laws against trafficking in Moldova. Are they not being enforced?

Nadya: These laws are not effective because the police are getting paid by the pimps to protect *the pimps!* We have a lot of corruption. And if you are a woman, it is very unlikely that the police will help you. Just yesterday, as we were coming home from my son's school, I saw a policeman just beating a woman on the street. Not here in Chisinau but in my hometown, Orhei.

Do people in your town know what happened to you?

Nadya: No. No. No. I didn't even tell my mother, but she is beginning to figure it out. I live with her in her apartment. Things are not so good between us.

How has this experience changed you?

Nadya: I simply no longer trust men. That's the main thing. Now I am just waiting for my son to get a little older so that I can get a job. I hope for nothing beyond that. I no longer hope for a nice family. I have no dreams for the future. I just want my children to be healthy so that everything will be okay with us. Nothing else.

Is there anything you want the people reading this book to know?

Nadya: Yes. There are young girls who are seventeen, eighteen, nineteen, up to twenty years old who are simply naïve. They don't understand that men will tell them anything. Some men will come up to them and say, "I will take you away and you can find a good job, and everything will be all right." Tell them they simply must not trust these guys. Do not trust, even if you think you know them. I will never trust again [*begins to cry*]. I have seen that to trust someone is simply foolish. Well, maybe I will trust someone one day, but so far, I cannot. [*She becomes very agitated and upset.*] I am sorry that I just can't.... I wanted to give you a lot of information.... I am sorry.... I can't.... Maybe Lilya can tell you more about my case.

No, don't apologize. Thank you so much for talking to us. That was very brave of you. Please take care of yourself. Thank you.

* * * *

When Nadya and Maxim leave the room, the psychologist, Lilya, takes a few minutes to talk to me about Nadya.

Lilya: Nadya is having a really hard time reintegrating. She came to us with so much trauma it was difficult to help her. One of her issues, and something she has in common with a lot of victims who have a hard time reintegrating, is that she is looking for a savior. She grabbed onto this second man, the Turkish john, so fast, as if he could save her. And he has betrayed her again. I am afraid that this sequence will repeat over and over again. This is a typical situation for some of our survivors.

She really needs therapy, but she has not had any yet. This is the first time she has even been to the IOM offices. She left the program without getting any real psychological help. That is why I was glad that she decided to come talk to you. I sensed that she is ready to accept more help, so I wanted her to come to these offices. She really needs some emotional support. This is very important. Nadya doesn't have any family support, she is basically alone. She lives with her mother, but they barely talk to each other. It is a very difficult situation. Other women who have the support of family or friends are able to draw upon their own inner strength. But people like Nadya are always looking for someone to grab onto to save them.

I will go get the second girl, Viorika. She was trafficked to the United Arab Emirates [UAE]. She was a construction worker and her recruiter promised her a good-paying construction job abroad. She left a small child behind with her mother when she left Moldova. Now her mother knows something is wrong and is really worried. But Viorika will not tell her mother what happened to her, like in Nadya's case. Nonetheless, Viorika's family has embraced her in a very supportive way. She stayed at the Center and went through psychotherapy. Now she has found a job and is working steadily. She has had a totally different recovery. Nadya is depressed and keeps very much to herself. You'll see the difference with Viorika. I'll go get her now.

* * * *

Viorika is a fair-skinned, freckle-faced, twenty-seven-year-old woman. Her long brown hair is pulled back into pigtails and clasped with a barrette. She looks somewhat like a tomboy—cute and sweet looking. She was a victim of debt bondage. The traffickers who bought her forced her into prostitution to repay them for expenses that they incurred in purchasing her.

Hello, Viorika. What a lovely name.
Viorika: Thank you. It is the name of a spring flower, one that blooms just after the snow.
Lilya: It's blue and beautiful like *you* [*to Viorika*] because you have such beautiful blue eyes.

Do you mind telling me a little about what happened to you?
Viorika: [*Sighs*] I had many difficulties back then and I am still having them now. Well, I made the acquaintance of a woman who was sending girls abroad to work. She offered to help me find a job abroad, and I agreed. So, I went. That's it—that is the story in short.

She sent me to the United Arab Emirates. When I got there, the traffickers took me right away. They … [*long pause*] taught us what we had to do and how to do it. It was really hard. I was forced into it right away … [*long pause*] into the brothel. They told us that first we had to work to pay them back for the airline ticket. Once we paid off our debt, then we could send the money we earned home to our families. But it happened that during the most difficult time, while I was still working off my debt, we got caught by the authorities. I was glad that this nightmare ended so soon and that we were sent back home, but I never got any money. I went through all that for five months and never got a penny.

When did this happen?

Viorika: Last year. In November [2009] the recruiters sent us abroad, and in April this year [2010] we got rescued and I flew back to Moldova.

How did that happen? Who rescued you?

Viorika: The authorities raided the brothel, and we got caught in the raid. They turned us over to an NGO that they have in the UAE.[6] Those people really helped us both emotionally and financially. They also helped us get back home. They notified the IOM here in Chisinau, Moldova, and people from the IOM met us at the airport when we arrived. So, our fellow countrymen greeted us and gave us a really warm welcome. There were two of us women returning—an acquaintance and myself. We both felt so good to be back home and to be greeted so warmly.

Lilya: I think I was one of the people who met you at the airport.

Viorika: Yes. Yes, you were. And you brought us back here to the IOM Center. We were so glad to be home and yet we did not know how to talk openly about our experience. On the one hand, we were so ashamed and in so much pain it was difficult to speak. On the other, we were so grateful.

Lilya: I remember when we got to the IOM Center, Viorika wanted to go home right away, to see her child. She said, "I don't want anything. I just want to go home. Home!" But I told her that it was already late and that she would be much better off spending the night at the Center. So, you spent the night at the Center, and left the next morning, right, Viorika?

Viorika: No, we left right away. You showed us around the Center and then we left for home. I came back a few days later with my little girl and we had tea and a chat with you. Then I returned to stay for a while so I could get some medical treatments and let my health improve before I went back home to stay.

Are you working now, Viorika?

Viorika: Yes. I have a job in Chisinau, in construction. It is difficult, but the main thing is that I have work *and* I am able to see my daughter. She lives with my mother about 100 kilometers from Chisinau [about 62 miles]. I work during the week in Chisinau, and on the weekends I go live with my mother. Of course, there are difficulties, but such is life.... Such is my fate.

I have a very good relationship with my mother. We have a loving family—very friendly and nice. My mother, my sister, and my younger brother and I all live together.

Do they know what happened to you?

Viorika: No. Only my sister knows. I could not tell her everything, but I told her where I was and that I was in a brothel. She understands me and supports me. As for my mother ... [*long pause, sighs*]. I cannot tell my mother about this, it would hurt her too much. For a mother, this kind of thing is too painful. In the past, we have had a lot of conversations about prostitution and women who work like that ... in that field. Both she and I were categorically against anyone working like that. Well, after this ... [*long pause*] I cannot tell her that, well, that I.... [*pause*]. You know.

How has this experience changed you?

Viorika: Practically everything has changed. Well, for one, I now appreciate having my family around me so much more than I ever did before. Even though I am having some difficulties right now, it is important to be close to my family. In the evenings we get together with my mother and discuss how the day went, or what our plans for the future are, or what we are hoping to accomplish. This feels right. But when I was so far away.... [*deep sigh*].

I have a daughter and I would like a family of my own someday. Every woman wants her own hearth, and so do I. But my experience has changed the way I look at men. I don't really trust them. I cannot fully relax and trust any man. I always have a lot of suspicions that are hard to overcome. So, my relationships now are ... [*deep sigh*]. Even if a man were an excellent match for me, you know, I already have this fear and mistrust. I would think that he only wants to use me, that he only wants ... what a man wants from a woman.... that's it. I can no longer trust any man to want a serious relationship.

My man left me—the father of my daughter. I was pregnant and we were engaged to be married, but he just left. And now, after all that has happened to me, I cannot look at anyone as a potential husband. I can work around men, and I can talk to them. That is okay. But as for a serious relationship? No. I am not ready for that. Perhaps with time I will change and heal. Time is the best healer. I just want my daughter and my mother to be happy. That's it.

You said that you wanted your mother and your daughter to be happy. I am wondering if there is anything that you wish for yourself.

Viorika: If they are happy, if I see that they are happy, then I will also be happy. Is this not so? Isn't it possible that I can find happiness through their happiness? You know, I have not yet thought about what my future might be like. I am not even dreaming of the future. For me the main thing is the present moment, that today and tomorrow my family will be well. Maybe someday I will be able [to] think about the future, and maybe then, gradually, I will begin to dream again. But right now, all I can really do is try to solve some of these problems that I have. But I am very grateful that the IOM is here and that you are writing this book. You all are helping people to come back and to start believing in themselves again.

Speaking of my book, is there anything you would like to tell the people reading it?

Viorika: Yes. Stay together with your friends and family. They are the only real source of support one has. All these problems that life gives us? We can face them with our heads up and we can keep on believing in ourselves if we have the support of people who love us. They help us live with hope. Today is today. Tomorrow may be better. But the main thing is that you have people close to you that understand you and that you can trust. This is the main thing for me. It enables me to continue living and to have hope.

Life tests all of us. It gives us obstacles so that we can prove to ourselves that we can overcome them and see what our worth is in this life. Are we capable of making mistakes and recovering from them? Can we learn not to repeat these mistakes and to help others because of these mistakes? This is what is important so that we can look others in the eyes and treat them with honesty and kindness.

Viorika, thank you for talking to us. You are a very strong woman—I can see that. Thank you.

* * * *

When Viorika leaves the room, Lilya begins to tell me about the next woman that I am to interview.

Lilya: Lida was also trafficked to the United Arab Emirates. She is basically an orphan. She has no one except her aunt. Her father is still alive, but he is a bad alcoholic living in Russia somewhere. Her mother is dead. When she returned to Moldova she tried living with her aunt, but there were too many nieces and nephews living there. There was no room for Lida, and her aunt could not afford to feed her. So, she moved to Chisinau. This is a girl with an excellent eye for aesthetics. She can do a lot with her hands. She can design and sew clothes, she can knit beautiful things. It is rare that you meet someone her age with such an amazing sense of culture and such a rich sense of beauty. Well, Lida is such a special girl, but she has absolutely no family support. She is entirely by herself.

It is very difficult for her to get a job. She has worked many places that she will tell you about. And each time, they would hire her illegally, without the proper documents or forms, without registering her as an employee, and then they would not pay her. Well, now again she is out of work. But this time she has found a solution. She bought an old sewing machine from an old lady. This lady allows her to pay a small amount every month until she can pay it off. So now, Lida sews and knits and sells her things wherever she can. She says, "I don't know what else to do. I really have no choice," because no matter where she went, *everyone* cheated her by not paying her. One time when she came in, she was literally starving. So, we paid the rent on her apartment. We helped her because we could see that she had a very strong desire to make it on her own, but at that time she just couldn't make it. It was too hard.

I will go get her now and she can tell you herself.

* * * *

Lida walks with great confidence and composure as she enters the room. She is very pretty and looks younger than her twenty-six years. Her short dark hair is pulled back, and she is wearing a lovely teal knit cap and matching scarf. Her long nails are manicured and painted, and she is very stylishly dressed. Everything about her is chic and composed. I find out later that she designed and sewed her entire outfit. Over the course of the interview, it becomes clear that she is very bright and has a wonderfully warm sense of humor.

Hello, Lida. Nice to meet you. Can you tell us a little about yourself?

Lida: Well, I am from Moldova. In 2002, I was trafficked to the UAE—the United Arab Emirates. I got back here a year or so ago [2008] with the help of the Chisinau Assistance and Protection Center. They helped me a lot. I am now trying to find employment somehow, but it is not working out so well. It is easy to find work. But to find work that will actually pay you is very difficult.

How is it that you can work and not get paid? Is this here in Chisinau?

Lida: Yes. Well, at first, I was employed in our Trading Center here in Chisinau. They hired me for a probationary period. They said that after the probationary period, I would get full-time employment. However, during probation that lasts sometimes twenty days, sometimes ten, you do not get paid. They can make you work eleven, twelve, even fourteen hours a day. So, for twenty days I worked fourteen hours a day for free. At the end of the probationary period, they told me that I did not meet their qualifications and would not get hired. They do this to everybody. That is how they get free workers.[7]

Next, I got a job in my profession. I was studying to become a fashion tailor in Moscow, Russia, and was hired to work in a sewing factory here in Chisinau. It is a joint Moldovan–Italian venture. They bring fabrics from Italy and have Moldovan girls sew them. [Labor is much cheaper in Moldova than in Italy]. They offered to pay me a portion of my salary, 500 Moldovan *lei* a month [US$26], until they could afford to give me my whole salary.[8] They asked me to wait and keep working until they could pay me the rest of my wages, but they didn't say how long I should wait. I left that job over two months ago and still have not gotten any money from them.

And they can get away with this? Can you take them to court to get your money?

Lida: First of all, I was working without official registration, so I have no recourse. They told me it would take two to three months before they could officially register me as an employee. I was working there unofficially. I quit after one month. No one can live on 500 *lei* a month. I was not surviving, so I left. I keep calling them, but they say they have no money. And since they never registered me, I cannot file a claim against them.

The girls who were working there with me are still there, hoping to get paid somehow. They will not testify on my behalf because they are afraid that they will never get paid if they do. Of the twelve girls who were working there with me, only three of us left. The rest have some other means, either a husband or parents, that can support them until they get paid. But I have no one, so I had to find a job that paid something.

Well, the last place I worked at was also in the Trading Center. I was selling jewelry there. I worked for a month and when I asked to get paid, they fired me. Not only did they fire me, but they also said I owed them 5,000 *lei* [US$281]. Their accounting is all wrong. They always have a lot of girls who work there for only a month or two, three months at most, because they do not pay their workers. The owners claim that money was missing from the till, and they accused me of stealing it. Maybe they blame everyone, I don't know. But they wanted me to sign a note saying I owed them this money. I refused, so they kicked me out. So, you can see the work situation here is very difficult here in Moldova.

Yes, I can see that. When did you come back home from the UAE?

Lida: I think July sometime last year [2008]. I was gone six years. I was trafficked in 2002. At first, I was forced into a brothel. But after eight months, one of the johns bought me for his own personal slave. I was lucky that he wanted me to live with him and take care of him rather than force me to be a prostitute. For five years I lived with him. But then the police found me and arrested me for living in the country without legal documents. They sent me first to prison and then back to Moldova.

What happened that day when you got back to Moldova? Who met you? What were you feeling?

Lida: Because I was returning from prison, Nadezhda, a special assistant from the IOM Center, met me at the airport [along with the others]. They took me with them back to the Center. But since I had been gone for so many years, after two days I asked them to let me go home and they agreed. But a week later some representatives from the Center came to visit me to conduct a medical and physical checkup. Well ... [*long pause as she stares at the table in front of her*].

At first, I lived with my aunt. But we don't communicate anymore because ... because my cousin ... well, I am not on the best terms with her. And I don't really have any parents. Well, my dad lives in Moscow. I went there for a while, but I can only handle him for about a half an hour because he is a terrible drunk. He was drinking really heavily, and he was physically abusive. He is always drunk, so what's the point of listening to him? I don't really talk to him much anymore. I am on my own and I don't have any children.

What do you do now?

Lida: Now, I am working from home. As I mentioned, I am a fashion tailor by profession. I have several people for whom I sew and knit things. That is how I am making a living right now. Later, I will see whether I can find work with a firm or if I can continue on my own. I have already worked for a few months without a salary. I can't do that anymore. I need to earn money in order to live. One time the Center helped me pay my rent. Another time they helped me buy food. But I cannot keep doing this. I need to find another way. I am not really making enough money. It is okay for the moment and hopefully things will get better.

Do you have dreams for the future?

Lida: Well ... my dreams.... For some reason I am pretty sure that within the next five years I will have my own sewing shop. And then we'll see. That is my aspiration.

How has this experience changed you? Has it influenced the way you think about people?

Lida: Well, in general, I think there are good people and bad people. Not just in Moldova or in the UAE, but everywhere. You have them in the U.S.

as well [*laughing*]. This is why ... well, what are you going to do? One needs to learn how to forgive. Forgive and then forget it—that's all.

And as for the men? [*Laughing*] I don't have time to think about them. I am working and not thinking about men [*laughing again*]. I have decided that I need to rely on myself, and to build my own career rather than to find some man to help me. I want to become accomplished and not have to depend upon anyone else.

Is there anything you might like to tell the people reading this book? Anything you want them to know about your experience or how you survived it?

Lida: You know, if all this hadn't happened to me, all those years in the Emirates, and even what I am experiencing now, I would not be as strong as I am. It all made me stronger. It literally steeled me, made me into steel. And.... I don't know ... maybe if I hadn't been trafficked, I would be sitting at home crying for someone to help me. But now if there is a problem, I sit down, calm myself, and know that I will be able to solve it on my own. I do not regret that I have gone through all this. It might even be better that I have, I don't know. No one can escape the difficulties life presents. No one has insurance against troubles. So, maybe I am better because I now know how to handle difficult things.

Lida, thank you so much for talking to us. You are truly inspiring. Thank you.

* * * *

When she leaves the room, Lilya stays to talk to us a bit more. Lilya's dark hair frames a face that is etched with stress lines, and there are bags under her dark eyes. I wondered if this was a result of trying to help so many traumatized women. She was present during all three of the interviews. Her demeanor was warm and maternal. It is obvious that she respects and cares very deeply for her charges. I had a sense that she would move heaven and earth to help one of her clients. She seemed very professional and dedicated.

Lilya: Lida was there for six years but was forced into prostitution for only eight months. It often happens that way, that a john will take a fancy to a girl and try to "save" her by getting her out of the trafficking situation and making her his girlfriend. One reason Lida is so strong now is because many years have passed since her trauma. Lida's john gave her a somewhat normal life for five years.

When she came back to Moldova, we met her and helped her. It is hard for her, but she has gained such strength. So much time has passed that her pain and disappointment has faded a little. And she will have a good profession. She has golden hands, so she is able to earn a little money. She went to college and that also works in her favor. Not everyone has that. Some of our clients only have a second- or third-grade education. They have a very difficult time integrating after being trafficked. Without an education or a profession, or family acceptance, most of these people break down. These are the ones who are likely to kill themselves, or go into prostitution, or get lost in drugs or alcohol. There are quite a few of those cases.

Can you say approximately what percentage of your clients end up breaking down in some way or killing themselves?

Lilya: It is hard to say because we have been working for twenty years now, and each year is different. But the first years we were working with trafficking victims, quite a few of them had college and university degrees. They quickly found internal reserves of strength to help them. But these last few years, especially this year, many people with very little education are being trafficked, as well as children and orphans [social orphans]. It is much more difficult for them. A few years ago, we had a 60 to 70 percent recovery rate.[9] Now, it is about 55 percent. We observe them for a year. By the end of the first year under our care, only a little over half get settled into a normal kind of life. So many of them are so desperately searching for an end to the pain and fear that they die. They simply die.

We had one woman who came to us a year ago. She is now pregnant, and I am afraid that she will simply abandon her child because she doesn't have anyone to help or support her. Her mother died and she has no father. She feels lost and confused.

How many clients do you have at the Center? Is it a residential center?

Lilya: We have room for twenty-two residents. However, we don't always have twenty-two. Right now, for example, we have eighteen. We have a very interesting program because we don't just work with trafficking victims. We also have a prevention program. And for us, prevention isn't just saying, "Don't go there, it's dangerous." We do so much more. Because when a person has nothing to eat, you can't just tell them, "Don't go there." It doesn't work.

We provide social, economic, and psychological support for at-risk people, just like we do for victims. We help them find a profession or help them find work. We will buy them tools if they need them. For example, if it is a hairdresser, we will give her money for scissors, a hairdryer, etc.

What can a hairdresser do without tools? Nothing. So, this way, even if she can't find a job, she can work from home cutting hair and earn a living.

We also have a very specific training for children from orphanages and boarding schools. We try to help them get a profession or find work. Also, if we have a mother who is raising a child on her own and is struggling, we try to help her, too. If we don't help her, she is very likely to go abroad looking for work. But right now, if we can give her diapers and some food for her child, then she will have a little hope and be more prone to stay in Moldova.

We also help victims of domestic violence and sexual violence, because a woman who is getting beaten or raped will do just about anything and go anywhere just to escape her abuser. Also, as you know, rape is a serious trauma. And quite frequently, trafficking victims start considering themselves dirty, or damaged goods, or having no worth, so they easily go into prostitution. But if they get timely psychological help, we can still help them patch their lives back together.

Thank you, Lilya. I know you must go now. Thank you so much for your time and for introducing me to those three very courageous women.

12

LILA

Victim of sex trafficking
NGO: La Strada
Chirca, Moldova
October 25, 2010

Of all the forms of modern-day slavery, sex trafficking is by far the most lucrative. Enslaving persons for sexual exploitation earns traffickers an estimated US$99 billion in profits annually. Despite the fact that only 19 percent of the world's trafficking victims are used in commercial sexual exploitation, sex slaves generate 66 percent of the annual profits.[1] Economist Siddharth Kara estimates that a single sex slave can earn an annual profit of between US$19,000 and US$36,000 for the brothel owner, depending upon geographical location of the brothel and ethnicity of the slave.[2] With such immense profitability, there is little wonder why human trafficking is the fastest growing illegal activity in the world today, and that traffickers fit no single profile.

The reality of human trafficking is often blurred by stereotypes that are presented in films such as *Taken* and *Eastern Promises*. These stereotypes portray traffickers as scary-looking men in BMWs with tinted windows, shiny suits, and gold chains around their necks preying on young girls. One main misconception is that human trafficking is a man's business. This could not be further from the reality. While that may have been true in the early aftermath of the collapse of the Soviet Union, since the turn of the twenty-first century human trafficking is a lucrative business that attracts all kinds of people willing to dehumanize and degrade others to make high profits with minimal risk. Recruiters (those who make initial contact with the victim), traffickers (or slavers—those who buy, sell, or own the slave), and pimps (often the middleman between the owner and the john) can be women, family members, middle-class businessmen and women, wealthy government officials—virtually anybody.

According to La Strada in Chisinau, Moldova, recruiters in most trafficking cases are female. They can be old or young, they can be a neighbor, a friend, or, as in Lila's case, a trusted family member. Recruitment relies on manipulation and the willing participation of the victim. That is what makes prosecution of trafficking cases so difficult. As Tatiana Fomina of La Strada said, "How do you prove trafficking when the victim willingly goes abroad, sometimes even buying her own ticket?"[3] Lila's interview highlights how thousands of women participated in their own enslavement simply by trusting a friend or relative. Her experience also underscores the sad fact that, once sold, a woman's fate is entirely in the hands of others. Lila tried to escape many times and ended up paying a high price for it. Finally, her cousin, the woman who recruited her, pressured her owner to release her.

As we drove from Chisinau to the village of Chirca to meet Lila, I was again struck by how fertile the empty fields looked. "How can this be?" I wondered as we drove past miles of abandoned farms in some of the richest black-earth areas of the former Soviet Union. Chirca is one of hundreds of Moldovan villages that have been emptied by the cascade of economic crises since 1991. With no jobs to be had, up to 60 percent of village populations have left to find work somewhere else—in Russia, or Italy, or Cyprus, or any of a myriad of places. Indeed, Chirca, like all the villages we visited, seemed devoid of people between the ages of eighteen and fifty.

Finally, my driver stopped on the side of a very potholed dirt road. It was 6:30 p.m. on a fall evening and the light was starting to fade. There were only a few houses nearby and I wondered what was going on. The driver made a call on his cell phone and in a minute a young woman approached the car. She appeared to be in her late twenties, with very long, thin hands. She wore a simple white-gold wedding band on her right hand. It was Lila. She quickly opened the car door and got into the back seat where I was sitting. As she climbed into the car, she started talking very quickly and looking around nervously. Explaining that her husband was sick of her talking about being trafficked, Lila said that she only had forty-five minutes to talk to me before her husband would come home from work. She was clearly agitated at the prospect of him coming home and finding her talking to me. I suggested we meet another time, or that we simply cancel the interview. She was adamant that she wanted to talk to me, claiming that each time she talks about her experience, she feels a little relief.

She launched immediately into her story. During the interview, several old women and children walked past the car, peering into the windows, trying to see us in the fading light while the driver paced outside the car as if he was guarding us. It all felt very clandestine. Toward the end of the interview, a young girl handed Lila's two-year-old daughter over to her through the open car window. The child was clearly tired, hungry, and too shy to interact with me.

Lila, were you born in this village?

Lila: No, but I was born in this district, Anenii Noi *raion*.[4] We lived a few villages further south of here, but then we moved here in 1980. My mom lived on the other side of the railroad tracks. There is a train that runs just there [*points across the dirt road to the far side of a field*]. Behind there is the railway station in a big yellow house. That's where we grew up. My husband is also kind of from here. I got married here.

When did you get married?

Lila: [*Deep sigh*] I have been living with my husband for twenty years already. I turn forty years old next year. I am thirty-nine now. I was born in 1971. Life in Moldova is very difficult. You know it yourself. Earlier … when the Russians were here, life was easier.[5] Life here is not sweet, and thousands of young women are leaving to find a better life. My story is just one of those.

My mother had five sisters and two brothers. One of her sisters' daughters, my cousin, was the one who sold me. Zhenya is her name. Why did I trust her? I trusted her because she was my cousin. She was like a sister to me, a close blood relative.

How did it happen that she was able to sell you?

Lila: She left to find work in Turkey. She was working in Turkey for two years. I didn't know exactly what she was doing there. When she came back, she asked me, "Do you want to get out of poverty, or what?" I said, "Yes, I have a desire to make a better life, of course. But I am not young, so if I must work as …" [*long pause*]. I had heard that when girls go to Turkey they only work as … you know in what profession.… I am not young. I am not of the age to work like that. I told her that I would only be a housekeeper or domestic worker. My cousin said, "No problem. When I was there, I lived at one man's house. He is of such-and-such an age and has two children and a wife. Why don't you go there? You can be their house cleaner—vacuum, dust, and the like." I said that would be OK, but only for a month because my first daughter was only two years old at the time. Anything longer than a month I cannot agree to. She said, "Fine. I can get you work there for a month." So that is how I went abroad.

And when was that?

Lila: That was in 2003. It was February 13, 2003. I managed to get back at the end of April, so I was there two and a half months … just about … [*long pause*]. That is how I found myself in Turkey. I trusted my cousin. We were really close. Why would I not trust her? But by the time I got to Turkey she had already sold me. The man I went to work for, the one who bought me, told me that he paid my cousin US$1,000 for me, and that he now owned me. She called him to make sure I got there okay, so I begged him to let me talk to her. I told her I wanted to go back home. She said, "You know what, my dear? You are already there. The Turk told me that you are already in demand there."[6] And how was that? From the very first day I was forced to work as a housekeeper. I also served tea. They drink a lot of tea in Turkey. Every time someone came over, I had to serve tea. And lots of people came to the house—*a lot*. My cousin said, "You are in demand. People like you." What did I know? They asked me for tea, so I would bring them tea and then leave. I was kind of like a servant.

I worked as a housekeeper and served tea there for only a week and then they took me away. The Turk took me to another house—I think he might have sold me. At this new place there was a girl who worked there, but she was not a slave like me. She was from out of town. I trusted her when she said that she could help me run away. But then, before I could run away, I got sent to yet another place. I ran away from that third place, but the Turk was able to catch me. He brought me back and beat me severely. That was when I knew that I could never leave.

When did you first realize that your cousin had sold you into prostitution?

Lila: You know, I found out as soon as I got to Turkey. The Turk met me at the airport. He was younger than me. He met me and took me to the house. As soon as we got to his house he said, "Get undressed." I was horrified! I said, "What for?" I told him that I could not … that I did not come there to be a prostitute. I told him that I had a husband and a child at home. He just said, "Hurry up if you do not want to get a beating." I said, "No! No! No! What are you doing?" I don't even know how he got me undressed so quickly. I was begging him, "What about my cousin?" I told him my cousin promised me that I would not have to do that! He told me that my cousin knew exactly what she had done to me.

And I trusted her! How could I have trusted her? This guy, the Turk, had a wife and children. But apparently, they have polygamy over there. That is what they are accustomed to. My cousin was his second wife. I was to be another wife, I guess.[7] I told him, "I will tell your wife about this, or my cousin." He just laughed.

He raped me, brutally, that night. Then he took me to the house where he lived with his wife and children. I was crying and I could not stop. His wife kept asking me why was I there? How did I get there? When I told her about my cousin, she just ... [*pause*] got very quiet and shrank. That was the end of the conversation. I figured the Turk probably beat his wife too.[8]

His wife was.... I could tell that his wife was afraid of him. In Moldova, our husbands beat us quite frequently, so I can see it if a woman is getting beaten.[9] A victim of domestic violence has a certain look. I can tell just by looking. And the Turk's wife had that look. She also let me know that when her husband was not home, we could talk. And we did. His wife was a *good* woman, a normal person. She helped me as much as she could.

This might be a stupid question, but how did it feel to be trapped there?
Lila: Oh! You know, it was so scary.... I was even more scared because I could not understand what they were saying about me. I don't understand the Turkish language. They would look at me and I didn't know what they wanted. These men would come over, drink tea, and talk back and forth with each other, pointing at me, saying, "Moldavia, Moldavia!" so I knew they were talking about me. It really frightened me. My God, what were they talking about? What were they going to do to me? But then they seemed to lose interest in me.

But the next day these same men came and talked about me again. Only this time the Turk grabbed me by the collar, drug me to the car, and pushed me in, you know, as if I were a dog or an object.... I got really scared thinking he was going to take me somewhere and rape me again. I was thinking, "What does he want from me?" At that moment, my cousin called him on his cell phone. I was crying and screaming, "I want to go home!" He let me talk to her. She said, "Just go to work! You wanted to make money, didn't you?" I did want to make money, but not *this* way.

It was even more frightening because my husband did not know anything. You know, the day I left for Turkey I just closed the door behind me and didn't tell him anything. I have no idea how my husband found out that I had been sold, but he found out something bad had happened to me. He called Interpol.[10] Thank God for that. If he hadn't called Interpol ... oh! I am too frightened to even think about what might have happened to me.

Anyway, after they shoved me in the car, they took me to a tall apartment building and imprisoned me on the eighth floor. I could not look out the window or wave for help because there were police downstairs. When I managed to run away, I didn't go to the police. I don't know why. I was just too afraid, I think. But my owner caught me anyway and beat me.

When the Turk sold me to these guys he kept saying "problem, problem," meaning that I was a problem for him. I was constantly crying and saying, "I want to go home! I want to go home!" But he kept bringing men to rape me and I couldn't take it any more ... especially at my age. Even one of the johns got worried about me. I heard him explaining to the Turk, "We can't do her anymore. She is already bleeding all over. Everything is bleeding, even her anus. She is exhausted and her body is worn out. You could kill her this way...." The Turk replied, "So what? If she dies, I will just take her and wrap her in a carpet and throw her body in the trash." I know this because one of the other girls that was also enslaved there translated the conversation for me. But *there* ... oh ... there were *so* many girls. They would bring these girls at night and then several men would rape them.[11] On occasion a girl would get a chance to tell me that she is from Odessa, Russia, or Moscow ... one girl was from the Caucasus in Russia, another from Ukraine. He kept reselling them constantly.

How many women cycled through while you were there?

Lila: Oh, many! Sometimes he would bring three girls a night, sometimes two. I remember one girl had slashed her wrists trying to kill herself. He beat her viciously for that. She was so badly beaten, I regretted that I did not go to the police when I ran away, just so that he couldn't beat her anymore. He beat her so very harshly.

And then I think he sold me again. Anyway, I got sent to a new place, a Turkish woman's place. She was the pimp.[12] She had a daughter who was eighteen years old. This female pimp told me she would help me run away. She told me to keep working for her, and she would tell the Turk that I was not making any money. This way, she would be able to save money for me to buy an airline ticket so I could fly away. I trusted her ... why not? I had nothing to lose, so I did what she told me. Evidently, she *did* tell the Turk that I was not making any money, because he would come and beat me and spit on me. He would yell at me, "You bitch! You are not making any money." But I kept quiet. The older woman told me to keep my mouth shut, so I thought she was indeed saving money for me. But she wasn't, she was keeping the money for herself. After I tried to run away from there, the Turk came and got me. He beat me so badly that I was all black and blue. When this old woman saw me, she said, "My God, what have I done?" She felt sorry for me and wanted to approach me, but the Turk motioned for her to stay back.

I remember one day the Turk brought in this one girl. When we were alone, she begged me to help her if I ever got free. She said she had been in Turkey for ten months already and had been passed to nine pimps.[13] The one she was working for when I met her made her service sixteen clients a day. After she made so much money for that pimp, he sold her to a client so that *he* could pimp her out. She was making a lot of money, but she never got any of it. It all went to her owners. She was desperate and exhausted. She said she had a seven-year-old daughter at home and that her mother was sick. She would do anything to get back home. She gave me all her information. I memorized it because we could not write anything down. When I got back to Moldova, I gave the information to the Moldovan police. They checked it out and said that yes, they knew about her but that she was still in Turkey. She had not gotten home yet. After that I do not know what happened to her. [*Lila was shaking, and her voice was trembling quite a bit.*] I asked the police to let me know if they found her, but I have heard nothing yet. I felt so sorry for her.

When you were black and blue from beatings, how did the johns react? Did they notice something was wrong?

Lila: Oh, the men would still come even when I was in bad shape. They would come in as clients, see me and feel sorry for me, but they couldn't do anything. Some gave me money and said, "Here, hide it!" But that money stayed at the brothel, because when the police came, they would search everything and keep whatever they wanted, especially money. No matter where I hid the money, the police would find it and keep it. The johns could see that I wouldn't last much longer, so they would try to make a plan to help me escape. One said that he would change me into men's clothing, and I could just walk out with him. What ideas did we not come up with? But the Turk checked everything carefully, and he was a violent man. Even the clients were afraid of him. Everyone was afraid of him except the police. The police would come, and they would rape me, too [*her voice trembles*]. Even the police!

One policeman who came in, he had two stars on his uniform. I think it meant that he was a colonel or something. Some kind of higher rank. So, how did he dare?! I trusted him because he was an officer, so I asked him to help me get out of there. After he left, the Turk came in and beat me senseless because the officer had told him what I said. I couldn't take it anymore. Who could protect me?

I just kept crying. I was too afraid to ask anyone for help again because the Turk would find out and beat me. Also, once because I had asked some clients for help the Turk stopped feeding me. He withheld food as punishment. I really thought I was going to starve to death, and I was afraid to die. He kept threatening me, saying he would let me die and then wrap my body in a carpet and throw it in the trash. He said no one was looking for me, and no one would find me.

But then my cousin started calling the Turk to complain about my husband. My husband told me later that he was putting pressure on my cousin to find me. Remember, when I left, he was not home, and I did not tell him where I was going. He began looking for me by asking those people I had recently spent the most time with. He started to put pressure on my cousin because he thought that she knew something and wasn't telling him. In fact, he threatened to beat her up if she kept saying she didn't know anything. Finally, she said, "Yes, I know where Lila is."

And how did you get home? Did he get you out of there?

Lila: My husband contacted Interpol and the Moldovan police. I know this because my cousin began calling the Turk saying that she was afraid the Moldovan police were going to arrest her. She told the Turk to let me go. But instead, the Turk started hiding me in different brothels. The police came to his house looking for me. When they searched his place, they found my passport. When the police questioned him, the Turk said that I was his cousin's lover.

With this kind of pressure, the Turk became even more psychotic and violent. He would grab me and shake me violently and scream, "Moldavia, I am going to kill you if anyone harms my favorite girl [meaning Lila's cousin]. I will kill you." But my husband kept threatening my cousin, and she kept calling the Turk, begging him to let me go—she was afraid that she would end up in jail. Finally, one day he beat me, saying, "Fine, Moldavia, get the f**k out of here!" He loaded me up in the car and I thought to myself, "This is it. This is the end. He is going to kill me and dump me somewhere and that will be that." So, while he drove, I just sat silently, terrified, trying to figure out how to get out of the car. But then I noticed that we arrived at an airport. I thought, "Oh my God, can this be real? Can I really be going back home?" [*Lila's voice was shaking, and she was holding back tears.*]

But this was *just* before Easter, and all the plane tickets to Chisinau, Moldova, were sold out that day. So, the Turk took me back to his place. When we got back to his place, his wife was there. She grabbed my hand and just held onto it. She told me that my cousin was making problems for her husband because my husband was threatening my cousin. She said, "It is too much trouble, so my husband is going to send you back home. Don't worry, just try to hold onto that right now, that you are going to go home soon." [*Lila imitates the wife's voice and intonations, speaking quietly and softly.*]

That evening, I was really, really quiet. I tried to disappear. I wanted to just stay invisible until I could go home... [*pause*] But then I had to use their bathroom and it just so happened that the bathroom door slammed shut. Oh, my God! That made him crazy. He raped me so violently that night ... it was so very frightening.... He hurt me very badly and he knew it.

Afterward, he kept saying, "Moldavia, Moldavia, peace." Things like that. He kept asking me to forgive him and forget everything that happened. I walked out of the room where he raped me, and his wife saw how badly I was hurt. She grabbed me and held me, saying, "Forgive him. Please forgive him. I also have two children. Forgive him for me, for me and the children. How could your cousin have sent you here? She *knew* what a beast he is. How could she do that to you?"

And that was it. The next day, he drove me back to the airport. He took back roads and kept looking out for the police. When we got near the airport, he gave me my plane ticket and then pushed me out of the car. He said, "Now, get the f**k out of here so I never have to see you again. But, because I am letting you go, tell your cousin that in exchange for you, *tell her she must bring me twelve new girls here.*" [Lila imitates his harsh, threatening voice.]

So, what happened when you arrived back in Chisinau?

Lila: My husband and my cousin met me at the airport. First thing she said was, "How *could* you cause so much trouble in Turkey? What have I ever done wrong to you? What? Did he touch you or something? I don't belieeeve you!" [Lila imitates her cousin in a whiny voice that conveys hurt and disbelief.]

I told her that everyone knew what a beast the Turk was, even the police. I asked her, "How could *you* do this to me?" My husband said, "Don't talk to her anymore. The police will be talking to her instead. That's it. Let's go." So, we went home. And I have tried to live a normal life since then. But you know, after all that happened … for many years I could not be with my husband sexually. He would beat me frequently because I could not have sex with him, even though he swore to the police that he was not beating me. But when he got drunk, he would beat me. I left him many times [*deep sigh*]. But I always came back and forgave him. I don't know why. And we are still together. Maybe I love him. He quit drinking recently. And, you know, he is already a different man.

What happened to your cousin?

Lila: Well, at first, she was arrested, and I was going to testify against her in court. She was in jail. But I dropped all charges against her. I signed a paper relieving her of all guilt. I should not have done that, but I forgave her. Why? Because her mother is my aunt, and my daughter knows her. Her mother threatened to kill my daughter if I testified against her. I just couldn't take the stress from all the threats coming from my aunt. I was afraid she would really kill my child if I testified! I filed a restraining order with the police to try to get protection for my child and me. But it was clear that the police were not going to do anything to protect us. So, I figured it was better to let my cousin out of jail than risk the murder of my child. Otherwise, I would not have dropped the case against my cousin. What she did should not be pardoned.

Once you got back, did you receive any assistance? Any rehabilitation services?

Lila: I went to our district for help, but they did not help me. However, La Strada has helped me so much! I want to write a thank-you letter, but I don't know to whom to write it. La Strada is some kind of miracle for people like me because they help a lot. They have a lot of wonderful people working there.

Yes. It was Svetlana at La Strada who arranged this interview. Why did you agree to do it?

Lila: Because I want people to know this. I want them to know what happens to people who go abroad. I believe it is *right* to talk about this. It is important to reach those young girls so that they understand that they shouldn't go abroad to find work. Whatever is going on over there [in Turkey], there are no normal relationships. I don't know why girls still believe that they won't get hurt.

It's just that.... I don't know ... there is just such *filth* there, it is such an abomination. I don't know how to say it.... After I returned home, I took so many baths. All the time I was taking baths and even after all these years of bathing, it still feels like I have not cleaned myself of all that filth. Years have passed and I still feel that filth inside me, like I have not been able to wash myself clean.

How are you now? How do you think about your experience?

Lila: When I got back, I was scared all the time. I could not sleep with my husband for a long time.... I don't know for how long. And everything inside me hurt. I was sick of the filth, and my body hurt. I thought I would never be able to recover from that. Yet, you do recover. Very slowly you return from that state. I did not believe that I could ever sleep with my husband again.

It was very hard to recover, because here people have no value. A human being here is treated like some stray dog. Even worse than a dog. When I came back, a lot of my neighbors in the village were gossiping behind my back. They would say things like, "What, have you sucked enough of it over there?" Such cruel and rude comments. I stopped paying attention. It was good when my husband was by my side. He only had to turn his head and the gossips would shut up. But when he was not around, I was too ashamed to even go out of the house. Sometimes, some of the villagers would even throw rocks at me.[14] So, for a long time I would sneak around the back alleys so that I would not run into so many people. I was afraid that my sister and brothers were ashamed of me, too. But no, just the opposite. They said, "She is our sister, and we love her just as she is." They defended me and told people, "She is just as good a person as she was when she left. She left a good person, and she came back the same way." That was so important.

People just don't understand. There is a lot of ignorance here. Plus, there are so many shortages [that] people are really hurting. Because there is so much poverty, people feel a lot of tension and they tend to fight each other. They think that if someone went abroad, they must have lots of money. But as you know, it is just not true.

You know, I never thought this would happen to me. When I got back, I received some help from UNICEF. They gave me medicine and medical treatment.[15] I had head trauma because when the Turk beat me, he would pound my head with a heavy telephone. So, in that sense UNICEF was helpful. But they did not seem to understand what happens to a woman who gets trafficked. But then someone told me about La Strada. I felt so warm and welcome at La Strada, unlike the other organizations. There are such good people there, at La Strada. Kate, I didn't know we had such good people in Moldova! When I started working with them, I couldn't believe it. Where do people like this come from? They were kind and generous. They even gave me free shampoo!

Has this experience changed you?

Lila: I found out that it is better to be home in Moldova and make a few pennies however you can, than to seek big money abroad. There is no big money for we Moldovan girls abroad. It only *looks* like there is a way out of poverty somewhere else. But that is a lie. One should not seek happiness somewhere else. A woman needs to make her own happiness and then hold onto it. There is too much filth out there. It destroys your body and your soul. It is horrible.

You have been home seven years now. Do you continue to have problems related to being trafficked?

Lila: [*Long pause*] Yes. You know, at first it was very difficult. But time is a sort of healer. I slowly got better mostly thanks to La Strada and those people who supported me.

You are a very strong woman. I can see your strength and determination.

Lila: I am trying to be strong, yes. I must be strong; otherwise, how could we survive? I have a family with two children. I need to raise them. They are girls, so I want them to know that they need to be careful. You know, I was offered a job in Israel. There is a firm that will get you a job there and arrange everything. But my daughters tell me not to do it, not to go anywhere. So, somehow, I will find a way for us to survive here. I just don't know how.

* * * *

It is hard to believe that Lila even considered taking another risk. But she told me that jobs are not available, and she had to borrow money just to bury her parents, who had died. She had pressures from debt, no food, and if the fundamental economic problems do not get resolved, the desperation continues.

13

SASHA AND ANDRE

Victims of labor and sex trafficking
with psychologist Marina
NGO: Revival of the Nation (Ternopil, Ukraine)
IOM Offices, Kyiv, Ukraine
October 28, 2010

At the time of this interview, in the press, in policy discussions, and in public opinion, trafficking in persons was still most commonly associated with trafficking of women for sexual exploitation. There was a growing awareness that children were being trafficked for sexual exploitation, forced labor, or begging, but the issue of the enslavement of adult males, especially from Eastern Europe, was most conspicuous in its absence from trafficking discussions.[1] There were some indicators that men were also being trafficked, but the scope of the issue was not yet understood.

One likely cause for the focus on trafficking of women is gender bias. Especially in Eastern Europe, there is a generalized assumption about the vulnerability of women. Men who migrate are seen as adventurous and brave, whereas women who do so are considered naïve and foolish, deserving of punishment or rescue.[2] These views function to structure opinions about human trafficking—that women who are exploited are trafficked and hence vulnerable victims, while men under the same exploitative conditions are seen as illegal migrants and even criminals, but not trafficking victims.

Early on, most anti-trafficking efforts in Europe and Eurasia focused on women and children. Public awareness campaigns and trainings for law enforcement and other officials that focused on women and children reinforced the notion that men were generally not vulnerable to trafficking.[3] Further, sex trafficking depends upon attracting johns and therefore requires an element of visibility. Labor trafficking occurs in hidden locations, so it is much less likely to be discovered by authorities. In 2006, a report by the Organization for Security and Co-operation in Europe noted that trafficking for forced labor was the least recognized aspect of human trafficking.[4]

These fundamental gendered assumptions were held by the victims themselves. Men are much less likely to seek help after being trafficked. They do not identify as having been trafficked, whereas women seek help at much greater rates. Men tend to internalize their experience and blame themselves for being foolish, stupid, or weak. Consequently, NGOs that provide services to survivors report an overwhelming number of female trafficking victims, to the near exclusion of men. For example, an IOM trafficking database in 2010 revealed that less than 20 percent of trafficking victims receiving assistance were male.[5] But does this mean that only 20 percent of trafficked persons were male? Probably not—each year, countless men leave their homes searching for work or a better life and fall prey to traffickers.

Sasha's interview underscores the push factors that lead men to go abroad to seek better employment. His story is typical of men trafficked from post–Soviet states to Russia. Most male victims had some kind of technical training or university education. Well over half already had a job when they decided to go abroad for a better job. And all of them were held in subhuman conditions hidden from the public eye—crammed into filthy living spaces, given substandard food, and threatened with violence to keep them compliant. Sasha's traffickers took his documents and passport and forced him to work in a locked and guarded compound for several months until he managed to escape.

The interview took place in the offices of the International Organization for Migration (IOM) in Kyiv, Ukraine. Marina, psychologist and director of the NGO Revival of the Nation in Ternopil, Ukraine, brought three survivors of trafficking to Kyiv to meet me. They took the overnight train from Ternopil and arrived in Kyiv in the morning. With a population of about 230,000, Ternopil is one of the largest cities in western Ukraine. Located on the Seret River about 128 km (80 miles) east of L'viv and 836 km (520 miles) west of Kyiv, Ternopil was once a lively trade center. At the time of the interview, it was the economic heart of western Ukraine, specializing in light industry, machine engineering, metalworking, and some food production. It was also a vibrant college town, home to several universities, academies, institutes, and trade schools.

We made our introductions with Marina and exchanged pleasantries. Sasha was my first interviewee of the three. At twenty-five years old, he looked like a college student. Throughout the interview, his cheeks quivered as if he was on the verge of tears. At several points, he had to stop talking in order to hold back the tears. His Russian was halting and broken; he was much more comfortable speaking Ukrainian. He also seemed quite unsure of himself and lacking in confidence. Perhaps it was his language skills, or perhaps it was trauma. He often looked to Marina for encouragement.

Before the interview, Marina gave me a brief history of trafficking in Ternopil and of her NGO, which operated throughout western Ukraine. In the first years of its existence, 1998–2002, Revival of the Nation had only female clients who had been sold into sexual slavery. As elsewhere, women constituted the first wave of persons trafficked from Ukraine. There was a flow of women and girls to Turkey, the United Arab Emirates, the Czech Republic, Poland, and finally to Russia. Beginning in 2002, the NGO began seeing male victims who had been trafficked for labor exploitation. Because Ternopil is relatively close to Central Europe, many people head west to find jobs in Spain, Portugal, Italy, Greece, Czechia, and Poland, making them vulnerable for trafficking. Over the last two decades, however, Russia became the prime destination country for Ukrainians seeking work abroad.[6] Before Russia annexed Crimea in 2014 and a separatist war erupted in eastern Ukraine, Russia was appealing for several reasons: the language is quite similar; one didn't need a passport or visa to go there from Ukraine; and the culture is quite similar. Consequently, people trusted that they were going to a legitimate job and ended up trafficked. However, since the 2014 Russian occupation of eastern Ukraine and the more recent 2022 invasion, voluntary migration to Russia has all but stopped.[7]

In the first decade of the twenty-first century, despite the increased number of male victims, the majority of those helped by Revival of the Nation were female—about 76 percent. Between 1999 and 2010, the NGO helped over 2,000 trafficking victims from western Ukraine. For the most part, it is young people who get trafficked while seeking employment abroad. Typically, individuals who end up exploited for labor do not go abroad by themselves. Most of the time, they travel as a group that gets recruited by the same "employment" agency or organization, and the whole group is trafficked. So, if one person of the group manages to get help, they will refer other members of the group to the NGO that helped them. This is how Revival of the Nation got a lot of their clients—through word-of-mouth referral.

I began this interview by asking Marina a few questions about her organization. Marina had a pleasant and engaging demeanor, and I could see that she had a calming influence on her clients. She was there to help translate and to protect her clients from retraumatization. During the interview she remained very attentive to the interviewees, watching for signs of increasing stress, facial tics, excessive nervousness, and the like. I am glad she was there—it helped me relax a bit, too.

What happens when a client comes to you for help?

Marina: The first thing we do is get them a medical examination to assess their health and then get them whatever medical treatments they may need. This examination takes place in Kyiv, provided the client is willing to travel that far. If not, we have an agreement with a medical university in Ternopil that will conduct medical examinations and health assessments for us. The clinic in Ternopil can also provide most medical treatments.

We also have psychologists give them a mental health evaluation, followed up by psychological counseling. We have a psychiatrist that works with our clients and have had several people who have needed hospitalization for extreme psychic trauma and mental illness.

Finally, we provide vocational rehabilitation for our clients. Many of our clients have higher education degrees, but finding a job as an engineer or a teacher might be very difficult in today's market. So, we help them learn new skills. Beginning in 2000, we implemented a business training and microloan program to help clients start their own businesses. It has been very successful. To date, thirty-five of our clients have opened their own businesses, and they have in turn created seventy-six jobs. I will let Sasha tell you about it. He has opened his own business and now has two people working for him. We also have agreements with local employment agencies, so that once victims are rehabilitated and have received job training, we can help them find a job. This is what we do to help our clients. Of course, it costs them nothing.

[I turn my attention to Sasha, who has been sitting quietly as Marina and I chatted.]

Hi, Sasha. Are you ready to begin the interview?
Sasha: Yes.

What kind of education do you have?
Sasha: I have a higher technical education. I got a degree at Ternopil's Polytechnic University in 2007—just over three years ago.

After you finished your studies at the university, what happened?
Sasha: [*Looks a bit lost, looks for help from Marina*]
Marina: He got trafficked while he was going to university. It happened during his studies.
Sasha: During my last year of studies at the university, my mother got really sick. [*Long pause. He looks at Marina, who nods.*] I needed money because I was studying at a private university.[8] My mother, who was fifty-one years old at the time, had lost her job and was not working. My

father had a state job, but the salary was very small—1,000 *griven* a month [approximately US$47]. So, I needed money. Many people I knew were working on construction sites in St. Petersburg and Moscow in Russia. They found the jobs through job announcements. I think some employment agencies were recruiting people from the university.

Where were these announcements? In a magazine? A newspaper?
Sasha: No, they were posters glued to poles all over campus. They were everywhere. I thought I could get a job on a construction site, but … hmmmm…[*long pause as he looks down at his hands*]. I ended up working in stone masonry, cutting granite. It was very difficult work, with a lot of granite dust. They didn't give us any safety equipment, no eye protection or dust masks. We were making gravestones and monuments for graves.

So, you saw these announcements on the light poles on campus. What did you do next?
Sasha: [*Looks at Marina, who nods.*] Ummmm, there was a phone number on the poster, so I called it. A woman answered and she said they needed people to work in Russia. She said I could make good money there.

How much money did she promise you?
Sasha: $600–$700 a month. This was a good salary for Moscow at the time, but for here, for us in Ternopil, it was huge. So, I agreed to meet with them. I met the two of them, a man and a woman, downtown by a department store. They didn't have a regular office that I know of. They were Russians, but I don't remember what they said their names were. They were very friendly and seemed nice.

There were about five or six other Ukrainian students who came to the department store looking for jobs. The Russians brought contracts and official-looking paperwork for us to sign. We all signed the papers. It seemed legitimate and they looked like legitimate contracts. So, I took an academic leave of absence from my university for a year. I figured I would work one year in Russia and then have enough money to finish school.

Then what happened?
Sasha: Well, we took the train from Ternopil to Moscow. They paid for our tickets.[9] When we arrived, someone met us at the train station. They took us to a place outside of Moscow. I don't know exactly where, but it was not far from Moscow. We were told at first that we would work eight to ten hours a day…… Ummmm…. But … then later they said there were many

orders to fill so we would have to work twelve hours a day, then fourteen, and then sixteen hours a day.

Marina: They were making those marble slabs and granite monuments that people buy for graves. It was an underground enterprise. It was not an official, legally licensed shop.

Sasha: They needed really strong people to handle the stone. But soon I began having problems with my lungs. All the granite dust ruined my health.

Where did you live?

Sasha: S-s-s-s... [*he stutters, looks at Marina, who nods*]. In that shop there were two rooms. Tiny rooms like broom closets. There were ... hmmm.... Two women in one of them, and we men lived in the other one. Hmmmm.... There were ten of us altogether in those two tiny rooms—two women and eight men. Plus, there were always guards and watchmen around who told us what to do.

I had only worked there a short time, I think two weeks or so, when I told them that this job was not for me. I told them I wanted to leave. They ordered me to keep working. They said it would go badly for me if I didn't work.

What went through your mind when you realized that you couldn't leave?

Sasha: I have a nervous condition, and this really affected my nerves. I broke out in a rash all over and started suffering physical symptoms. They did nothing and would not let me get medical treatment. We just had to keep working and they would not let us leave the premises. [*Long pause as he struggles to control his emotions. He looks at Marina, who nods.*]

And they only gave us something to eat two, or sometimes three, times a day. Most of the time they fed us only twice a day, just some thin gruel or nearly rotten meat. And they forced us to work sixteen hours a day.

Did they physically abuse you?

Sasha: No. Well, they didn't beat me personally. But they beat some of the other guys who resisted them. I am generally calm and compliant. I don't like to cause problems. So, I did what they told me. But some of the other guys would refuse to do something and then the guards would beat them ... ahh ... beat them very badly. It was terrible. I was there four months before I was able to escape.

How did you escape?

Sasha: In ... [*long pause as he struggles with his emotions. Looks at Marina,* *who nods*] ... In our tiny room there were bars on the windows. We took a file from the shop that we worked out of. And we s-s-s-s.... [*he stutters*] filed the bars until we cut through them and then we ran away. We ran away without our passports or documents since the guards took them from us the very first day.

Did you run to the local authorities or the police?

Sasha: The local authorities get paid by the traffickers to keep quiet about abuses like this, so they just look the other way. I knew that they would not help. And the police are just as bad. If we had gone to the police, they would have just returned us to the traffickers. Here in Ukraine, we have similar kinds of police who are totally corrupt.

After I escaped, I hitchhiked rides on large long-haul trucks. The long-distance truck drivers helped me. They transport freight from one country to another. Many of the drivers are Ukrainian and they helped me. When I got to the Ukrainian border, I flagged a truck down and the driver hid me in the sleeping compartment of his truck. He smuggled me back into Ukraine since the traffickers had my ID and passport. Then I caught another ride to Kyiv, where a good friend of mine gave me some money and helped me get back to Ternopil.

How did you feel as you were hiding in that sleeping compartment on your way back to Ukraine?

Sasha: Well.... I was numb, indifferent. It was like I no longer cared what happened to me. My heart and soul were broken, and I believed that it could not get any worse. Whatever happened, it could not be any worse. So, I didn't really feel anything.

You arrived in Kyiv and met your friend?

Sasha: Yes. We were classmates in Ternopil and now he is getting his PhD here in Kyiv. He is a really good friend. Well, I told him what happened to me, and he helped me get back home.

Once you got home, how did you find Marina's organization?

Sasha: My mother found an announcement in the paper.... Well, it was not an announcement really, but an article. It was about this organization that helps people who get trafficked.

So, you told your mother what happened?

Sasha: Of course. She could see it, and she feels everything. She knew something was terribly wrong. Then she found this article and wanted me to call for help. At first, I was too ashamed. You understand? I really didn't want to call them. I no longer cared about anything. But my mother convinced me to call. I had some very difficult health problems and needed medical attention. Especially my stomach. My stomach was destroyed by stress. Most of my physical ailments are from nerves.

Marina: Yes. He has severe stomach and intestinal pain caused by stress—PTSD. Nonetheless, he finished his studies at the university. Once he returned to Ternopil, he was able to complete his degree.

Sasha: Well.... I *had* to. I only had one year left, I had already completed four years.[10] After I got my degree, I got a part-time summer job working as a glass cutter in a small shop. It was really interesting work and not too difficult or strenuous. And it was creative work. I cut mirrors in all sorts of artistic designs. I *really* liked the work, and Marina's organization told me they could help me open my own glass-cutting business. They helped me with licensing, a microloan, and some work training. Now I have a small business and lots of work—work that I enjoy. It is enough for me.

So, how has this experience changed you?

Sasha: Well.... [*Long pause as he struggles with his emotions. He looks to Marina, who nods.*] Ummm, I still trust people a little, but nothing like I did ... before.... It is just the way I am. I just wanted to earn some money.... I [*laughing with irony*] earned something, all right—experience, illness, nerve problems. And I got this rash. At first, I thought it was an allergy, that maybe I had eaten something and got a reaction. But it didn't go away. The doctors told me it was a type of neurosis that is caused by stress, something like neurodermatitis. Well, I will have it for the rest of my life. It's just that it is so ugly. So, I guess this has made me abnormal. Because of this experience, I am no longer a normal human being.

Marina: No, it is *normal*, Sasha—it is all *normal*. These are normal reactions to what you went through.

Sasha, what are your dreams now? What do you want your life to be like?

Sasha: I want to get married next year. I have been dating my girlfriend for over five years now, and I want to marry her. She knows what happened to me and she understands my problems.

First, we need to save enough money to buy an apartment so that we will have a place to live. Being married and living with one's parents is too difficult. Now that I have this business and work is good, it is possible. Also, I want children. I want two or three, but my girlfriend only wants one. She is afraid of having more than one [*laughs*].

As you know, I am writing a book about human trafficking to be published in the U.S. Is there anything you would like to say to people who might read this book?

Sasha: [*Clearing his throat. Very serious.*] Do you have such problems with slavery in America?

Yes. Unfortunately, we do. Most commonly it is women and children who are sold into sexual slavery. But we also have labor exploitation.

Sasha: That is sad. Well, I would tell people that if they must get work somewhere, they should go only through friends or close relatives. Rely only on people you know and trust to find you work. Because if you go somewhere without knowing where you are going to ... [*pause*] you can get really hurt. For men it is dangerous because there is labor exploitation. But for women it is really, really dangerous, well, because... [*pause*] you know.

Yes, I know. Those women who were there with you, are they still there? Or did they escape too?

Sasha: I don't know what happened to them—if they ran away or not. They did not escape with us. They were still locked in their room. There was nothing we could do to help them escape. I hope they got away and scattered. But all that is already in the past for me. Now I must look ahead.

* * * *

At this point, Marina reminded us that there were two more people waiting to talk to me, so it seemed like a good time to end the interview. As Marina went out to bring Andre in, I reflected on how globalization and the slave trade work symbiotically. Andre was a victim of both.

Migration and the exploitative conditions that arise from it are in large measure a result of globalization.[11] One obvious reason for this is the massive movement of goods and people across international borders. But a darker aspect of globalization that feeds the slave trade is the increasing inequality of economic and political power. To be sure, whether during the historic slave trade or slavery in today's world, relations of oppression and coercion have always been rooted in economic and political inequality. However, such inequality has never reached the scale that it has in the twenty-first century. According to an Oxfam report in 2018, twenty-six people hold the same amount of wealth as the poorest half of humanity—3.8 billion people.[12] Put another way, the combined incomes of the richest 5 percent of the world's population are 114 times the incomes of the poorest 5 percent.[13]

Further, factors linked to globalization, such as internationalization and liberalization of economies, coupled with advanced transport and communication technologies, has allowed for a great deal of mobility. Indeed, according to the International Labour Organization, labor migration is one of the hallmarks of the twenty-first-century global economy.[14] The extreme polarization of standards of living and economic opportunities is the main driver of contemporary migration, facilitated by the increasing mobility of resources, technologies, and people.

Andre's interview highlights the impetus of migrants on the bottom end of economic inequality to immigrate in order to find better economic opportunities. And his experience is directly linked to the globalized economy: He was recruited in Ukraine by Russians to work in Italy, where he was enslaved and exploited. Further, until 2008 he had no trouble finding work in Ternopil and was perfectly content with his life there. However, the global economic crisis hit Ukraine particularly hard. In 2008–09, Ukraine's gross domestic product fell by 15 percent, exports fell by 25 percent, and the consumer price index rose by over 12 percent.[15]

With production falling and prices rising, unemployment in Ukraine jumped to nearly 9 percent.[16] Those who were able to hold onto their jobs often faced significant pay cuts. It was in this atmosphere of uncertainty and frustration that Andre began to explore employment options abroad. Before leaving Ukraine, Andre had achieved the equivalent of a master's degree in education, at the Ternopil National Pedagogical University.[17] He also completed training at a trade school as a tailor and gained certification as a Master of Cutting and Sewing (*zarko* in Russian). His third degree is as a teacher of labor skills.[18]

I arranged this interview with Andre via the IOM office in Kyiv. I asked if they had any clients who might allow me to interview them for this project. The psychologist, Marina, later explained that she thought Andre needed to talk about his experience in order to not suppress it, but to come to accept it and move on. Indeed, many survivors told me that they wanted to talk about their experiences—they said that it helped minimize the pain and brought them a little peace.

Andre opted to have Marina, who was helping him reintegrate, present during the interview. Not only did she provide him with support during the interview, but she also helped with translation. Andre primarily spoke Ukrainian. Since he was from western Ukraine, he did not grow up speaking Russian, as those living on the eastern side of the country did. Indeed, his Russian language skills were quite limited, as were my Ukrainian skills. At various times throughout the interview, Marina stepped in to help Andre understand a question I asked or explain something to me that Andre said.

Andre is a muscular, very masculine thirty-year-old man. As he sat across the interview table from me, I was struck by how emotionally fractured he seemed. At first glance he appeared to be quite confident and physically strong. However, once the interview began it became quite clear that he was struggling with very deep emotions. His speech was halting and hesitant. I got the sense that he really did not want to discuss his ordeal, even though he voluntarily agreed to let me interview him. Often as he responded to my questions, he would stammer and break eye contact. He had a slight tremor in his hands. Andre displayed many of the characteristics typical of trafficked victims. He suffered gastrointestinal disorders, physical pain, fatigue, and anxiety. As is common, he also internalized his abuse, blaming himself for being tricked and getting trafficked. He later intimated that he was raped more than once during his ordeal. While he did not want to discuss any of the details, he said that he was also exploited for sex by his captors. He was forced into slave labor in Italy for ten months and had been back in Ukraine a little over a year at the time of this interview.

With all your education and qualifications, it would seem that you could find good employment in Ukraine. Yet at some point, you decided to leave the country. Why?
Andre: Well, I wanted to improve my finances. That is, I wanted to earn more money.[19]

When was this?
Andre: It was late in 2008.

And what happened?
Andre: Wellll, it happened so that ... [*long pause as he tries to control his emotions*], well, I was promised one thing, but in fact received something totally different. That is.... I was forced to work and did not receive any wages.

Here in Ukraine? Or somewhere else?
Andre: I was a slave in Italy. I was hired in Ukraine to work in Italy. I thought I would earn pretty good money there—they promised me I would.

Who promised that to you? And what did they promise?
Andre: It was an employment agency. Well, they promised a decent salary and *good* living conditions as well as *good* working conditions. In reality,

hmmm, that is … [*long pause as Andre struggles to hold back tears*] … I read their … ohhhh … advertisement in the paper…. It sounded like a legitimate employment agency, so I called them. They told me that they could arrange to get me a good job in Italy. They said this service would cost me, hmmm…. US$200 including the visa and the cost of traveling there. I signed a contract, paid the money, and was taken to Italy.[20] Some guys met me at the airport in Italy and they took me to the construction site. They just dumped me there at the construction site in Italy. Well, they took me to … hmmm…. [*long pause*] to the boss for whom I was supposed to be working. And they left me there. I didn't really know where I was. I could not speak Italian and I never got paid any money. They fed me really very little with very poor-quality food. The living conditions … hmmm … were also very bad. We were living right in that place, where the owner lived. Well, where the boss lived, that guy we were working for. He had his own house. We lived in a little carport, like a little car garage. Hmmm … and we had to work twelve to fifteen hours every day.

You say "we." How many people were with you there?
Andre: Three men. We were doing construction. He made us work every day building houses with very little food. We were not allowed to leave, and we rarely got a day off. Then, in September, the rainy season started. It was cold and wet and there was no more work.

Were you able to escape or run away?
Andre: No. They just let us go. The rainy season started. It was not profitable for them to keep feeding us with no work for us to do. They gave us enough money to buy an air ticket home and they let us go. So, on September 6 [2009] I flew back here to Ukraine. That was a year ago.

What happened when you came home? Who met you at the airport?
Andre: Nobody met me there because nobody even knew I was flying back. And I didn't come straight to Ternopil. We don't have an international airport at Ternopil. So, I flew into L'viv—that is a city in western Ukraine. To get back home I had to take a train from L'viv.

And how did you feel when you arrived home? Were you relieved?
Andre: Let's just say I felt poorly. It was horrible. But I am … hmmm … an optimist in life, so that for me … it is easier … easier than for others, perhaps. I had some very bad experiences, but I like to believe that things will get better, so I can tolerate some very bad things.

And what happened next? You were at the train station in Ternopil—then what?

Andre: Then I went home to my parents' house. I live with my parents. I had to pretend that everything was okay. I didn't tell them what happened to me. Why would they need that extra suffering? I made it back; I was alive and healthy. Why would I want to cause them pain? No. I did not tell them. I pretended like I had a great time and spent all my money in Italy. But then, one day, I was looking through the newspaper and I saw an advertisement for this organization. This organization—yes, "Rebirth of the Nation." That is what it is called.

Not IOM?

Andre: No. Rebirth of the Nation. [*At this point, Marina intervenes and translates into English, "Revival of the Nation."*].²¹ This organization said that it could help people who had troubles abroad, like me. So, I went there for a consultation, and they *did* help me. They sent me here, to Kyiv, to the medical clinic to get checked out. I developed a lot of health problems during the nine months I was enslaved in Italy. I had joint pain and back problems. I hadn't seen a doctor or had any kind of medical exam. I also had ... ahhh, uummm [*pause while he struggles for a word*].

Marina: "Stomach"?

Andre: Yes, severe stomach problems. So, Revival of the Nation sent me to Kyiv and arranged for me to have a complete physical examination. They treated me and gave me a little financial help, too. They also fixed my teeth. My teeth got very bad in Italy from all the beatings. When they would beat me in the face, they knocked out a lot of my teeth.

Marina: You see, Andre was suffering from the effects of ten months of extreme stress resulting from his captivity, as well as physical abuse, overwork, and poor diet.

So, was it a year ago approximately that you got back home?

Andre: Yes, on September 6. A little over a year.

How had this experience changed you?

Andre: Well ... hmmmm [*long pause as his emotions arise again*] ... let's say that, probably, after what happened, I think that people are not to be trusted. Hmmm.... I am still an optimist; I still think that everything will be okay. Mentally, I am pretty healthy.

Marina: Andre, may I interject? [*Andre nods, showing relief for her stepping in.*] When Andre came to us, he was still in a depressed state, you see. Anyone would feel insulted and hurt for being used like a thing. He trusted them and they sold him like an object. They treated him horribly, and it was hard for him to accept that anyone could treat him so badly. I remember at his first interview at Revival of the Nation, when we first met, he could not come to terms with the fact that he had been sold. He kept saying, "How can this be, that somebody *sold* me when we are the *same*? We are both human beings, they are like me, how could they *sell* me? [Emphasis is Marina's.] How can one person sell another?" And it was quite horrifying to him—he had not accepted that.

Andre: Yes. How was that even possible? Because I trusted them, they abused me. They promised me, and then treated me like I was not human.

Marina: Especially that over there, in Italy, there was also a lot of physical abuse. They would viciously beat the workers, and sometimes even assault them sexually. They did not let Andre and the others out of the compound and watched them constantly so that no one could escape.

Andre: Yes, we were constantly being watched. We were forced to work sixteen hours a day, and even then, they would beat us. If you refused to work…. [*long pause*] if you refused to go to work—they would beat us mercilessly.

At first, I tried really hard to forget what happened to me. I wanted to just throw this part of my life away. It is hard. It is very hard. But now … hmmmmm … let's just say that everything has ended. I am an optimist, so I want to think that everything is okay now. I have gotten medical treatment and counseling, so I think maybe it will be better. Through this organization I received a six-day business training. They are helping me write my business plan. I will be… [*long pause while he formulates his thoughts*], let's say, I would like to try my hand at being a small business owner. Yes. This organization also is giving me the opportunity and the money, little by little, to put together what I need to create my own sewing shop. Hmmm…. That is my plan for the future. This is what I would like to do. I no longer want to leave my city or my country.

As you know, I am writing a book, and it will be published in the United States. Would you like to say something to the people who might read it?

Andre: To the people who have helped me, I want to say thank you. And to the people who want to leave their … hmmmm [*he pauses as he struggles with his emotions*], that is, who want to go somewhere to earn money…. [*pause*] outside their country, I want to tell them to be a little more careful. I would advise them to be a little more careful than I was. If there is an opportunity to consult with someone, or to obtain legal documents—it's better that they take time to verify the legal documents and never dash headlong into the unknown.

That is good advice, Andre. Thank you.

Conclusion

If slavery is not wrong, nothing is wrong.—Abraham Lincoln
in a letter to A.G. Hodges, 1864

What I have seen and experienced in gathering the stories reported in this book has affected me deeply and will remain with me the rest of my life. I sat with dozens of survivors, looking into their eyes, hearing their stories and bearing witness to their suffering as each one told me how easily and rapidly they were enslaved. Their courage and resilience have left me with a profound desire to work to end this unspeakable crime. While the stories have often broken my heart, I refuse to avert my gaze. It is my hope that you, too, will have discovered in this book a passion and a commitment to become an advocate for those who cannot advocate for themselves.

A little over two hundred years ago, Europe and the United States adopted laws to ban slavery. Most of the world followed suit over the course of the nineteenth century. However, as one abolitionist remarked at the time, the laws may have gotten rid of the slaves but they did nothing to get rid of the slavers. Indeed, since the middle of the twentieth century, international slavery has returned with a vengeance. Hundreds of thousands of persons are trafficked across international borders and enslaved each year for the purpose of exploitation for economic gain. Many millions more are enslaved within their own countries.[1]

In the twenty-four years since the adoption of the Palermo Protocol and the Trafficking Victims Protection Act of 2000, the number of governmental and nongovernmental agencies that define, track, and monitor human trafficking has exploded. Consequently, our understanding of modern-day slavery has deepened, estimates and statistics related to human trafficking have gotten more precise, and advocacy for vulnerable populations and victim services has spread globally. Public awareness of modern slavery has also exploded. There is now an abundance of movies, television shows, news programs, documentaries, conferences, papers, articles, books, and websites addressing human trafficking and modern-day slavery. Further, most countries, except for a relative handful, have signed onto the Palermo Protocol and/or adopted anti-trafficking legislation and conventions.[2] Nonetheless, despite a significant expansion in prevention and prosecution of human trafficking, the crime has gotten worse. Nearly all international agencies that provide annual reports on human trafficking document a steady rise in the number of victims, without a concurrent steady rise in the number of prosecutions.

As several of the service providers in this volume noted, human trafficking is growing, and the traffickers change tactics and strategies in response to law enforcement policies and market forces. The demand for young, beautiful Eastern European women overwhelmingly fueled the trade for sexual exploitation in the early 1990s as the Soviet Union ceased to exist and new post–Soviet states emerged. In the first decade of the twenty-first century, as law enforcement focused on monitoring women crossing international borders, traffickers targeted an increasing number of Eastern European men and women for servile labor exploitation.

Later in the new century, as Covid-19 swept the globe, traffickers once again adjusted their strategies. Countries and borders may have shut down, but the traffickers did not. According to an International Labour Organization blog post, the 2020 global shutdown affected 81 percent of the world's labor force and 90 percent of the world's students.[3] The huge financial hardship on families, the closing of schools, and the millions of people who lost parents, caretakers, or primary wage earners to the disease placed billions of people at risk for human trafficking. At the same time, in order to respond to the pandemic, states shifted resources away from human trafficking prevention and victims' services, and NGOs faced critical staffing and resource shortages, creating an ideal environment for human trafficking to flourish.

While trafficking in human organs slowed owing to the nearly complete cessation of transplant surgeries during the pandemic, all other forms of trafficking expanded. Around the world, as children spent more time on the internet for school and social interaction, traffickers increasingly targeted them for sexual exploitation online.[4] For migrant workers, mass layoffs led millions to accept risky jobs, making them more vulnerable to labor exploitation. Vast numbers of female domestic workers, and women in general, reported a dramatic increase in sexual violence and exploitation during the Covid shutdowns. Homelessness, poverty, isolation, and domestic violence are key factors in making persons vulnerable to human trafficking and slavery. The Covid-19 pandemic greatly exacerbated all these factors, and recruiters and traffickers have been quick to take advantage.

Russia's invasion of Ukraine in February 2022 also led to a significant increase in human trafficking. Anywhere there is mass chaos—economic, environmental, social, or military—large numbers of the population become vulnerable to exploitation. According to the U.S. Department of State, when Russia invaded Ukraine in 2022, eight million people, overwhelmingly women and children, were forced to flee the country and an additional 5.5 million people were internally displaced—nearly one-third of the Ukrainian population. Traffickers allegedly sought to exploit refugees at border crossings and transit centers.[5] Observers documented thousands of unaccompanied children evacuated from nearly two hundred facilities who were at very high risk of trafficking. Even those Ukrainians who aren't displaced are at risk of trafficking owing to the economic impacts of the war. The State Department survey noted that over 50 percent of the Ukrainian population is at risk of exploitation and slavery.[6]

These trends in the post–Soviet world mirror global trends. Although most victims remain women and girls, the proportion of men and boys being trafficked has increased dramatically.[7] In part, the increased numbers could reflect improvements in detecting, recording, and reporting data on human trafficking. At the same time, such large increases in trafficked persons reflect a real increase in the number of slaves.

As is abundantly clear in these interviews, contemporary slavery is more diverse, complex, and pervasive than its nineteenth-century counterpart. Researchers Kevin Bales and Siddharth Kara were among the first scholars to draw attention to this new form of modern slavery not based on legal ownership of human "property." The exercise of property rights over human beings has been replaced by a wide array of mechanisms slavers use to exert control over victims, resulting in de facto ownership. Such mechanisms include violence, threats, indebtedness, isolation, physical captivity, confiscation of documents, emotional or mental abuse, and myriad other forms of coercion and manipulation. Yet, despite formal legal prohibitions against slavery, extralegal slavery has endured in various forms throughout the modern era.[8] What we are seeing in the twenty-first century, and what is documented in these pages, is simply the current incarnation of involuntary servitude and human trafficking. Like most forms of commerce, the nefarious trade in humans is versatile and adapts to local opportunities and market forces the world over.

However, despite regional variations, the general characteristics of human trafficking are remarkably similar. Fraudulent recruitment, whether in advertisements, employment agencies, or in person, is one tactic used in nearly all trafficking cases. Most of the survivors I interviewed were lured into slavery through promises of a good job. The so-called Romeo pimp is another form of fraudulent recruitment some of my interviewees experienced, using the false promise of a romantic relationship to manipulate young women. Once he gains her trust, she is raped and sold.

Another consistent factor in most trafficking scenarios is the vulnerability of marginalized groups. Race, ethnicity, socioeconomic status, and gender often determine who is targeted by the traffickers and who is not. Whether it is social orphans in Moldova, unemployed single mothers in Ukraine, the Roma in Eastern Europe, or people left behind as economies change, the most disadvantaged and marginalized people in a society are the most vulnerable. Additionally, traffickers profit from wars and natural disasters. In the chaos of these events, huge numbers of children are orphaned and people are displaced, becoming easy prey for the traffickers.

It is clear from the experiences of the survivors interviewed here, and from the cases recounted by the service providers, that the traffickers will not, and cannot, see the humanity of their victims. To the exploiters, they are not human, but a commodity to be bought, sold, exploited, and discarded. Indeed, in every country today, at this moment, human beings are being bought and sold, dishonored and degraded for profit, enduring unimaginable misery and oppression. The primary motivation of slavers the world over now, as always, is greed. As long as slavery can generate substantial profits with very little risk for the exploiters, this crime against humanity will endure.

What, then, can be done? Scholars, activists, survivors of slavery, law enforcement professionals, international anti-trafficking organizations, national agencies, and specialists in think tanks have already produced a large and detailed literature on how to combat human trafficking regionally, nationally, and internationally. Hundreds of thousands of pages have been written on policy recommendations: expanding legislative approaches, fostering international cooperation, implementing better victim assistance programs, and improving data gathering and outreach efforts. Unfortunately, too few of these recommended programs have ever been implemented.

The primary obstacles to ending slavery in the twenty-first century are a lack of public awareness, a lack of political will, and a lack of resources. These three obstacles are interrelated. Greater awareness among the general public will lead to increased pressure on politicians to fund anti-slavery efforts. As one human rights lawyer told me, "Where public opinion goes, legislation flows." The public must be made aware of the dehumanizing and oppressive nature of slavery, as well as its prevalence around the world today. People need to know that it is happening right here, right now: in the suburbs of California; in the brickyards of India; in the tomato fields of Florida; in the brothels of Thailand and Belgium; in the factories of Bangladesh; in the construction sites of Eastern Europe; and in all places in between, even in your own neighborhood.

When I was a kid and I read about Harriet Tubman and the so-called Underground Railroad, I marveled at the courage and humanity of the abolitionists. I imagined that if I lived in the time of slavery, I would also be an abolitionist. But I do live in the time of slavery. The stories in this volume give the lie to the notion that slavery ended two centuries ago. In the nineteenth century, a handful of committed abolitionists started a movement that resulted in the end of legal slavery nearly worldwide. And they did it without cell phones, social media, or the internet. While slavery in the twenty-first century is more diverse, convoluted, and complicated than its nineteenth-century counterpart, we have the tools and the technology to address this "old monster" in its myriad forms. There are countless local, regional, national, and international anti-slavery organizations. Now is a very good time to become a modern-day abolitionist.

Appendix:
What You Can Do

It is tempting to talk about slavery and abolition in universal terms—that there are slaves and there is an abolitionist movement to free them. Unfortunately, that is not the case. Slavery today takes multiple forms: forced prostitution, labor exploitation, slavery in corporate supply chains, debt bondage, irregular migrants trapped in systems of exploitation, child soldiers, child labor, begging, illegal organ trafficking, hereditary bondage, the exploitation of prison populations—and the list goes on. And there are numerous abolitionist movements. For example, what is needed to free Ukrainian children from Russian labor and sexual exploitation is very different from what is needed to address forced labor in Ghana's cocoa fields or Brazil's agricultural sector. It is useful to understand that there are very different causes and conditions for slavery and that there must be different anti-slavery responses.

And yet, as noted above, there seem to be three overarching obstacles to at least limiting, if not ending, human trafficking and slavery: a lack of public awareness, a lack of political will, and a lack of resources. If you start from this premise, there are concrete steps you can take that will counter these obstacles and support abolition.

First in importance is raising public awareness. If people do not know that slavery exists, how can they work to erase it? To that end, you can educate yourself and your friends about the prevalence of human trafficking in your own area. The U.S. Department of Health and Human Services has a number of great recommendations in its "Look Beneath the Surface" campaign: *https://www.acf.hhs.gov/otip/partnerships/look-beneath-surface*. The Polaris Project has several industry-specific toolkits for educating and training yourself and others in spotting and responding to slavery: *https://humantraffickingsearch.org/learn*.

The second thing you can do is to bring political and economic pressure to bear on corporations and elected officials. Consume wisely and demand more transparent supply chains. Talk to stores in your area and ask them to carry a variety of fair-trade items. Ask your public officials where they stand on funding survivor networks and services. Ask them if human trafficking is a priority or even on their horizon. Support as much as possible local businesses with transparent supply chains, or companies that sell fair trade products. Finally, you can donate your money or your time to anti-trafficking organizations. The U.S. State Department has numerous projects to end slavery: *https://www.state.gov/program-to-end-modern-slavery*. There are also many NGOs that focus on prevention and rehabilitation. The best ones are survivor-led organizations. You can find one in your area through a cursory Google search.

In the end, it is up to us to help those who are trapped in desperate conditions of servile exploitation. Each of us profits, in some way, from slavery—most notably through cheap goods and foods, or through metals in our phones and computers, or from cheap services. But we can change this. As Margaret Mead reminds us: "Never doubt that a small group of thoughtful committed citizens can change the world. Indeed, it's the only thing that ever has."

Chapter Notes

Preface

1. For some examples of collections of modern-day slave narratives, see Kevin Bales and Zoe Trodd, eds., *To Plead Our Own Cause: Personal Stories by Today's Slaves* (Ithaca: Cornell University Press, 2008); Laura T. Murphy, *Survivors of Slavery: Modern-Day Slave Narratives* (New York: Columbia University Press, 2014). For excellent studies that draw on firsthand accounts, see Mary Buckley, *The Politics of Unfree Labour in Russia: Human Trafficking and Labour Migration* (Cambridge: Cambridge University Press, 2018); Siddharth Kara, *Modern Slavery: A Global Perspective* (New York: Columbia University Press, 2017); E. Benjamin Skinner, *A Crime So Monstrous: Face-to-Face with Modern-Day Slavery* (New York: Free Press, 2008); Louisa Waugh, *Selling Olga: Stories of Human Trafficking and Resistance* (London: Phoenix, 2008).

2. One exception is Mary Buckley's pathbreaking work, where she relies on interviews with law enforcement and service providers to understand anti-trafficking efforts in Russia. See Buckley, *The Politics of Unfree Labour in Russia*, especially chapter 6.

3. In its simplest form, documentary prose is nonfiction storytelling such as practiced by the author Svetlana Alexievich, who writes predominantly in the oral history tradition to record significant events in the USSR and post–Soviet states. Documentary prose is not the same as oral history in that it can include memoirs, autobiographies, and interviews. In my work I rely on an interpretation of documentary prose by the Russian writer Verlam Shalamov, who defined it as "not the prose of the document but the prose of the ordeal borne out as a document [*proza vystradannaya kak dokum*]," quoted in Leona Tokar, "Toward a Poetics of Documentary Prose—From the Perspective of Gulag Testimonies," *Poetics Today* 18, no. 2 (Summer 1997): 188.

4. Anya (trafficking survivor), interview by the author, a village near Chisinau, Moldova, November 18, 2008.

Introduction

1. *John* is slang for a man who pays prostitutes for sex (see glossary).

2. What I didn't know at the time was that in 1997 alone, an estimated 175,000 women from Eastern Europe were trafficked and forced into prostitution. See Elena V. Tiuriukanova and Ludmila D. Erokhina, eds., *Torgovlia Liud'mi: Sotsiokriminologicheskii Analiz* (Moscow: Izdatel'stvo Akademia, 2002), 141.

3. "6 Are Accused of Forcing Girls from Mexico into Prostitution," *New York Times*, 26 March 2002.

4. "Contraband Women—Traffickers' New Cargo: Naïve Slavic Women," *New York Times*, 11 January 1998.

5. According to the Global Slavery Index 2023 report, there were nearly 50 million people enslaved in the world in 2023. See https://www.globalslaveryindex.org, accessed 20 January 2024.

6. See U.S. State Department Trafficking in Persons Report (TIP), https://www.state.gov/reports/2023-trafficking-in-persons-report, accessed January 2024.

7. Global Slavery Index 2023 Report,

https://cdn.walkfree.org/content/uploads/2023/05/17114737/Global-Slavery-Index-2023.pdf, accessed January 2024.

8. Heikki Mattila, "Combating Human Trafficking," *INTERSEC Journal of International Security* 14 (February 2004). For more on human trafficking from Eastern Europe, see Lauren McCarthy, *Trafficking Justice: How Russian Police Enforce New Laws, from Crime to Courtroom* (Ithaca: Cornell University Press, 2015); Sally Stoecker and Louise Shelley, eds., *Human Traffic and Transnational Crime: Eurasian and American Perspectives* (Lanham: Rowman & Littlefield, 2005).

9. See, for example, Jennifer Lynne Musto, "What's in a Name? Conflations and Contradictions in Contemporary U.S. Discourses of Human Trafficking," *Women's Studies International Forum* 32 (2009): 281–287.

10. The "Protocol to Prevent, Suppress, and Punish Trafficking in Persons, Especially Women and Children" was approved by the United Nations in 2000. The entire text of the protocol can be found at www.ohchr.org/EN/ProfessionalInterest/Pages/ProtocolTraffickingInPersons.aspx, accessed January 2023.

11. Trafficking Victims Protection Act of 2000, Public Law 106–386, October 2000, www.state.gov/documents/organizations/10492.pdf, accessed January 2023. For an excellent overview of terminology debates and problems of statistics, see Elzbieta M. Gozdziak and Elizabeth A. Collett, "Research on Human Trafficking in America: A Review of the Literature," *International Migration* 43 (2005): 99–129.

12. Some good examples of this include David Brion Davis, *The Problem of Slavery in the Age of Emancipation* (New York: Vintage, 2015); William S. Kiser, *Borderlands of Slavery: The Struggle Over Captivity and Peonage in the American Southwest* (Philadelphia: University of Pennsylvania Press, 2017); William D. Phillips, Jr., *Slavery from Roman Times to the Early Transatlantic Trade* (Manchester: Manchester University Press, 1985); Lowell J. Satre, *Chocolate on Trial: Slavery, Politics, and the Ethics of Business* (Athens: Ohio University Press, 2005).

13. Debt bondage is a form of exploitation by which an individual's labor is appropriated to "pay off" a debt (real or purported) that is virtually impossible to repay, due to the low wages and/or the imposition of interest and additional indebtedness (sometimes for items whose costs are assessed at more than market value). See, for example, Buckley, *The Politics of Unfree Labour in Russia*, 11–13; Siddharth Kara, *Bonded Labor: Tackling the System of Slavery in South Asia* (New York: Columbia University Press, 2012); Stephanie Barrientos, Uma Kothari, and Nicola Phillips, "Dynamics of Unfree Labour in the Contemporary Global Economy," *Journal of Development Studies* 49, no. 8 (2013): 1037–1041.

14. For an excellent discussion on usage of various terms, see Beate Andress, "Why Definitions Matter," available from the International Labour Organization at https://www.ilo.org/global/about-the-ilo/newsroom/news/WCMS_234854/lang—en/index.htm, accessed January 2023. See also Andrea Nicholson, Minh Dang, and Zoe Trodd, "Full Freedom: Contemporary Survivors' Definitions of Slavery," *Human Rights Law Review* 18, no. 4 (December 2018): 689–704; Rebecca J. Scott, "Under Color of Law: Siliadan v. France and the Dynamics of Enslavement in Historical Perspective," in *The Legal Understanding of Slavery from the Historical to the Contemporary*, ed. Jean Allain (Oxford: Oxford University Press, 2012): 152–164.

15. For a comparative study of the differences between chattel slavery in the American South and Russian serfdom, see Peter Kolchin, *Unfree Labor: American Slavery and Russian Serfdom* (Cambridge, MA: Belknap Press of Harvard University Press, 1987). See also Andres Resendez, *The Other Slavery: The Uncovered Story of Indian Enslavement in America* (New York: Houghton Mifflin Harcourt, 2016); Debra Blumenthal, *Enemies and Familiars: Slavery and Mastery in Fifteenth-Century Valencia* (Ithaca: Cornell University Press, 2009).

16. Michael Dottridge, "Eight Reasons We Shouldn't Use the Term 'Modern Slavery'" (speech, Vienna, Austria, 29 September 2017), Open Democracy, https://www.opendemocracy.net/en/beyond-trafficking-and-slavery/eight-reasons-why-we-shouldn-t-use-term-modern-slavery/, accessed July 2019. See also Karen E. Bravo, "The Role of the

Transatlantic Slave Trade in Contemporary Anti-Human Trafficking Discourse," *Seattle Journal for Social Justice* 9, no. 2 (2011): 555–597.

17. Kevin Bales, *Disposable People: New Slavery in a Global Age* (Berkeley: University of California Press, 2004).

18. Laura T. Murphy, *Survivors of Slavery: Modern-Day Slave Narratives* (New York: Columbia University Press, 2014), 14–17.

19. Siddarth Kara, *Modern Slavery: A Global Perspective* (New York: Columbia University Press, 2017), 8.

20. The essential element of slavery is the forced extraction of labor for another person's profit. As regards sexual slavery and prostitution, some commentators see an element of coercion and violence in all sex work, others do not. Some commercial sex workers feel themselves to be exploited, but they willingly tolerate it because they can make a living with their bodies. Therefore, any discussion of sexual exploitation bumps into the thorny issue of "choice" when it comes to commercial sex work. I do not wish to engage in these debates. If a person does not profit from her own labor, and is not free to leave, I consider that person a slave. For a thorough discussion of the debates about the relationship of trafficking to voluntary prostitution, see Joyce Outshoorn, "The Political Debates on Prostitution and Trafficking of Women," *Social Politics* 12, no. 1 (2005): 141–155.

21. The obligatory residency permit, or *propiska* system, was officially instituted in the Soviet Union in 1932. Until 1996 every citizen 16 years or older was required to carry an internal passport with a *propiska* stamp that identified the region of the bearer's legal residence. Through this system an individual's movement and migration patterns could be controlled.

22. In 2000, the International Institute of Finance estimated that in a seven-year period over US$140 billion left Russia in capital flight. See Donna Hughes, "Supplying Women for the Sex Industry: Trafficking from the Russian Federation," in *Sexualities in Post-communism*, ed. A. Stulhofer et al. (Philadelphia: Haworth, 2002). See also David Hoffman, *The Oligarchs: Wealth and Power in the New Russia* (New York: PublicAffairs, 2002); Karen Dawisha,

Putin's Kleptocracy: Who Owns Russia? (New York: Simon & Schuster, 2014); Anders Aslund, *Russia's Crony Capitalism: The Path from Market Economy to Kleptocracy* (New Haven: Yale University Press, 2019).

23. See James O. Finckenauer and Yuri A.Voronin, "The Threat of Russian Organized Crime," *Issues in International Crime* (June 2001): 2–6.

24. The complicity in human trafficking of local officials is a theme repeated in numerous interviews that I conducted with service providers. Neli Babcinci, Alina Budeci, Stella Rotaru, and Ion Vizdoga all claimed to have firsthand experiences with corrupt officials.

25. Mary Buckley notes that many authorities, as well as the public, believed that the trafficked women were either so incredibly stupid or naïve that they deserved what they got. Buckley, *The Politics of Unfree Labour in Russia*, 62–63.

26. Chief of the International Trafficking Task Force in Riga, interviewed by the author in Riga, Latvia, February 25, 2009.

27. Donna Hughes and Tatyana Denisova, "The Transnational Political Nexus of Trafficking in Women from Ukraine," *Trends in Organized Crime* 6 (2001): 6.

28. See Donna Hughes, *Trafficking for Sexual Exploitation: The Case of the Russian Federation*, IOM Migration Research Series, no. 7 (Geneva: International Organization for Migration, 2000).

29. See Ludmila Erokhina and Mariia Buriak, *Torgovlia Zhenshchinami I Det'mi v Tseliakh Seksual'noi Ekspluatatsii v Sotsial'noi I Kriminologicheskoi Perspektive* (Moscow: Profobrazovanie, 2003); Louise I. Shelley, "The Changing Position of Women: Trafficking, Crime, and Corruption," in *The Legacy of State Socialism and the Future of Transformation*, ed. David Lane (Lanham: Rowman & Littlefield, 2002): 207–222.

30. I was living in Moscow; Russia; and Kharkiv, Ukraine, that year. In those cities, and in every city and town I visited, the main streets were lined with *babushky* (grandmothers) selling everything and anything you could imagine, from tired, well-worn clothes, old bottles, and nice jewelry to dildos and sports equipment, in order to get a little money for food.

31. Natasha, interviewed by the author, Chico, California, May 16, 2016.

Natasha was recruited and agreed to take a job abroad as a model. Luckily for her, the morning she was to meet and travel with several other young women who had been "hired" by this "modeling agency," she was sick and did not go. A good friend of hers did go and was enslaved and sold several times over a three-year period.

32. Hughes and Denisova, "The Transactional Political Nexus," p. 5.

33. Ruth Rosenberg, "Trafficking of Adult Men in the Europe and Eurasia Region: Final Report" (Washington, DC: United States Agency for International Development, 2010), http://lastradainternational.org/lsidocs/Trafficking%20of%20Men%20Draft_final.pdf, accessed July 2019; Rebecca Surtees, *Trafficking of Men—A Trend Less Considered: The Case of Belarus and Ukraine*, IOM Migration Research Series, no. 36 (2008), https://www.iom.int/sites/default/files/our_work/ICP/IDM/MRS-36.pdf, accessed July 2019.

34. Ghenadi Cretu (Migration Specialist), interviewed by the author, Chisinau, Moldova, November 12, 2008.

35. Amnesty International, "Russian Federation: Nowhere to Turn to—Violence Against Women in the Family" (London: Amnesty International, 2005), 7–8; see also Janet Elise Johnson, *Gender Violence in Russia* (Bloomington: Indiana University Press, 2009), 32.

36. United Nations Population Fund, "A House Divided: Domestic Violence in the Russian Federation," 28 November 2007, https://www.unfpa.org/es/node/6563/.

37. EU/UN Development Program, "Ten Unknown Facts About Domestic Violence in Ukraine," 15 January 2010, http://www.ua.undp.org/content/ukraine/en/home/presscenter/articles/2010/01/15/ten-unknown-facts-about-domestic-violence-in-ukraine-a-joint-eu-undp-project-releases-new-poll-results.html.

38. Ibid.

39. Alina Budeci (psychologist at La Strada), interviewed by the author, Chisinau, Moldova, October 25, 2008.

40. Stella Rotaru (repatriation specialist at IOM), interviewed by the author, Chisinau, Moldova, November 5, 2008.

41. Alexei (trafficking survivor), interviewed by the author, Chisinau, Moldova, November 5, 2008.

42. Ibid.

43. Sveta (trafficking survivor), interviewed by the author, Chisinau, Moldova, November 10, 2008.

44. See, for example, Lucia Ovidia Vreja, "Human Trafficking in South Eastern Europe," *Connections* 1, no. 4 (Winter 2005): 49–62.

45. Helena (psychologist), interviewed by author in L'viv, Ukraine, February 12, 2009.

Part I

1. Stella Rotaru (repatriation expert), interview by the author in Chisinau, Moldova, November 5, 2008. Stella was referring to the lasting trauma survivors endure. Many survivors get re-trafficked or commit suicide largely because the circumstances that led to their trafficking had not changed, or they could not live with the trauma of slavery.

2. Recently there have been a few studies and articles that criticize the work of the so-called "rescue industry." These largely critique the discourse around sex trafficking or the competition to get funding from international organizations for "rescue" work. See, for example, Laura Maria Agustin, *Sex at the Margins: Migration, Labour Markets and the Rescue Industry* (London: Zed Books, 2007); Anne Elizabeth Moore, "The American Rescue Industry: Toward an Anti-Trafficking Paramilitary," *Truthout* (8 April 2015), https://truthout.org/articles/the-american-rescue-industry-toward-an-anti-trafficking-paramilitary/; Laura LeMoon, "The Groups 'Rescuing' Sex Trafficking Victims Are as Bad as the Pimps," *Intersectional Feminist Media* (28 April 2017), https://www.wearyourvoicemag.com/more/social-justice/sex-trafficking-rescue-industry; Dana Bruxvoort, "The Untold Side of Raids and Rescues: Rethinking Anti-Trafficking Efforts," *Human Trafficking Center Blog* 29 (January 2014), https://humantraffickingcenter.org/the-untold-side-of-raids-and-rescues-re-thinking-anti-trafficking-efforts/, accessed 23 July 2019.

Chapter 1

1. An *oblast* is a type of administrative division in former Soviet lands. It is analogous to "region."

2. In 1934–38, Joseph Stalin launched a brutal purge of "enemies of the people." Hundreds of intellectuals and artists from Kharkiv were arrested and killed as part of the Stalinist regime's efforts to wipe out Ukrainian nationalism.

3. In 2010, with a population of 1.5 million people, Kharkiv was home to sixty scientific institutes, thirty universities and colleges, six museums, seven theaters, and eighty libraries.

4. Elina Beketova, "Behind the Lines Special Edition: One Year On," Center for European Policy Analysis, 22 February 2023, https://cepa.org/article/behind-the-lines-ukraine-after-russias-invasion/; Michael Schwirtz, "Kharkiv Got Some Breathing Space, But Still Doesn't Breathe Easily," *New York Times*, 20 January 2023.

5. Lena is referring to Article 15 of the Council of Europe Anti-Trafficking Convention that provides for victims of human trafficking to receive compensation from the perpetrators as well as the State. See *Report Concerning the Implementation of the Council of Europe Convention on Action Against Trafficking in Human Beings by Ukraine* (2014), 43.

6. Mariupol is in southeastern Ukraine on the north coast of the Sea of Azov. With a population of nearly 500,000, Mariupol is the tenth largest city in Ukraine and second largest in the Donetsk region. It is a significant industrial, educational, and business center. It was also the first city to fall to the Russians in the 2022 invasion. It was the scene of intense fighting and horrific human rights abuses. See Becky Sullivan, "Mariupol Has Fallen to the Russians: Here's What It Means for Ukraine," NPR, 19 May 2022, https://www.npr.org/2022/05/18/1099885151/mariupol-falls-ukraine-russia-what-it-means.

7. She is referring to boys who cross-dress as girls.

8. These three *oblasts*, or regions, constitute nearly the entire eastern border with Russia. The majority of the population identifies as ethnic Russian. These areas also have a lot of poverty. Luhansk was one of the areas of heavy fighting during the Russian–backed separatist war of 2014–15 and has been occupied by Russia since the 2021 invasion.

9. It is important to note that Lena was working with victims trafficked to Russia at precisely the time that the Russian government claimed there was no trafficking in Russia and closed down nearly all of the anti-trafficking NGOs.

10. Kursk is in southwestern Russia, near the border with Ukraine. It is an important industrial area, as well as an important highway and railway junction.

11. Krasnodar is in the south of Russia, near the Black Sea and the Sea of Azov—about 300 km north of Sochi, site of the 2014 Winter Olympics.

12. Belgorod is located about 700 km south of Moscow and 40 km from the Ukrainian border.

13. Lena participated in the Open World Leadership Program. Established by the U.S. Congress in 1999, the Open World Leadership Program enhances capabilities for cooperation between the U.S. and countries of the former Soviet Union on issues such as human trafficking and child exploitation crimes. See www.openworld.gov, accessed January 2024.

14. According to the UN Global Initiative to Fight Trafficking, survivors of human trafficking have much higher rates of HIV/AIDS than voluntary sex workers. In addition to being exposed to forced and unsafe sex with multiple partners, victims are often injected with drugs to assure their compliance. Victims may also receive medical or surgical procedures, including forced abortions by unqualified practitioners in unsanitary conditions using contaminated instruments. See http://www.ungift.org/knowledgehub/en/about/human-trafficking-and-hiv-aids.html, accessed January 2023.

15. Prostitution is legal in most cities in Belgium. Sex workers in legal brothels must register with the tax authorities and receive official ID. These are the documents that the traffickers faked for Lena. Obviously, she did not register with the tax authorities or the police.

16. Because prostitution is legal in Belgium, brothels and prostitutes are regulated. However, it is very easy for traffickers to get around the authorities and avoid regular checks. Some people argue that legalizing prostitution will alleviate forced prostitution, but Lena's experience is a powerful indication that this is a fallacious argument.

17. According to Siddharth Kara in

2009, one Eastern European woman in a brothel in Europe netted for her owner an average of US$67,300 a year. See Siddarth Kara, *Sex Trafficking: Inside the Business of Modern Slavery* (New York: Columbia University Press, 2009).

Chapter 2

1. This argument is advanced in Andreas Schloenhardt and Mark Loong, "Return and Reintegration of Human Trafficking Victims from Australia," *International Journal of Refugee Law* 23, no. 2 (July 2011): 143–173.

2. Allison Jobe, "The Causes and Consequences of Re-trafficking: Evidence from the IOM Database," International Organization for Migration, 2010, https://publications.iom.int/system/files/pdf/causes_of_retrafficking.pdf, accessed January 2024.

3. This interview took place in 2008—well before 2014 when Russia annexed the Crimea and started a separatist war in eastern Ukraine. Russian cooperation with Ukrainian organizations ended dramatically in 2014 when Russia invaded and occupied portions of Ukraine.

4. Quite often victims don't even know what country they are in, let alone in what city or on what street.

5. Donetsk is an industrial city to the southeast of Kyiv. It is the site of some of the worst fighting in the war between the Russian separatists and Ukraine that began in 2013. Since 2022 it is totally under Russian occupation.

6. Founded in 1896, the ITF is an international federation of over 700 trade unions representing 4.5 million transport workers from 150 countries. They have a special branch dealing with seamen and maritime issues.

Chapter 3

1. Laura Dean and Anastasia Dovgaia, "The Politics of Russia's Approach to Human Trafficking," *The Russia File* (blog), Kennan Institute/Woodrow Wilson Center, 18 January 2017, https://www.wilsoncenter.org/blog-post/the-politics-russias-approach-to-human-trafficking, accessed 3 November 2018.

2. The U.S. State Department has a ranking system for how countries deal with the issue of human trafficking in its annual Trafficking in Persons Report (TIP). Tier 3 comprises countries whose governments do not fully comply with the minimum standards and are not making significant efforts to do so.

3. U.S. Department of State, *2023 Trafficking of Persons Report: Russia*. https://www.state.gov/reports/2023-trafficking-in-persons-report/russia/, accessed January 2024.

4. For more on forcible separations of children, see Human Rights Watch, "'We Had No Choice': 'Filtration' and the Crime of Transferring Ukrainian Citizens to Russia," 1 September 2022, https://www.hrw.org/report/2022/09/01/we-had-no-choice/filtration-and-crime-forcibly-transferring-ukrainian-civilians, accessed November 2022.

5. See Mary Buckley, *The Politics of Unfree Labour in Russia: Human Trafficking and Labour Migration* (Cambridge: Cambridge University Press, 2018), 86–91.

6. See U.S. State Department TIP Report, 2010, Country Profile, Russia, https://2009-2017.state.gov/j/tip/rls/tiprpt/2010/142761.htm, accessed July 2023.

7. *Ibid.*

8. The Primorsky, or "maritime," krai is the furthest southeastern administrative region of Russia, wedged between China's eastern border and the Sea of Japan.

9. Laletina grew up during the Sino–Soviet split. Throughout the 1960s ideological and political tensions between Moscow and Beijing grew and intensified. In 1969 those tensions escalated into a shooting match over a border dispute. Armed skirmishes were short-lived, but tension remained high between China and the Soviet Union until Mikhail Gorbachev visited Beijing in 1989.

10. Created in 1961 by President J.F. Kennedy, USAID provided civilian foreign aid consistent with U.S. foreign policy goals. However, President Trump's 2018 budget cut 80% of the funding for USAID, thereby ending such programs.

11. Unfortunately, the shelter turned out not to be sustainable. In 2013 it was still funded locally but by 2015 it had to close due to lack of funding. Buckley, *The Politics of Unfree Labour in Russia*, 88.

12. *Taiga* refers to the dense forests (boreal forests or snow forests) of Siberia. It is the world's largest terrestrial biome.

13. Khabarovsk is the largest city in the Russian Far East. It is 800 kilometers (500 miles) north of Vladivostok and 30 kilometers (19 miles) from the Chinese border at the confluence of the Amur River.

14. Guangzhou, formerly called Canton, is a busy transport and trade hub in South China on the Pearl River.

15. In Russia, only the top 1 percent of students are admitted into "free" departments of state universities—no tuition or fees. Admission is based solely on merit, academic achievement, and entry test scores. Under the Soviet Union, all universities were free. When the Soviet Union collapsed in 1992, most universities created "paid" programs that anyone could get into if they had the money. These "commercial" departments are quite expensive and corrupt.

16. Permsky krai is located in the east of the European part of Russia, in the Volga Federal district. The capital city, Perm, is 1,445 km (718 miles) due east of Moscow. The area is rich in minerals, precious metals, oil, and timber, making it a prime location for exploited labor.

17. Krasnodarsky krai is one of Russia's "states" or regions in the south. Sochi is a well-known beach resort on the Black Sea and site of the 2014 Winter Olympics.

18. Tajiks are citizens of Tajikistan, located in Central Asia.

19. A cowshed is like a lean-to: it has a tin roof and is open on one or two sides. It is just enclosed enough for the animals to get out of the sun or the rain.

20. U.S. State Department TIP Report, 2017, https://www.state.gov/j/tip/rls/tiprpt/countries/2017/271269.htm, accessed 16 September 2017.

Chapter 4

1. Several of my informants cited this statistic, which I believe comes from an International Labour Organization report.

2. See U.S. Bureau of International Labor Affairs, "Child Labor and Forced Labor Reports: Moldova" U.S. Department of Labor, 2017, https://www.dol.gov/agencies/ilab/resources/reports/child-labor/moldova, accessed 23 July 2019.

3. La Strada International is a European NGO platform that works from a human rights perspective in support of trafficked persons. The platform aims to prevent human trafficking and to protect and realize trafficked persons' rights. For more information and a history of La Strada, see their website, https://www.lastradainternational.org/history-la-strada.

4. Internal trafficking is when the victim is trafficked within the country of origin.

5. Svetlana was the child psychologist at La Strada in Chisinau.

6. Cyprus has been divided since 1974, when Turkey invaded in the north in response to a coup backed by the Greeks. Following a brief war, the island was partitioned by the UN, with the northern third occupied by Turkish Cypriots and the southern two-thirds by Greek Cypriots.

7. It is common for traffickers and pimps to get women addicted to drugs and alcohol in order to be able to better control them. Addicts often become both emotionally and physically dependent on their suppliers.

8. New Jersey millionaire Anthony "Mark" Bianchi was arrested for sex tourism in Moldova. He went to small villages in Moldova and Romania and bought young boys for sex, raping nearly a dozen boys under the age of sixteen. He was found guilty and in 2009 was sentenced to 25 years in a U.S. federal prison. To date, two of his appeals have been rejected by the courts.

9. Balti is located 132 km (about 81 miles) north of Chisinau.

Chapter 5

1. *Khrushchevky* are named after the Soviet leader Nikita Khrushchev, who oversaw the rebuilding of the USSR following WWII. These buildings are three to five stories high, made of low-cost concrete panels, and they usually have leaky gas and water lines and no elevators.

2. See Al Jazeera, *Slavery: A 21st Century Evil*, March 2012, http://www.aljazeera.com/programmes/slaverya21stcentury evil/2011/10/20111010134454998749.html; William Finnegan, "The Countertraffickers:

Rescuing the Victims of the Global Sex Trade," *New Yorker*, 5 May 2008, http://www.newyorker.com/magazine/2008/05/05/the-countertraffickers, accessed 27 July 2019.

3. *Makler* is a popular classifieds newspaper published twice weekly in Moldova. It is the primary medium for posting false advertisements. In any issue, one can find hundreds of help wanted ads for work abroad, study abroad, marriage services, etc. It is a valuable tool for recruiters.

4. This is still a trend. Therefore, most trafficking arrests are of recruiters, who themselves were victims of trafficking at one time.

5. Because of poverty and a lack of schools in most of rural Moldova, it is quite common for students to attend state boarding schools, especially if their parents are working abroad or if the families are too poor to feed them. In 2005 there were sixty-three such schools, with a population of over 11,000 children. However, in most cases, once a child turns fourteen years old, he or she can no longer live at the school. Traffickers are known to hang around boarding schools, just waiting for kids to age out.

6. Debt bondage is a very common form of trapping a person in slavery. Victims are offered a job abroad, but when they arrive, they are told they must work without pay until they pay off the debts incurred for their travel. These sums are usually overinflated, so a woman going to Cyprus, for example, may end up "owing" her trafficker upwards of US$6,000. She must work off the debt before she is allowed to go free.

7. The Civil Registry and Migration Department of Cyprus grants temporary residence and work permits to alien artists engaged in dance or musical performances in public places that provide entertainment. These visas are very easy to obtain, requiring little documentation.

8. In December 2003 the Russian Federation adopted its first criminal statutes on human trafficking. In April 2004, Russia ratified the Palermo Protocol.

9. This is no longer the case. Russia has consistently been listed in the annual U.S. TIP Reports as engaging in state-sponsored trafficking since 2018. Vladimir Putin and others in the Russian government have not only denied the existence of trafficking in Russia, but they have actively worked to conceal the problem and weaken the rule of law regarding trafficking. See Leah Waid, "Human Trafficking: The Secret to Putin's Economy," *Harvard International Review*, 25 November 2020, https://hir.harvard.edu/putin-and-human-trafficking, accessed July 2022.

10. Stockholm syndrome is a psychological response wherein captives develop a psychological alliance, or identify closely, with their captors. First named in 1973 following a bank hostage situation in Stockholm, the syndrome is a survival strategy people develop during captivity. The most infamous example of the Stockholm syndrome was the kidnapping and recruitment of Patti Hearst by the Symbionese Liberation Army in 1974 in the U.S.

11. The state agencies involved in the MOU are the Center for Combatting Trafficking in Persons (which falls under the jurisdiction of the General Prosecutor's Office in the Ministry of the Interior) and the Ministry of Social Protection.

12. A city in the breakaway region of Transnistria.

Chapter 6

1. The Bolshevik Revolution took place on October 25, 1917, according to the Julian calendar that was followed by Russia at the time. That date on the Gregorian calendar was November 7. Shortly after the Revolution, Russia adopted the Gregorian calendar in order to keep in step with the rest of the world.

2. This is a holdover from the Soviet past. All citizens must carry an internal passport and register it in their city of residence.

3. According to the 2004 census, Moldovans made up 75.8% of the population in Moldova, whereas in Transnistria Moldovans made up 32%, followed by Russians (30%) and Ukrainians (29%). See Moldova Population, *World Population Review*, 14 June 2019, http://worldpopulationreview.com/countries/moldova, accessed 20 June 2019.

4. While the interview was in Russian, Oksana used the English words "human

rights," indicating that there really isn't an equivalent Russian term for the concept.

5. In 2018, two policemen from Transnistria were indicted for sex trafficking, so it does happen. See *2018 Trafficking in Persons Report—Moldova*, UN High Commissioner for Refugees/Refworld, 2018, http://www.refworld.org/docid/5b3e0acea.html, accessed 20 June 2019.

6. While it is impossible to give exact data, experts estimate that as many as 90 percent of women who have been trafficked for sexual exploitation were victims of domestic violence or sexual abuse before they were trafficked. One possible explanation is that women, seeking to flee a violent situation at home, become vulnerable to trafficking.

7. Bender (in Russian, *Bendery*) is located eight miles from Tiraspol, on the west bank of the Dniester River—the Moldovan side. It is in the buffer zone established in the 1992 ceasefire, but Transnistria has de facto control over the area.

Chapter 7

1. *OSCE Trial Monitoring Programme for the Republic of Moldova: Final Report*, Organization for Security and Co-operation in Europe, 28 July 2010, https://www.osce.org/moldova/70945, accessed 26 July 2023.

2. See William Finnegan, "The Countertraffickers," *New Yorker*, 5 May 2008, http://www.newyorker.com/magazine/2008/05/05/the-countertraffickers, accessed 27 July 2019.

3. While researching this project in Chisinau in 2008, I had my own encounter with corrupt officials. Late one evening, two policemen showed up at our apartment with the express intention to harass and intimidate me and my husband. They told us to abandon our research project in Moldova. Friends at the IOM and La Strada confirmed that we had attracted some unwelcome attention and advised us to leave the country immediately, which we did. We had no such problems in 2010.

4. He is talking about the *propiska*—a residence permit required of all Soviet citizens. The Soviet state required everyone to register their place of residency with the local police. By law, each citizen was only allowed one place to live. Housing was owned and distributed by the state, which determined the square footage of a domicile according to family size. Even citizens who went to live somewhere else temporarily—for example, to attend university—had to apply for a new resident permit.

5. ZAGS stands for *Zapis aktov grazhdanskogo sostoyaniy*, or civil registry. Also known as the Wedding Palace, it was a Soviet-style bureau that registered all weddings and births. Once a union was registered with ZAGS, a civil marriage ceremony was performed.

6. *Makler* in Russian means "Broker." It is a weekly paper of classified ads, including help wanted ads.

7. At that time the average monthly wage in Moldova was less than US$100 a month.

8. In the 1990s the term "trafficking of persons" did not exist in legal terminology; it was called "exporting people."

9. The very first high-level statement on trafficking came in 1997 in Strasbourg by the Council of Europe. However, the final declaration was worded as violence against women and not human trafficking. See Anne T. Gallagher, *The International Law of Human Trafficking* (Cambridge: Cambridge University Press, 2010), 110.

10. Ion used the French word *soutenuer*—one who lives off the earnings of prostitutes.

11. Ion used the word plan, harkening back to the Soviet system of five-year plans. The state would plan all production quotas for the next five years, including the production of solved criminal cases. Heads of enterprises that didn't meet their planned quotas were often punished.

12. In Russian, Ministerstvo vnutrennikh del (MVD).

13. The Communist Party was the ruling party in Moldova between 1998 and 2009.

14. Petru Lucinschi was the general secretary of the Moldovan Communist Party from 1989 to 1991. After winning the presidential elections in 1996, Lucinschi became the second president of independent Moldova beginning in January 1997 through 2001.

15. Karamalak, often using the alias of Grisha Bulgarul, was accused of numerous serious crimes including extortion,

robbery, murder, and criminal attacks. He was arrested several times before 1998, but each time he was released owing to a "lack of evidence."

16. In 1998, Karamalak left Moldova for Russia, where he remained wanted by international law enforcement. Russia refused to extradite him, despite numerous extradition pleas by the Moldovan state.

17. 1 hectare equals 2.47 acres.

18. Ion Bejan was the deputy director of a new police unit, the Center for Combatting Trafficking. It was founded by a $1.9 million grant from the U.S. Bejan was indicted for protecting Alexander Covali, a significant trafficker of minor girls for sexual slavery; Bejan was subsequently fired.

19. Historically, Moldova was a Romanian principality, and Moldovans still speak Romanian. So, when the Soviet Union collapsed in 1991–92, Moldovans could easily get Romanian citizenship. In 2007 Romania joined the EU, so Romanian citizens can travel and work freely within the EU. Moldovans cannot.

20. Gheorghe Papuc was the minister of internal affairs in Moldova from February 2002 to March 2008 and then again from October 2008 to September 2009.

21. Here Ion used the Romanian word *nanash*, which implies a trusted associate—like a brother in a mafia family.

22. In 2001 the Communist Party won a majority in Parliament and party leader Vladimir Voronin became president. Prior to this, the previous democratic administration divided the Moldovan court system up into regional and district courts—much like our state and federal system. The Communist reform was intended to dislodge non–Communists, who largely worked in the regional court system.

23. In 2010, Reshetnikov, then a Communist Party candidate for Parliament, claimed that he was kidnapped, beaten, tortured, and drugged by unknown assailants wanting him to give incriminating evidence against President Voronin. Physicians at the hospital said that Reshetnikov's injuries were "extremely superficial." See Marek Jan Chodakiewicz, *Intermarium: The Land Between the Black Sea and the Baltic* (New Brunswick: Transaction Press, 2012), 368, fn. 132.

24. At the time of the interview, the International Labour Organization estimated that one-third of the Moldovan workforce was working out of the country, sending back remittances.

25. Balti (in Russian, *Beltsi* or *Beltsy*) literally means "swamp" and is the second largest city in Moldova. Situated 132 km (81 miles) north of Chisinau, it is considered Moldova's northern capital. Because of its location, it also is an important hub for trafficking drugs and people east through Ukraine to Russia, or west through Romania to Europe.

Part II

1. Global Slavery Index, 2016 report, https://www.globalslaveryindex.org. See also International Labour Organization (ILO), http://www.alliance87.org/2017ge/modernslavery#!section=4; United Nations Office on Drugs and Crime (UNODC), *Global Report on Trafficking in Persons 2016* (United Nations Publication, E.16.IV.6, 2016).

2. ILO, *Profit Estimates: The Economics of Forced Labour*, http://www.ilo.org/global/topics/forced-labour/statistics/lang—en/index.htm. The illegal drug trade generates around $60 billion each year in the U.S. alone. See Oriana Zill and Lowell Bergman, "Do the Math: Why the Illegal Drug Business Is Thriving," *Frontline*, PBS.org.

3. Amnesty International, "Killer Facts: The Scale of the Global Arms Trade," https://www.amnesty.org/en/latest/news/2015/08/killer-facts-the-scale-of-the-global-arms-trade.

4. Kevin Bales, *Disposable People: New Slavery in a Global Age* (Berkeley: University of California Press, 2004).

Chapter 8

1. Preceding the Arab Spring in 2010, thousands of Moldovans used Twitter and other forms of social media to bring down a corrupt and unpopular Communist regime. Until 1991, the Soviet–sanctioned Communist Party of Moldova was the only legal political party. Then, in August 1991, as the Soviet Union was disintegrating, Moldovans voted to suspend all activity of the Communist Party. Within two years, under the leadership of Vladimir

Voronin, the old Communist Party of Moldova became the newly reconstituted Party of Communists of Moldova (PCM). However, little changed but the name. In 1998 the PCM emerged as the largest political party in Moldova. With the backing of Russia, in 2001 the PCM won a majority of seats in Parliament and elected Voronin president. One of Voronin's first acts as president was to dismiss the heads of the state-run radio and television stations and appoint his own people. Observers argue that this move is what allowed the Communists to consolidate their hold on society. Voronin and the PCM stayed firmly in power until they were forced out in the "Twitter Revolution" of 2009.

2. According to Transparency International's Corruption Index, Moldova ranks 123 out of 176 nations assessed for corruption. Thirty-seven percent of Moldovans report paying bribes routinely, and the police are perceived to be the most corrupt institution in Moldova. See https://www.transparency.org/country/MDA, accessed 10 December 2017.

3. Not until 2015 did the Council of Europe adopt a convention against trafficking in human organs. See Council of Europe Treaty Series, no. 216, https://rm.coe.int/16806dca3a, accessed 10 December 2017.

4. "Organ trafficking" refers to the illicit trade in organs, while "human trafficking for organ removal" refers to the trafficking in persons for the purpose of removing an organ, typically a kidney. I use the terms interchangeably because organ trafficking is presumed to be preceded by human trafficking for the purpose of removing an organ from a body.

5. United Nations Convention Against Transnational Organized Crime: Protocol to Prevent, Suppress, and Punish Trafficking in Persons, article 3.

6. UN Global Initiative to Fight Human Trafficking, *Trafficking for Organ Trade* (Geneva: United Nations, 2011), http://www.ungift.org/knowledgehub/en/about/trafficking-for-organ-trade, accessed 10 December 2017.

7. "Illegal Kidney Trade Blooms as New Organ Is 'Sold Every Hour,'" *The Guardian* (27 May 2012), http://www.theguardian.com/world/2012/may/27/kidney-trade-illegal-operations-who, accessed 26 August 2014.

8. This "emptying out" of Moldovan villages continues today. Recently the *New York Times* reported on a similar village that is left with only one inhabitant. See Patrick Kingsley and Laetitia Vancon, "And Then There Was One: Three People Lived in This Village Until Two Were Murdered," *New York Times*, 14 July 2019, https://www.nytimes.com/2019/07/15/world/europe/moldova-eastern-europe-population-decline.html?searchResultPosition=2, accessed 15 July 2019.

9. See, for example, Juan Gonzalez et al., "Organ Trafficking and Migration: A Bibliometric Analysis of an Untold Story," *International Journal of Environmental Research and Public Health* 17, no. 9 (5 May 2020): 3204, doi:10.3390/ijerph17093204.

10. UNODC, *Assessment Toolkit: Trafficking in Persons for the Purpose of Organ Removal* (Vienna: United Nations, 2015): 11–12. https://www.unodc.org/documents/human-trafficking/2015/UNODC_Assessment_Toolkit_TIP_for_the_Purpose_of_Organ_Removal.pdf, accessed 27 July 2016.

11. Siddharth Kara, *Modern Slavery: A Global Perspective* (New York: Columbia University Press, 2017), 112.

12. UNODC, *Assessment Toolkit*, 14.

13. Donating a kidney to a relative is not a crime in most countries. That is why Anatoli claimed the recipient was his uncle.

14. Marin seems to be the main recruiter for the village.

15. I have encountered this many times in Russia. In all post–Soviet countries, the currencies went through numerous reforms. Banks would not honor bills that were issued before the reforms. Further, banks would only accept new foreign bills that were in pristine condition. So, if you had old bills, or if they were torn or tattered, there was nowhere you could exchange them.

Chapter 9

1. Tatiana Fomina, Viorelia Rusu, and Daniella Misail-Nichitin, *Trafficking in Persons in Moldova: Comments, Trends, and Recommendations* (Chisinau: La Strada, 2005): 13–29.

2. Anya deviates from this profile in that she completed three years of high school and then attended vocational school, learning how to make shoes and clothes.

3. Fomina et al., *Trafficking in Persons in Moldova*, 28. For more on the connection between trafficking and domestic violence, see Stephen Warnath, *Examining the Intersection Between Trafficking in Persons and Domestic Violence* (Washington, DC: USAID, 2007), 11.

4. *Ibid.*

5. Push factors are exactly what they sound like—conditions such as poverty, war, drought, famine, domestic violence, lack of opportunity, discrimination, and the like, that push people to leave their home countries in search of a better living situation.

6. For details on Moldova's economic struggles since independence, see Jenny Bryson Clark and Denese McArthur, "The Political and Economic Transition from Communism and the Global Sex Trafficking Crisis: A Case Study of Moldova," *Journal of Intercultural Studies* 35, no. 2 (2004): 128–144.

7. Transnistria is on the eastern side of Moldova, sharing a border with Ukraine. In 1992, Transnistria declared independence from Moldova. A brief civil war ensued, with Russia aiding Transnistria with troops and war materiel.

8. Neli Babcinci, interview by the author in Chisinau, Moldova, 2010.

9. See Maria Otarashvili, "Moldova and the Global Economic Crisis," *Foreign Policy Research Institute* (May 2013), https://www.fpri.org/research/eurasia/recent-findings/moldova-global-econ-crisis/.

10. In 2013–14, in advance of Moldova signing political reform and trade agreements with the EU, Russia again placed bans on Moldovan wine, meat, and fruits. Although Moldova has developed new markets for its wine, the bans still have a huge effect on Moldova's economy. See *ibid.*

11. Stella Rotaru interviews by the author in Chisinau, Moldova, 2008 and 2010.

12. Myriam Meloni, "The Country That Was Orphaned by Emigration," *Narratively* (8 January 2016), https://narratively.com/the-country-that-was-orphaned-by-emigration/. See also Henry Foy, "Moldova's Left-Behind Children," *Financial Times*, 19 June 2015, https://www.ft.com/content/bf5d6278-152f-11e5-a587-00144feabdc0, accessed 23 July 2018.

13. This is known as the shuttle trade, which arose simultaneously with *perestroika*. In the lag time between the state cutting production in order to privatize and privatized industries producing enough to meet demand, thousands of ordinary items were in deficient supply and store shelves were bare. One could make a good living by buying cheap goods in Turkey or elsewhere and reselling them at a higher price in the former Soviet Union. Shuttle traders also bought goods in cities and sold them in villages where such items were in scarce supply. Or they bought goods in industrial areas (like Moscow) and sold them in agricultural areas (like Moldova). Typically, shuttle traders were women. They shuttled across rather porous borders, buying and selling. It was dangerous and illegal, but it could be quite lucrative. See, for example, Irina Mukhina, *Women and the Birth of Russian Capitalism: A History of the Shuttle Trade* (DeKalb: Northern Illinois University Press, 2014).

14. By this time, it was Serbia. Yugoslavia broke up in the early 1990s, but Anya remembered it as Yugoslavia.

15. The Serb authorities dumped the group back in Romania with no charges filed.

16. Timisoara is a Romanian city located about 85 kilometers [53 miles] from the Serb border.

17. A white passport is a temporary passport that allows the holder to enter their home country.

18. About US$500—a small fortune in Moldova at the time.

19. Pimps or traffickers who had bought the girls from "the fat Russian" must have made arrangements to collect them at specific bus stops.

20. Tiraspol is the capital of Transnistria, about 70 kilometers (43 miles) from Chisinau.

21. At the time that Anya was in Turkey, there was no Moldovan embassy in Istanbul. A Consulate General of the Republic of Moldova opened in Istanbul on March 1, 2008, but Anya was trafficked to Turkey in 1999. Who the officials were who came to see her remains unclear.

Chapter 10

1. Ruth Rosenberg, "Trafficking of Adult Men in the Europe and Eurasia Region: Final Report" (Washington, DC: USAID, 2010), 6.

2. Article 2(1), International Labour Organization Forced Labour Convention (no. 29), 1930.

3. This is the equivalent of being a junior in high school in the U.S.

4. Prior to 1990, military training departments functioned at all higher education institutions in Moldova, while younger schoolchildren had basic military training as a compulsory discipline. After Moldova declared its independence in 1991, military training departments were abolished.

5. By 1991, the Soviet Union and the Soviet Bloc were coming apart at the seams. In less than a year, the USSR would cease to exist.

6. *Perestroika* (literally meaning *restructuring*) was a program implemented under Soviet leader Mikhail Gorbachev in the mid-1980s as an attempt to restructure Soviet political and economic policies. He proposed reducing the direct involvement of the Communist Party leadership in the country's governance and increasing the local governments' authority. Seeking to bring the Soviet Union up to economic par with capitalist countries, Gorbachev decentralized economic controls and encouraged enterprises to become self-financing.

7. *Perestroika* included shifting the huge central-command Soviet economy to one more responsive to market forces. Consequently, the state rapidly privatized many of its industries and services. The result was shortages, factory closures, unemployment, and hyperinflation.

8. This is known as the shuttle trade, which arose simultaneously with *perestroika*; see chap. 9, note 13.

9. Perm is located 1,072 km (666 miles) east of Moscow, near the Ural Mountains. From Perm to Tajikistan is over 3,000 km (1,864 miles).

10. Kamskiy avtomobilny zavod, KAMAZ, is the largest producer of heavy-duty trucks in Russia. Kamaz trucks are widely used by the Russian military, as well as by long-haul trucking companies throughout Russia and Eastern Europe.

11. It is unclear where Alexei actually was. He used the words "Char Dara" and "Cherdara." Cherdara is a small town 123 km (76 miles) southeast of Dushanbe in Tajikistan. There is also a Char Dara (also known as Chahar Dara and Chahar Darreh), which is one of seven districts in the Kunduz Province of northern Afghanistan on the border with Tajikistan. The district center is the village of Char Dara. It is approximately 3,354 km (2,085 miles) from Perm, Russia. This is probably where Alexei was first taken.

12. In the Russian army, the three-star rank is a colonel-general (*general-polkovnik*). This rank is typically a steppingstone to becoming a full general.

13. The AKM is most commonly known as a Kalashnikov. Used by the Soviet military since 1959, it is the most ubiquitous of the entire AK series of automatic rifles. It is used widely in the former Soviet Union, Africa, and Asia.

14. Alexei is referring to the Soviet–Afghan War, 1979–89. The 2001 U.S. invasion of Afghanistan had not happened yet. During the Soviet war, northern Afghanistan, along the Soviet border, was under the control of the People's Democratic Party of Afghanistan, and hence supported by the USSR. During the Soviet occupation, the fighting took place mainly to the southeast.

15. In 1991, Tajikistan declared independence from the Soviet Union, ending Soviet control of the long border with Afghanistan. Within a year, Tajikistan was plunged into civil war and economic and political chaos. Consequently, the border between Tajikistan and Afghanistan was quite porous and remains so to this day.

16. This might be a nickname. *Anasha* is a slang Uzbek word for cannabis.

17. Sergiev Posad (called Zagorsk under the Soviets) is located 75 km (46 miles) from Moscow. It is an industrial center with a population of around 100,000. It is named for the famous Trinity Monastery of St. Sergei located there.

Chapter 11

1. For a thorough discussion of the health and psychological consequences of modern-day slavery, see Louise Shelley,

"The Diverse Consequences of Human Trafficking," chap. 2 of *Human Trafficking: A Global Perspective* (New York: Cambridge University Press, 2010), 59–82.

2. Interview with unnamed service provider by the author at the IOM offices in Chisinau, Moldova, October 2010.

3. Vitoria, interviewed by author in Orhei, Moldova, October 28, 2010.

4. In the Soviet school system, which is still used today, children start first grade at age seven. There is no kindergarten.

5. Nadya was very vague as to the location of her home with her Turkish john. I think she was afraid that he would find out where she was now. She did not say where the consulate was located; I assume it was in Istanbul.

6. Viorika didn't remember the name of the NGO.

7. There is some disagreement among policymakers on whether unpaid internships qualify as trafficking or slavery. While some "internships" or probationary work certainly qualify as exploitative, if the worker is free to leave and not under threat, it is not trafficking.

8. At that time, the average monthly salary in Moldova was 3,413 *lei* or US$192.

9. "Recovery" here means successful reintegration, where the client can resume a normal life and full-time employment within a year of treatment.

Chapter 12

1. International Labour Organization, *Profits and Poverty: The Economics of Forced Labour* (Geneva: ILO, 2014): 26–28.

2. Siddarth Kara, *Sex Trafficking: Inside the Business of Modern Slavery* (New York: Columbia University Press, 2009), 234–241.

3. Tatiana Fomina, interview by the author at La Strada in Chisinau, Moldova, November 12, 2008.

4. Anenii Noi *raion* is in central Moldova in the Nistra river basin. It is predominately rural, with only 10 percent of its 83,000 inhabitants living in the district's one town. Another 89 percent live in villages and communal-type farms. The land itself is primarily orchards, vineyards, and pastures.

5. Lila is referring to the time when Moldova was part of the Soviet Union. In 1991, Moldova gained independence from the USSR and since that time the economy has been in chaos. Between high tariffs placed on Moldovan exports by the EU and Russia's greatly diminished importation of Moldovan wine and agricultural products, the Moldovan economy declined to the point where, by 2003, Moldova became the poorest country in Europe.

6. Lila calls the man who initially bought her "the Turk."

7. Polygamy was abolished in Turkey in 1926, as part of Atatürk's secular reforms. Polygamy is illegal and carries up to a two-year prison sentence. In some rare cases polygamy is still practiced, mainly in the Kurdish areas in the southeast.

8. Lila's cousin herself might have been a trafficking victim and then later became the recruiter for the Turk in order to gain her freedom. This happens fairly often. To ensure loyalty, a trafficker will sometimes allow a victim to become a business partner after making him so much money or recruiting so many girls for him. This was likely the case with Lila's cousin and the reason why the wife knew of her.

9. According to a recent study, 40 percent of married Moldovan women are victims of physical domestic violence, 60 percent are victims of domestic psychological violence, and 19 percent are victims of sexual violence. See http://www.wave-network.org/sites/default/files/04%20 MOLDOVA%20END%20VERSION.pdf, accessed July 2019. So prevalent is domestic violence that there is a saying in Moldova: "A wife who is never beaten is like a house that is never cleaned."

10. The International Criminal Police Organization, Interpol, facilitates international police cooperation.

11. Lila might be referring to the process of "softening up" new girls. In Eastern Europe, newly bought girls are typically put through about two weeks of gang rape, sodomy, and sexual torture until they are "softened up" or so broken in spirit that they become compliant and are less likely to run away.

12. A pimp, who sells persons for sex, is usually some type of middleman working for the slave owner. Typically, in a trafficking bust, it is the pimps and recruiters who get arrested. Usually there is a degree

of distance between the slave owner and those who buy and sell the women for sex.

13. Some traffickers have a large stable of girls that they rotate among pimps and brothels so that the johns have access to new girls every so often. The Turk obviously had a large network of pimps, brothels, and girls.

14. It may be hard to understand, but village life in Eastern Europe is very conservative and depends upon communal obedience. Anyone who goes abroad is immediately suspect. One woman I interviewed, having returned to her village after being trafficked to Europe, was branded a prostitute by the village. Every time she left her house, the village boys would beat her and rape her. She finally had to move to a larger town where no one knew her or her past.

15. Lila initially got help from the Materna Centre in Chisinau, a UNICEF–supported center that helps trafficked women and victims of domestic violence. According to UNICEF, of the 1,706 victims they identified and assisted between 2000 and 2005, 70 percent had experienced violence in the home. Domestic violence is often a precursor to getting trafficked.

Chapter 13

1. One of the first in-depth studies of trafficking of men for slave labor from Eastern Europe is Rebecca Surtees, *Trafficking of Men—A Trend Less Considered: The Case of Belarus and Ukraine* (Geneva: International Organization for Migration, 2008).

2. *Ibid.*, 15. See also Mary Buckley, *The Politics of Unfree Labour in Russia: Human Trafficking and Labour Migration* (Cambridge: Cambridge University Press, 2018), 116–139.

3. Ruth Rosenberg, "Trafficking of Adult Men in the Europe and Eurasia Region: Final Report" (Washington, DC: USAID, 2010), 6.

4. *Ibid.*

5. *Ibid.*, 2.

6. Because the Russian economy is heavily dependent on energy and resource extraction, it flourishes when oil prices are high. This has been the case, for the most part, since the early 2000s.

7. Sadly, thousands of Ukrainian refugees fleeing the fighting headed east into Russia, where they are vulnerable to trafficking or worse. Further, evidence suggests that thousands of Ukrainian children have been separated from their parents and forced into "reeducation" camps in Russia. The U.S. embassy in Georgia reported on over 6,000 Ukrainian children held in Russian camps without their parents. See https://ge.usembassy.gov/russias-re-education-camps-hold-thousands-of-ukraines-children-report-says.

8. Sasha literally said, "at a commercial university." He was referring to is the change in higher education since the collapse of the Soviet Union. Under the Soviets, all universities were free. After 1992, only the best and brightest students could enter the university for free on a state scholarship, but there are very few of these available. Consequently, most students must pay tuition and there is no financial aid. Further, to take qualifying exams a student must pay a large fee and often must bribe the professor to administer the exam. It is a complicated, corrupt system that demands a lot more money than the U.S. counterpart.

9. It is 1,062 km (660 miles) from Ternopil to Moscow. The train takes a little over twenty-four hours.

10. A typical undergraduate degree in Ukraine takes five years (not four, like in the U.S.). The schedule is very rigid and cannot be changed. Everyone who begins a degree program has exactly five years to complete it. A student is allowed one medical leave of absence in their academic career. Any other absences for any reason will result automatically in expulsion. Students who are expelled and want to continue their education must start over from the beginning; they cannot pick up where they left off.

11. For excellent discussions on various views of globalization, see David Held and Anthony McGrew, eds., *The Global Transformation Reader* (Cambridge: Polity Press, 2005); Frank J. Lechner and John Bolti, eds., *The Globalization Reader* (Chichester: Wiley-Blackwell, 2015).

12. Oxfam International, "Five Shocking Facts About Global Inequality and How to Even It Up," Oxfam.org, https://www.oxfam.org/en/even-it/5-shocking-facts-

about-extreme-global-inequality-and-how-even-it-davos, accessed 23 July 2019.

13. United Nations Development Program, "The Real Wealth of Nations: Pathways to Human Development," *Human Development Report 2010* (New York: United Nations Development Program, 2010): 73–78.

14. As noted in Elena Tyuryukanova, *Forced Labour in the Russian Federation Today: Irregular Migration and Trafficking in Human Beings* (Geneva: International Labour Organization, 2005), 3.

15. Alexander J. Motyl, "Ukrainian Blues: Yanukovych's Rise, Democracy's Fall," *Foreign Affairs* 89, no. 4 (July/August 2010): 125.

16. *Ibid.*

17. In Russia and Ukraine, a five-year university program in education studies is what most K–12 teachers are required to complete. It is the equivalent of a master's degree in the U.S.

18. In Russia and Ukraine, students must take special gender-specific "labor skill" subjects as part of their mandatory curriculum. Boys normally take woodshop and girls are taught to sew, cook, and "keep a home." These labor education classes generally do not allow boys and girls to mix. They study separate skills in separate classrooms, reflecting the patriarchal nature of post–Soviet society. In some schools, very young girls may take a couple of weeks of woodworking, enough to learn how to cut a pretty shape out of thin wood. But boys are never taught how to cook or sew in secondary school. As a master of cutting and sewing, Andre was qualified to teach girls, but typically men teach woodshop and women teach home economics.

19. In 2008, as in the U.S., thousands of people lost their jobs. Andre was laid off and could not find a good-paying job.

20. The traffickers provided Andre with an airline ticket and all the travel documents he needed, as well as an escort to deliver him to Italy.

21. Revival of the Nation was one of the first five Ukrainian countertrafficking NGOs. Based in Ternopil, it was founded in 2000 and later developed ties with the IOM. Revival of the Nation operated the National Toll-Free Counter-Trafficking and Migrant Advice Hotline. It also served as a focal point for victim identification, referral, and reintegration.

Conclusion

1. The Walk Free Foundation estimates that between 40 million and 45.8 million individuals are enslaved in the world today. The Foundation provides yearly estimates of slaves around the world, ranking more than 160 countries according to the level of slavery there. See the Global Slavery Index at http://www.globalslaveryindex.org, accessed 30 July 2019.

2. The twenty-one countries that have not accepted the Palermo Protocol include Bangladesh, Iran, Fiji, North Korea, Pakistan, Somalia, and Yemen. For a full list, see the U.S. Department of State 2018 TIP report, https://www.state.gov/trafficking-in-persons-report-2018/, accessed 30 July 2019.

3. Christina Bain and Louise Shelley, "The Evolution of Human Trafficking During the COVID-19 Pandemic," *Council on Foreign Relations*, 13 August 2020, https://www.cfr.org/blog/evolution-human-trafficking-during-covid-19-pandemic, accessed 15 February 2024.

4. Jamille Gigio and Hayden Welsh, "As the Global Economy Melts Down, Human Trafficking Is Booming," *Foreign Policy*, 10 August 2020, https://foreignpolicy.com/2020/08/10/as-the-global-economy-melts-down-human-trafficking-is-booming, accessed 15 February 2024.

5. See U.S. State Department 2023 TIP Report, "Ukraine: Trafficking Profile," https://www.state.gov/reports/2023-trafficking-in-persons-report/ukraine/#:~:text=Russia's%-20full-scale%20invasion%20of%20Ukraine%20forced%20eight%20million%20people,population%2C%20and%205.5%20million%20returnees, accessed 15 February 2024.

6. *Ibid.*

7. IOM Global Migration Data Analysis Centre, *Migration Data Portal*, https://migrationdataportal.org/data?i=stock_abs_&t=2017, accessed 7 July 2019.

8. Andres Resendez, *The Other Slavery: The Uncovered Story of Indian Enslavement in America* (New York: Houghton Mifflin Harcourt, 2016), 319.

Bibliography

Agustin, Laura Maria. *Sex at the Margins: Migration, Labour Markets and the Rescue Industry.* London: Zed Books, 2008.
Allain, Jean, ed. *The Legal Understanding of Slavery from the Historical to the Contemporary.* Oxford: Oxford University Press, 2012.
Amnesty International. *Russian Federation: Nowhere to Turn To—Violence Against Women in the Family.* London: Amnesty International, 2005.
Aronowitz, Alexis A. *Human Trafficking, Human Misery: The Global Trade in Human Beings.* Westport: Praeger, 2009.
Aslund, Anders. *Russia's Crony Capitalism: The Path from Market Economy to Kleptocracy.* New Haven: Yale University Press, 2019.
Baker, Adele. "Growing Pains: Domestic Violence in the New Russia," *Surviving Together: A Quarterly on Grassroots Cooperation in Eurasia* 15, no. 1 (1997): 53–55.
Bales, Kevin. *Disposable People: New Slavery in the Global Economy.* Berkeley: University of California Press, 2004.
———, Zoe Trodd, and Alex Kent Williamson. *Modern Slavery: A Beginner's Guide.* Oxford: Oneworld Press, 2009.
———, and Zoe Trodd, eds. *To Plead Our Own Cause: Personal Stories by Today's Slaves.* Ithaca: Cornell University Press, 2008.
Banyard, Kat. *Pimp State: Sex, Money and the Future of Equality.* London: Faber, 2016.
Barrientos, Stephanie, Uma Kothari, and Nicola Phillips. "Dynamics of Unfree Labour in the Contemporary Global Economy," *Journal of Development Studies* 49, no. 8 (2013): 1037–1041.
Belser, Patrick. *Forced Labour and Human Trafficking: Estimating Profits.* Geneva: International Labour Office, 2005.
Bolkovac, Kathryn, with Cari Lynn. *The Whistleblower: Sex Trafficking, Military Contractors, and One Woman's Fight for Justice.* New York: Palgrave Macmillan, 2011.
Boris, Eileen, Stephanie Gilmore, and Rhacel Parrenas. "Sexual Labors: Interdisciplinary Perspectives Toward Sex Work," *Sexualities* 13, no. 2 (2010): 131–137.
Borsi, Mihaly. "Transnistria—An Unrecognized Country Within Moldova," *Journal for Labour and Social Affairs in Eastern Europe* 10, no. 4 (2007): 45–50.
Boychenko, Kirill A. "Istoricheskoe reshenie Evropeiskogo suda po pravam, cheloveka v otnoshenii Kipra I Rosii, kasaiushcheesia torgovli liud'mi," *Rossiiskii kriminologicheskii vzgliad*, no. 2 (2010): 13–18.
Bravo, Karen E. "The Role of the Transatlantic Slave Trade in Contemporary Anti-Human Trafficking Discourse," *Seattle Journal for Social Justice* 9, no. 2 (2011): 555–597.
Brennen, Denise. "Life Beyond Trafficking," *Contexts* 13, no. 1 (Winter 2014): 20–21.
Bruxvoort, Dana. "The Untold Side of Raids and Rescues: Rethinking Anti-Trafficking Efforts," *Human Trafficking Center Blog* 29 (January 2014), https://humantraffickingcenter.org/the-untold-side-of-raids-and-rescues-re-thinking-anti-trafficking-efforts/, accessed 23 July 2019.
Brysk, Alison, and Austin Choi-Fitzpatrick, eds. *From Human Trafficking to Human Rights:*

Reframing Contemporary Slavery. Philadelphia: University of Pennsylvania Press, 2012.
Buckley, Mary. *The Politics of Unfree Labour in Russia: Human Trafficking and Labour Migration*. Cambridge: Cambridge University Press, 2018.
Burke, Mary C. *Human Trafficking: Interdisciplinary Perspectives*. London: Routledge, 2012.
Clark, Jenny Bryson, and Denese McArthur. "The Political and Economic Transition from Communism and the Global Sex Trafficking Crisis: A Case Study of Moldova," *Journal of Intercultural Studies* 35, no. 2 (2014): 128–144.
Clark, Nick. *Detecting and Tackling Forced Labour in Europe*. York: Joseph Rowentree Foundation, 2013.
Corrin, Chris. "Transitional Road for Traffic: Analyzing Trafficking in Women from and Through Central and Eastern Europe, *Europe-Asia Studies* 57, no. 4 (June 2005): 543–560.
Council of Europe. *Report Concerning the Implementation of the Council of Europe Convention on Action Against Trafficking in Human Beings by Ukraine*. Strasbourg: Council of Europe, 2014.
Cyrus, Norbert. *Trafficking for Labour and Sexual Exploitation to Germany*. Geneva: International Labour Office, 2005.
Danailova-Trainor, Gergana, and Patrick Belser. *Globalization and the Illicit Market for Human Trafficking: An Empirical Analysis of Supply and Demand*. Geneva: International Labour Office, 2006.
Davidson, Julia O'Connell. *Modern Slavery: The Margins of Freedom*. Houndmills: Palgrave Macmillan, 2015.
Davis, David Brion. *The Problem of Slavery in the Age of Emancipation*. New York: Vintage, 2015.
Dawisha, Karen. *Putin's Kleptocracy: Who Owns Russia?* New York: Simon & Schuster, 2014.
Doezema, Jo. *Sex Slaves and Discourse Masters: The Construction of Trafficking*. London: Zed Books, 2010.
Erokhina, Ludmila D., and Mariia Buriak. *Torgovlia Zhenshchinami I Det'mi v Tseliakh Seksual'noi Ekspluatatsii v Sotsial'noi I Kriminologicheskoi Perspektive*. Moscow: Profobrazovanie, 2003.
Finnegan, William. "The Countertraffickers: Rescuing the Victims of the Global Sex Trade," *The New Yorker*, 5 May 2008. https://www.newyorker.com/magazine/2008/05/05/the-countertraffickers
Fomina, Tatiana, Viorelia Rusu, and Daniella Misail-Nichitin. *Trafficking in Persons in Moldova: Comments, Trends, and Recommendations*. Chisinau: International Center for Women's Rights Protection and Promotion, La Strada, 2005.
Freeland, Chrystia. *Sale of the Century: Russia's Wild Ride from Communism to Capitalism*. New York: Crown, 2000.
Friman, H. Richard, and Simon Reich, eds. *Human Trafficking, Human Security, and the Balkans*. Pittsburgh: University of Pittsburgh Press, 2007.
Gondolf, Edward, and Dmitri Shestakov. "Spousal Homicide in Russia Versus the United States: Preliminary Findings and Implications," *Journal of Family Violence* 1, no. 1 (1997): 63–74.
Gonzalez, Juan, Ignacio Garijo, and Alfonso Sanchez. "Organ Trafficking and Migration: A Bibliometric Analysis of an Untold Story." *International Journal of Environmental Research and Public Health* 17, no. 9 (5 May 2020): 3204.
Goodey, Jo. "Sex Trafficking in Women from Central and East European Countries: Promoting a 'Victim Centered' and 'Woman Centered' Approach to Criminal Justice Intervention," *Feminist Review* 76 (2004): 26–45.
Gozdziak, Elzbieta M., and Elizabeth A. Collett. "Research on Human Trafficking in America: A Review of the Literature," *International Migration* 43 (2005): 99–129.
Gross, Ariela. "When Is the Time of Slavery? The History of Slavery in Legal and Political Argument," *California Law Review* 98 (2008): 283–322.
Hemment, Julie. "Global Civil Society and the Local Costs of Belonging: Defining Violence Against Women in Russia," *Signs* 29, no. 3 (2004): 815–840.

Hepburn, Stephanie, and Rita J. Simon. *Human Trafficking Around the World: Hidden in Plain Sight*. New York: Columbia University Press, 2013.
Hughes, Donna M. "The 'Natasha' Trade: Transnational Sex Trafficking," *National Institute of Justice Journal* 246 (2001): 9–15.
_____. *Trafficking for Sexual Exploitation: The Case of the Russian Federation*. IOM Migration Research Series, no. 7. Geneva: International Organization for Migration, 2002.
_____, and Tatyana Denisova. "The Transnational Political Nexus of Trafficking in Women from Ukraine," *Trends in Organized Crime* 6 (2001): 6.
International Labour Organization. *Profits and Poverty: The Economics of Forced Labour*. Geneva: International Labour Organization, 2014.
International Organization for Migration. *Description of the State Systems for Collecting Analysis and Data Sharing on Migration Statistics in Ukraine*. Kyiv: International Organization for Migration, 2007.
_____. *Victims of Trafficking in the Balkans: A Study of Trafficking in Women and Children for Sexual Exploitation to, Through, and from the Balkan Region*. Geneva: International Organization for Migration, 2001.
Ivakhnyuk, Irina, and Vladimir Iontsev. *Human Trafficking: Russia*. Florence: CARIM East, 2013.
Johnson, Janet Elise. *Gender Violence in Russia*. Bloomington: Indiana University Press, 2009.
Jonsson, Anna, ed. *Human Trafficking and Human Security*. London: Routledge, 2008.
Kampadoo, Kamala, ed., with Jyoti Sanghera and Bandana Pattanaik. *Trafficking and Prostitution Reconsidered: New Perspectives on Migration, Sex Work, and Human Rights*. Boulder: Paradigm, 2012.
Kara, Siddharth A. *Bonded Labor: Tackling the System of Slavery in South Asia*. New York: Columbia University Press, 2012.
_____. *Modern Slavery: A Global Perspective*. New York: Columbia University Press, 2017.
_____. *Sex Trafficking: Inside the Business of Modern Slavery*. New York: Columbia University Press, 2009.
Karacheva, Ekaterina. "Krasavitsy-rabnyi," *Argumenty I fakty* (5 January 2004). www.aif.ru
Kay, Rebecca, ed. *Gender, Equality, and Difference During and After State Socialism*. London: Macmillan, 2007.
Kego, Walter, and Alexandru Molcean. *Russian Organized Crime: Recent Trends in the Baltic Sea Region*. Stockholm: Institute for Security and Developmental Policy, 2012.
Kelly, Elizabeth. *Journeys of Jeopardy: A Review of Research on Trafficking in Women and Children in Europe*. London: International Organization for Migration, 2002.
Kiryan, Tetyana, and Mariska N.J. van der Linden. *Trafficking of Migrant Workers from Ukraine: Issues of Labour and Sexual Exploitation*. Geneva: International Labour Office, 2005.
Klinchenko, T. "Migrant Trafficking and Human Smuggling in Ukraine," in *Migrant Trafficking and Human Smuggling in Europe*. Geneva: International Organization for Migration, 2000.
Kolchin, Peter. *Unfree Labor: American Slavery and Russian Serfdom*. Cambridge: Belknap Press of Harvard University Press, 1987.
Kostiukovskii, Artem. "Treffik bez granits," *Argumenty I fakty* (28 April 2004).
Lehman, Johan, and Stef Janssens. "Research Note: The Various 'Safe'-house Profiles in East-European Human Smuggling and Trafficking," *Journal of Migration and Ethnic Studies* 33, no. 8 (November 2007): 1377–1388.
LeMoon, Laura. "The Groups 'Rescuing' Sex Trafficking Victims Are as Bad as the Pimps," *Intersectional Feminist Media* (28 April 2017), https://wearyourvoicemag.com/more/social-justice/sex-trafficking-rescue-industry, accessed 23 July 2019.
Limanowska, Barbara. *Trafficking in Human Beings in South Eastern Europe*. Sarajevo: United Nations Development Programme, 2005.
Limoncelli, Stephanie A. *The Politics of Trafficking: The First International Movement to Combat the Sexual Exploitation of Women*. Stanford: Stanford University Press, 2010.

Magenta Consulting. *Issledovanie fenomena trudovoi migratsii v Rossiiu*. Chisinau: International Center for Women's Rights Protection and Promotion, La Strada, 2007.
Malarek, Victor. *The Natashas: The Horrific Inside Story of Slavery, Rape, and Murder in the Global Slave Trade*. New York: Arcade, 2011.
Masika, Rachel. *Gender, Trafficking, and Slavery*. Oxford: Oxford University Press, 2002.
McCarthy, Lauren. *Trafficking Justice: How Russian Police Enforce New Laws, from Crime to Courtroom*. Ithaca: Cornell University Press, 2015.
Mihailov, Eduard, Mariska N.J. van der Linden, and Shivaun Scanlan. *Forced Labour Outcomes of Migration from Moldova: Rapid Assessment*. Geneva: International Labour Office, 2005.
Mizulina, Elena B. *Torgovlia liud'mi i rabstvo v Rossii: Mezhdunarodno-pravovoi aspect*. Moscow: Iurist, 2006.
Mosneaga, Valerii. "Irregular Transit Migration of Moldovan Citizens to the European Union Countries," in *Transit Migration in Europe*, ed. Franck Duvel, Irina Molodikova, and Michael Collyer. Amsterdam: Amsterdam University Press, 2014.
Murphy, Laura T. *Survivors of Slavery: Modern-Day Slave Narratives*. New York: Columbia University Press, 2014.
Musto, Jennifer Lynne. "What's in a Name? Conflations and Contradictions in Contemporary U.S. Discourses of Human Trafficking," *Women's Studies International Forum* 32 (2009): 281–287.
Nicholson, Andrea, Minh Dang, and Zoe Trodd. "Full Freedom: Contemporary Survivors' Definitions of Slavery," *Human Rights Law Review* 18, no. 4 (December 2018): 689–704.
Olimpiev, Anatolii Iu. *Protivodeistvie Torgovle Liud'mi*. Moscow: Zakon i Pravo, 2013.
Outshoorn, Joyce. "The Political Debates on Prostitution and Trafficking of Women," *Social Politics* 12, no. 1 (2005): 141–155.
Patterson, Orlando. *Slavery and Social Death*. Cambridge: Harvard University Press, 1982.
Peters, Alicia W. *Responding to Human Trafficking: Sex, Gender, and Culture in the Law*. Philadelphia: University of Pennsylvania Press, 2015.
Pilkington, Hilary. *Migration, Displacement, and Identity in Post-Soviet Russia*. London: Routledge, 1998.
Poletaev, Dmitrii. "Izmenenie praktik povedeniia trudovykh migrantov iz Srednei Azii v Rossii," in *Vostok na Vostoke, v Rossii I na Zapade*, ed. Sergei Panarin. 177–193. St. Petersburg: Nestor-Istoriia, 2016.
Quayson, Ato, and Antonela Arhim. *Labor Migration, Human Trafficking, and Multinational Corporations: The Commodification of Illicit Flows*. Abingdon-Oxon: Routledge, 2012.
Racioppi, Linda, and Katherine O'Sullivan-See, eds. *Gender Politics in Post-Communist Eurasia*. East Lansing: Michigan State University Press, 2009.
Resendez, Andres. *The Other Slavery: The Uncovered Story of Indian Enslavement in America*. Boston: Houghton Mifflin Harcourt, 2016.
Rodriguez, Junius P. *Slavery in the Modern World: A History of Political, Social, and Economic Oppression*. Santa Barbara: ABC-CLIO, 2011.
Rosenberg, Ruth. "Trafficking of Adult Men in the Europe and Eurasia Region: Final Report." Washington, DC: United States Agency for International Development, 2010.
Satre, Lowell J. *Chocolate on Trial: Slavery, Politics, and the Ethics of Business*. Athens: Ohio University Press, 2005.
Schloenhardt, Andreas, and Mark Loong. "Return and Reintegration of Human Trafficking Victims from Australia," *International Journal of Refugee Law* 23, no. 2 (July 2011): 143–173.
Scott, Rebecca J. "Under Color of Law: Siliadan v France and the Dynamics of Enslavement in Historical Perspective." In *The Legal Understanding of Slavery from the Historical to the Contemporary*, ed. Jean Allain. 152–164. Oxford: Oxford University Press, 2012.
Shelley, Louise I. "The Changing Position of Women: Trafficking, Crime, and Corruption." In *The Legacy of State Socialism and the Future of Transformation*, ed. David Lane. 207–222. Lanham: Rowman & Littlefield, 2002.
———. *Human Trafficking: A Global Perspective*. New York: Cambridge University Press, 2010.

Skinner, E. Benjamin. *A Crime So Monstrous: Face-to-Face with Modern-Day Slavery*. New York: Free Press, 2008.
Stoecker, Sally, and Louise Shelley, eds. *Human Traffic and Transnational Crime: Eurasian and American Perspectives*. Lanham: Rowman & Littlefield, 2005.
Surtees, Rebecca. *Trafficking of Men—A Trend Less Considered: The Case of Belarus and Ukraine*. IOM Migration Research Series, no. 36. Geneva: International Organization for Migration, 2008.
Tavcer, Scharie D. "The Trafficking of Women for Sexual Exploitation: The Situation from Republic of Moldova to Western Europe," *Police Practice and Research* 7, no. 2 (May 2006): 135–147.
Tyuryukanova, Elena V. *Forced Labour in the Russian Federation Today: Irregular Migration and Trafficking in Human Beings*. Geneva: International Labour Organization, 2005.
_____, and Ludmila D. Erokhina, eds. *Torgovlia Liud'mi: Sotsiokriminologicheskii analiz*. Moscow: Izdatel'stvo Akademia, 2002.
United Nations Office on Drugs and Crime. *An Assessment of Referral Practices to Assist and Protect the Rights of Trafficked Persons in Moldova*. Chisinau: United Nations Office on Drugs and Crime, 2007.
_____. *Report on Trafficking in Persons*. Vienna: United Nations Office on Drugs and Crime, 2016.
_____. *Trafficking in Persons for the Purpose of Organ Removal*. Vienna: United Nations Office on Drugs and Crime, 2015.
_____. *Trafficking in Persons: Global Patterns*. Vienna: United Nations Office on Drugs and Crime, 2006.
United States State Department. *Trafficking in Persons (TIP) Reports*, 2001–2023. www.state.gov/j/tip/rls/tiprpt
van Liemt, Gijsbert. *Human Trafficking in Europe: An Economic Perspective*. Geneva: International Labour Office, 2004.
Vreja, Lucia Ovidia. "Human Trafficking in South Eastern Europe," *Connections* 1, no. 4 (Winter 2005): 49–62.
Walk Free Foundation. *Global Slavery Index*. www.globalslaveryindex.org/findings
Warnath, Stephen. *Examining the Intersection Between Trafficking in Persons and Domestic Violence*. Washington, DC: United States Agency for International Development, 2007.
Waugh, Louisa. *Selling Olga: Stories of Human Trafficking and Resistance*. London: Phoenix Press, 2008.
Winrock International. *Nationwide Survey on "Trafficking in Women as a Social Problem in Ukrainian Society": Summary of Findings*. Kyiv: United States Agency for International Development, 2001.

Index

abolition 214–215
abortion 50, 83
addiction (drug and/or alcohol) 90
Afghanistan 162, 164, 166
anti-trafficking: NGOs 13, 15, 19, 42, 53, 67, 75, 79, 100; prevention efforts 14, 57, 102
Association for Female Lawyers (Moldova) 124

Bales, Kevin 8, 130, 212
Brezhnev, Leonid 98
brothels in the Russian Far East, history 55

Center for Studies on Organized Crime (Russia) 54
Center for the Prevention of the Trafficking of Women (Moldova) 115–116, 124
Central Asia 63–64, 163–164
chattel slavery 7, 162
child sex tourism 66, 78; *see also* sex tourism
child trafficking (Moldova) 70–71
China 58
Chinese migrants in Russia 55
Chisinau (Moldova) 82–83, 90, 120, 126, 137, 145, 149, 163, 171, 176, 192
Chisinau Assistance and Protection Center (Moldova) 171, 176, 179, 181, 183–184
corruption of local authorities 29, 65, 66, 74, 85, 106, 116, 119, 120, 121–122, 125, 132; *see also* police and authorities
Covid-19 212
Cretu, Ghenadi 12
Cyprus 71, 74, 76–77, 86, 88, 105, 112, 171

Dean, Laura 52
debt bondage 64, 85, 161, 162, 167–168, 175
domestic trafficking *see* internal trafficking

domestic violence 13, 108, 110, 144, 147, 184, 189, 193
dual exploitation 28, 33, 49, 209
Dubai 103, 119

Eastern Promises (film) 185
economic crisis of 2008 25, 27
Erokhina, Liudmila 54
escape(s): difficulty 61, 155, 203, 162; with help from *johns* 87–88, 172–173, 180–181, 191; from forced prostitution 31–32, 74, 87, 119–120, 172, 189; from slave camps 58–59, 60, 61, 166–167

Far East (Russian) 54
Far Eastern Center for Development of Civic Initiative (Russia) 54
forced labor *see* labor exploitation
forced prostitution *see* sexual exploitation

gender bias (in assessing human trafficking) 197–198
Germany 137
globalization 12, 205
Gorbachev, Mikhail 98
Greece 150 trafficking to from Russia 57–58

harvesting of organs (for trafficking) 125
HIV\AIDS 36, 47, 77, 86, 88, 90, 170
hot line(s) for trafficking help 72, 75, 76–77, 103, 105, 109, 110, 157
Human Trafficking Center (Moldova) 76

ILO *see* International Labour Organization
Interaction (NGO) 100, 104, 114
internal (domestic) trafficking 70, 75, 87
International Labour Organization 129, 130, 162, 206, 212
International Organization for Migration

241

12, 14, 30, 89, 103, 198; in Moldova 81–82, 83, 89, 93–94, 100, 109, 125, 171, 176; reintegration 32, 33, 38; repatriation 59, 60, 76, 83, 125, 176; in Russia 56, 60, 75; in Transnistria 100, 109–110; in Ukraine 38, 60, 198
International Transport Workers' Federation 46
Interpol 59, 60, 189, 192
invasion of Ukraine (by Russia) 3–4, 21, 23, 52–53, 114, 199
IOM *see* International Organization for Migration
Italy 208–210

judiciary in Moldova 123–124

Kara, Siddarth 8, 134, 185, 213
Karamalak, Grigory 120–121
Kazakhstan 43, 44
Khabarovsk 57–58
Kharkiv 21–24, 27, 30, 32
kidney(s), trafficking 133, 135–139, 141, 142, 166

labor exploitation 28, 46, 57, 85, 161–162, 197–210, 212; in agriculture 53, 64, 164; for begging 90; of children 70, 90; in construction 57, 59, 61, 70, 90, 207–209; in fishing industries 53, 62; in Russia 28, 42–43, 52; 53, 57, 58–59, 61, 62, 198; from Transnistria 102–103
LaStrada International 13, 14, 67, 89, 100, 144; in Moldova 77, 144–145, 158–159, 162, 169, 194, 195; in Transnistria 100
Lucinschi, Petru 120

migrants: abuse 61, 62, 64
migration 91, 109, 111, 144–145, 163, 205, 206; from Moldovan villages 72, 144, 146, 149, 186
modeling agencies 26–27
Moldova 43, 66–79; child trafficking 70–71, 117; corrupt police and officials 119–123, 125, 126, 132; laws against pimping and trafficking 118–119; organ trafficking from 125, 132–134, 139–142; poverty 71, 81, 101, 117, 134, 140, 144–145, 146, 169, 187, 196; and reintegration 50, 191–195; trafficking from 68–70, 83–84, 144–145, 146, 154–159, 165, 170–182, 186, 188–195; trafficking of pregnant women 118
Murphy, Laura 8

national referral system (Moldova) 89
North Koreans trafficked to Russia 53

oral history 2–3
organ trafficking 125, 132–134, 135–139, 142, 142, 166; Covid-19 212
Organization for Security and Cooperation in Europe (OSCE) 115, 198
organized trafficking rings 58, 86, 118, 120; and human organ trafficking 134
OSCE *see* Organization for Security and Cooperation in Europe
Oxfam 205

Palermo Protocol 7, 119, 133, 211–212
Papuc, Gheorghe 122–123
perestroika 112, 163
pimp(s) 26, 35, 36, 50, 83, 86, 88, 89, 102, 119, 185, 190; in Moldova 122, 130; "Romeo" pimp 172, 212
pimping 78, 116, 118, 119, 124, 126
Polaris Project 217
police and authorities: Belgian 32–33; complicit in human trafficking 52, 58, 61, 62, 66, 72–73, 106, 125, 132, 191, 203; corruption 65, 66, 74, 85, 106, 116, 119, 120, 121–122, 125, 132, 167, 173; denial of human trafficking 56, 100, 113, 115–116; Greek 58; Moldovan 73–74, 113, 116, 120, 121–122, 125, 132, 173, 190–191, 193; in rescue and repatriation 74, 148, 173, 176, 191; Russian 52, 61, 62, 203; in Transnistria 100, 113; Ukrainian 33; and victim support services 63, 109; *see also* corruption of local authorities
post–Soviet female unemployment 11–12, 14, 85, 112
post-traumatic stress disorder 40, 41, 204, 207, 209
pregnancy of trafficked victims 50, 83, 182
Pretty Woman (film) 44
Primorsky Center for Social Services (Russia) 56–57
Primorsky krai 55, 59
prosecution of traffickers: corrupt authorities 29, 126, 132; difficulties 31, 57, 65, 74, 78, 89, 93, 102, 115–116, 173, 193–194; witness intimidation 31, 57, 78, 116, 126, 194
prostitution (voluntary) 63, 126, 130, 184; *see also* sex work vs. sexual slavery
PTSD *see* post-traumatic stress disorder

rape 13, 45, 49, 85, 86, 88, 92, 170, 184, 189, 191, 192
recruiter(s) 106, 107, 116, 130, 134, 149, 171, 175, 176, 185, 186, 212, 176, 185, 187
recruitment strategies 15–16, 26, 44, 45–46, 68–69, 71, 75, 79, 84, 112, 118, 149, 201, 213

rehabilitation 33, 44, 77, 171, 194, 200; difficulties 76, 77–78, 101, 194; of trafficked children 47, 57
reintegration 40, 51, 77, 183–184; problems 39, 41, 46–47, 51, 174, 194, 209; and public attitudes 82, 88, 92, 194–195
repatriation 82, 83, 89, 103, 176, 192; and Save the Children 83
rescue(s) 176; difficulties 75–76, 86; with help from *johns* 74; from hot-line calls 75, 82, 110
reselling of slaves 149, 165–169, 188–190
retrafficking 37–38, 40, 78, 95, 171
Revival of the Nation (NGO) 198–199, 209
Road to Life (NGO) 21–23, 24, 25–26, 27, 33
Russia: migration to 61, 63–64, 79, 117, 121, 146, 163, 199; and post-Soviet conflicts 98, 110; trafficking of minors to 45, 47, 53, 70, 74; trafficking of Moldovans to 109; trafficking from Transnistria to 101; trafficking of Ukrainians to 49, 53, 59, 60, 62, 199–210

sex tourism 66, 83; *see also* child sex tourism
sex work *see* prostitution
sex work vs. sexual slavery 48, 74, 130; *see also* prostitution
sexual exploitation 170–182, 185, 189–190; in the Balkans 49, 83, 84; in Belgium 21, 24, 30; of children 35, 44, 57, 66, 68, 212; in China 54, 58; in Cyprus 86; in Greece 58; in Moldova 66, 83, 118; in Russia 28, 44, 49, 86, 90; in the UAE 26–27, 175–177, 181–182; in Ukraine 90; *see also* child sex tourism
sexual slavery *see* sexual exploitation
slave auction 144, 153–154
slave-labor camps 53, 58–59, 60–61, 166
slavery: definition 7–8, 95, 129, 130, 162, 165, 205, 213; in Russia 52, 58–61; survivors 36, 37, 70, 77, 85, 88, 109, 170–171, 176–178, 180–182, 183, 193–194, 207, 211
Sochi Olympics (2014) 61
social orphans 66, 85, 89, 111, 146, 214
Soviet Union, collapse 9, 11, 12, 44, 55, 70–71, 98, 117, 145, 162, 185
Stockholm syndrome 87
suicide 77, 183, 190

Tajikistan 164, 166
Taken (film) 185
Ternopil (Ukraine) 198–199
TIP *see Trafficking in Persons Report* (U.S. State Department)
Tiraspol (Transnistria) 99, 109
Trafficking in Persons Report (U.S. State Department) 52–53, 65
trafficking of minors 45, 53, 57, 89, 214; for adoption 117
Trafficking Victims Protection Act (U.S.) 7, 211
Transnistria 97–98, 109–111, 113, 126, 145, 152
transport of victims 83, 102, 111, 147–148, 150
Turkey 74, 76, 84, 107, 108, 138, 141, 144, 151–152, 160, 172–173, 187–188

Ukraine: domestic trafficking 45–46; trafficking of minors 45; trafficking of professional women 41, 49, 51
United Arab Emirates 26; forced prostitution 42–43, 175, 180; trafficking to 42, 78, 85, 88, 175, 179
United Nations Global Initiative to Fight Human Trafficking 133
United Nations Office on Drugs and Crime (UNODC) 134
United States Agency for International Development (USAID) 53, 56
USAID *see* United States Agency for International Development
U.S.S.R. *see* Soviet Union
Uzbekistan 43

victim assistance programs: closures in Russia 52–53; lack of state funds 53; state funded 56
Victims of Human Trafficking Assistance Center (Russia) 54, 58–59, 65
violence: and lasting physical or psychological trauma 47–48, 76, 83, 134, 170, 193–194, 209; as a means of control 30, 35, 49, 69, 83, 161, 166, 188, 190, 202, 209, 210; sexual exploitation and 49, 83, 94, 189, 190–191
Vladivostok, Russia 53–54

wealth inequality 205–206
World Health Organization 133, 134
Wyss, Martin 81, 82, 89